THE
DICTATORSHIP
OF THE
PROLETARIAT

June 17, 1992

To Annette –

Maybe there's something
in it for us. Who knows?

– John Eberg

THE
DICTATORSHIP
OF THE
PROLETARIAT

MARXISM'S THEORY OF
SOCIALIST DEMOCRACY

JOHN EHRENBERG

ROUTLEDGE   NEW YORK   LONDON

Published in 1992 by

Routledge
An imprint of Routledge, Chapman and Hall, Inc.
29 West 35 Street
New York, NY 10001

Published in Great Britain by

Routledge
11 New Fetter Lane
London EC4P 4EE

Library of Congress Cataloging in Publication Data

Ehrenberg, John, 1944–
    The dictatorship of the proletariat : Marxism's theory of
socialist democracy / John Ehrenberg.
        p.   cm.
    Includes bibliographical references (p.   ) and index.
    ISBN 0-415-90452-8   ISBN 0-415-90453-6 (pbk.)
    1. Communist state. 2. Dictatorship of the proletariat.
JC474.E37   1992
321.9′2—dc20
                                                                              91-45717
                                                                              CIP

British Library cataloguing in publication data also available.

For my wife Kathleen and to the memory of my parents

Contents

Part III: Problems of Communism

Conclusion

Acknowledgments

In different ways and no doubt for different reasons, Kalman Silvert, Charles Drekmeier, and Nelson Peery helped me learn how important theory and ideology are in political matters. Steve Bronner, Al DiMaio, Jeff Frieden, Mark Naison, and Bertell Ollman stand out among many friends who have enriched my understanding over the years and who helped shape this book. Leona Singer's encouragement and the generous support of Long Island University's Research Time Awards Committee made completion of the manuscript much easier than it would otherwise have been. The same is true of Cecelia Cancellaro, my editor at Routledge, who was a pleasure to work with from first to last. My children, Cassie and David, contributed to this project in more ways than they can begin to imagine.

Introduction

Marxism took shape as part of the nineteenth-century effort to understand how capitalism worked and it came to maturity as the guiding theory of the world's first successful proletarian revolution. From its formative tests in the Paris Commune and the struggle against Bismarck to its continued development during the Chinese Revolution and the struggle against fascism, it has drawn strength from Lenin's claim that it is "a million times" more democratic than any theory connected to private property in the means of production. Yet it now stands at the same crossroads as does the political movement to which it has provided theoretical leadership for most of this century. The acute crisis in which it finds itself is intimately connected to the near-total collapse of "official communism" and its democratic pretensions. Unable to offer a credible alternative to the existing order in the advanced capitalist societies and powerless to lead a shrinking number of "actual existing" socialist societies toward the communist future, it seems destined to operate on the fringes of contemporary public affairs even as it breeds a bewildering array of *esoterica* from a self-marginalized Western intelligentsia. Much of Marxism's ideological appeal over the years has come from its commitment to the overthrow of capitalism in the name of political and social democracy. Now it stands, more vulnerable than at any time in its recent history, to attack on the very same grounds. After three quarters of

1

a century as the guiding ideology of a series of communist parties and putative workers' states, its democratic claims seem more problematical than ever.

More influenced by ideology than most political movements, communism's insistence that its theory and practice inform one another compels us to examine its real history and its theoretical projections in light of each other. Before we conclude that its undoubted crisis proves that Marxism is irrelevant to the modern world, let us be clear about the content of its democratic claims.

The political theory of orthodox Marxism—the work of Marx, Engels, and Lenin—is the best place to begin, for it is entirely possible that communism's problems stem from insufficient fidelity to its roots rather than from too much orthodoxy. Some version of Marxism-Leninism remains the professed theoretical foundation of much of the contemporary Left. Nearly every important leader of the communist movement has based his or her work on it or has been driven by tradition to claim as much. Uniquely driven to maintain at least the appearance of theoretical consistency, communists and socialists remain tied to the same thinkers whose works call so many of their current projections into question. Kautsky's social democracy, Stalin's strategy of socialist construction, Mao's Great Proletarian Cultural Revolution, and Gorbachev's *glasnost* and *perestroika* must be appraised in light of concrete conditions, but the theoretical legacy of Marx, Engels, and Lenin remains the only generally accepted internal standard by which they can be evaluated on their own terms.

It is well known that Marx and Engels devoted a very small portion of their enormous theoretical work to the postcapitalist future, and what little they did say was so speculative that it could be of only general assistance when the Russian Revolution confronted Lenin with the concrete problem of building a new society. Despite this, their work does contain the seeds of a full-fledged theory of communism, and Lenin elaborated it in circumstances very different from those they had anticipated. This book's central claim is that Marx's, Engels's, and Lenin's conceptions of both capitalism and communism were expressed most completely in the theory of "the dictatorship of the proletariat," a term which stands at the very center of their work and simultaneously represents their understanding of democracy. Their description of a class dictatorship as a democracy reflects an understanding of both defined in terms of class struggle and meant to serve a social revolution whose consummation guided everything they did.

Seen in this light, the theory of the dictatorship of the proletariat is one of the central problems of modern communist practice as well. Officially renounced in some quarters and quietly abandoned in others, its revolutionary and democratic core has become an embarrassment to the very groupings whose claims still lead them to Marx, Engels, and Lenin for ritualistic theoretical support. Mutilated almost beyond recognition by the same permanent crisis to which it was proposed as a solution, its bureaucratized incarnation has become the principal internal obstacle to the development of the very socialism which it is supposed to embody. Effectively consigned to the same "atavistic" limbo to which Eduard Bernstein relegated it almost a century ago, it is not honored even in the breach by a weakened and disoriented Left which cannot begin to imagine what it might look like in the modern world.

Many of the same inconveniences which the theory raises for socialists can be found in scholarly treatments of the Marxist theory of the state as well. Some observers profess friendliness but try to "save" Marx and Engels from themselves by denying that there is really any antagonism between their work and conventional individualistic rights-based understandings of democracy. Marx and Engels did not mean what they said about the dictatorship of the proletariat and can be rescued from their Blanquist, Jacobin, and terrorist roots because they were liberal democrats at bottom whose revolutionary talk resulted from either an excess of youthful zeal or willful ignorance of what their words implied.[1] A second strand of analysis, usually more overtly hostile than the first, acknowledges that Marx and Engels really were critical of liberalism but takes this as proof positive of an antipathy to democracy as such.[2] Yet a third tendency, to which I belong, takes them at their word and tries to uncover what they meant when they called the dictatorship of the proletariat a democracy.[3]

If anything, similar problems of interpretation surface more dramatically when it comes to Lenin. Originally shaped by *émigré* Menshevik scholars and nourished by decades of cold-war antipathy to the Russian Revolution, a powerful body of thought treats him as a voluntaristic deviation from Marx and Engels's more realistic, humane, and gradual approach to social change. A master tactician of insurrection in a backward society, Lenin bequeathed to his successors the impatience with the slow pace of change and suspicion of the undirected activity of the workers which contributed to his willingness to betray democracy and made Stalin possible.[4] A second school of thought acknowledges that Lenin was the foremost representative of Marxist orthodoxy in the specific circumstances of the Russian Revolution but suggests that this case was so unusual that his legacy is of little or no relevance to Marxism as such.[5] A third tendency sees Lenin as the most important Marxist of the contemporary period and considers his work to be of general theoretical importance.[6] Lenin's is no more a closed and unchanging system than was Marx's or Engels's, but when it came to clarifying the core of modern communism's political theory it was he who put his finger on its unique and authentic insight:

> It is often said and written that the main point in Marx's theory is the class struggle. But this is wrong. And this wrong notion very often results in an

opportunist distortion of Marxism and its falsification in a spirit acceptable to the bourgeoisie. For the theory of the class struggle was created *not* by Marx, *but* by the bourgeoisie *before* Marx, and, generally speaking, it is *acceptable* to the bourgeoisie. Those who recognize *only* the class struggle are not yet Marxists; they may be found to be still within the bounds of bourgeois thinking and bourgeois politics. To confine Marxism to the theory of the class struggle means curtailing Marxism, distorting it, reducing it to something acceptable to the bourgeoisie. Only he is a Marxist who *extends* the recognition of the class struggle to the recognition of the *dictatorship of the proletariat*. This is what constitutes the most profound distinction between the Marxist and the ordinary petty (as well as big) bourgeois. This is the touchstone on which the *real* understanding and recognition of Marxism should be tested.[7]

Lenin's characteristically forthright interpretation reveals the deep continuity between his work and that of Marx and Engels. The theory of the dictatorship of the proletariat is the central, defining mark of a Marxist political theory which is incoherent and irrational without it. It summarizes its theory of the state, concentrates its understanding of democracy, and expresses its theory of socialist revolution and of communism. Without it, Marxism is just another radical criticism of capitalism.

All their expectations and hopes to the contrary notwithstanding, Marx and Engels lived in a prerevolutionary period. The capitalism whose collapse they so confidently expected proved far more resilient than they had thought possible, and they never had the pleasure of confronting the complexities which a real revolution posed to Lenin. The revolutionary communist core of their work remained untested and partially hidden as a result, and this explains why they spent so much of their time on analyses of capitalist society and bourgeois politics. There can be no doubt that they would have been delighted if the real world had forced them to spend less effort on capitalism and more on communism.

"It is more pleasant and useful to go through the 'experience of the revolution' than to write about it," Lenin observed in 1917.[8] It was left to him to guide the Russian Revolution after the surprisingly easy seizure of power in October, and he had only the theoretical legacy of Marx and Engels to rely on. This is not to suggest that he was driven exclusively by ideology, for the objective press of past and present always exerted a strong influence on his work. But his insistence that Marx's revolutionary political theory be restored to its central place had made him a leader of Russian Social-Democracy by the turn of the century, and he knew better than most of his contemporaries that much of his work was shaped by specifically Russian conditions which would limit its usefulness elsewhere. But in his unique ability to grasp and use the theory of the dictatorship of the proletariat he illuminated how indispensable it is to Marxist political theory generally and to the socialist project in particular. It is what he said it was: a theory of socialist democracy and of proletarian dictatorship and a description of the indispensable political condition for the construction of a classless society. If Marxism has any contemporary meaning at all, it is as a theory of socialist revolution and of communism. Lenin's leadership helped enrich the theory by bringing it to bear on the practical problems of the first revolution of its type. His understanding and development of Marxism remains central to contemporary politics.

My account treats the theory of the dictatorship of the proletariat as Marx, Engels, and Lenin did—as an account of the political content of an historically unprecedented revolutionary transition whose meaning is to be found in its motion toward a classless society. Its foundations were identical to those of Marxism's general theory, remained intrinsic to its maturation, and were further developed by Lenin. Part I traces the emergence of a distinctly communist political orientation from the legacy of classical German idealism. Marx and Engels's early and decisive commitment to the "ultimate goal" of a classless society led to their discovery that politics would lead economics in a social transformation which only the modern proletariat could initiate and complete. Part II begins with the failure of the revolutions of 1848 and 1905 to "break" the existing state and focuses on the later discovery of the Paris Commune and the Soviet Republic as "the political form at last discovered" by the revolutionary French and Russian workers. Part III outlines the inherently contradictory and very difficult coexistence of capitalism and communism in the same transitional "socialist" formation and traces Lenin's deepening reliance on a workers' state to defend a vulnerable revolution in a besieged and backward society. I have tried to center the analysis on the development and enrichment of the theory over time, for definite and remarkably similar phases mark the lives of all three men. An early period of theoretical development ended with a spontaneous democratic revolution whose defeat precipitated important modifications of the existing theory. Following a period of relative inactivity and theoretical clarification, Marx and Engels's analysis of the Paris Commune helped Lenin guide the October Revolution and launch the difficult first stage of communism. The permanent crisis which has characterized and deformed much of twentieth-century communism was present at the very beginning of Lenin's effort and has given rise to the central problem in the theory of the dictatorship of the proletariat: the understandable but misleading tendency to equate it with the historical evolution of the Soviet Union.

As Marx, Engels, and Lenin understood the matter, the dictatorship of the proletariat *is* the democratic content of socialism. It describes the only way the working class can hold and use state power and oppose the class dictatorship of the bourgeoisie. Their fusion of democracy and dictatorship in communism's political theory underlines their conviction that only the massive and continuous application of working-class power from below could suppress inevitable attempts at counterrevolution and simultaneously make possible the construction of a new society whose social foundations were not yet in place. All three men were theorists of a revolutionary democracy and a communism which depended on each other, and the theory of the dictatorship of the proletariat is the concentrated and comprehensive expression of their political doctrine. Its renunciation by its erstwhile defenders notwithstanding, the theory's assertion that working-class democratic political power must be dictatorial in form and in content continues to raise a number of important issues for contemporary democrats and self-described Marxists which cannot be resolved by distorting or ignoring the nature of its challenge. Having said this, let us begin at the beginning: with the evolution of Marx and Engels's understanding of the proletarian revolution's "ultimate result" and "immediate aim" before 1848, after which we will be in a position to approach the role of politics and the nature of a democracy whose frankly revolutionary and dictatorial character makes it very different from the democracy with which we are familiar.

NOTES

1. See, for example, Shlomo Avineri, *The Social and Political Thought of Karl Marx* (London: Cambridge University Press, 1968); Richard N. Hunt, *The Political Ideas of Marx and Engels*, 2 vols. (Pittsburgh: University of Pittsburgh Press, 1974–84); George Lichtheim, *Marxism: An Historical and Critical Survey* (New York: Columbia University Press, 1982); Stanley Moore, *Marx on the Choice Between Socialism and Communism* (Cambridge, Mass.: Harvard University Press, 1980).

2. See, among others, Isaiah Berlin, *Karl Marx* (New York: Oxford University Press, 1978); Leszek Kolakowski, *Main Currents of Marxism*, 3 vols. (Oxford: Oxford University Press, 1978); Axel van den Berg, *The Imminent Utopia* (Princeton: Princeton University Press, 1988).

3. See Etienne Balibar, *Sur la Dictature du Prolétariat* (Paris: Maspero, 1976); Hal Draper, *Karl Marx's Theory of Revolution*, 3 vols. (New York: Monthly Review Press, 1977–86) and *The "Dictatorship of the Proletariat" From Marx to Lenin* (New York: Monthly Review Press, 1987); Ralph Miliband, *Marxism and Politics* (Oxford: Oxford University Press, 1977).

4. There are endless varieties of this sort of analysis. Among the most influential are Louis Fischer, *The Life of Lenin* (New York: Harper and Row, 1964); David Shub, *Lenin* (Baltimore: Penguin, 1966); Adam Ulam, *The Bolsheviks* (New York: Macmillan, 1965); Edmund Wilson, *To the Finland Station* (New

York: Doubleday, 1953) and Bertram Wolfe, *Three Who Made A Revolution* (New York: Dell, 1948).

5. See Edward Hallett Carr, *A History of Soviet Russia*, 7 vols. (New York: Macmillan, 1968), vols. 1–3; Rosa Luxemburg, *The Russian Revolution and Lenin or Marxism?* (Ann Arbor: University of Michigan Press, 1977); and William Henry Chamberlin, *The Russian Revolution*, vol. 1 (Princeton: Princeton University Press, 1987).

6. See Tony Cliff, *Lenin*, 4 vols. (London: Pluto Press, 1975–79) and Neil Harding, *Lenin's Political Thought*, 2 vols. (New York: St. Martin's Press, 1977–81).

7. V. I. Lenin, "The State and Revolution," *Collected Works* (Moscow: Progress Publishers, 1960–72), 25:416–7. Unless otherwise noted, all subsequent references will be to this edition.

8. "Postscript to the First Edition of 'The State and Revolution,' " 25:497.

Part I

The Politics of Social Revolution

Chapter 1

"Ultimate Results"

Like many of their generation's young intellectuals, Marx and Engels were trained to evaluate political affairs in light of Hegel's theory of the state and both turned to radical democratic journalism in an effort to make the public sphere realize its liberating potential. But real life soon made it clear that there was something fundamentally wrong with what they had learned in school and the confrontation between their theoretical training and their practical experiences forced them to appraise the former in light of the latter. Their reevaluation of Hegel helped set their understanding of the relationship between the state and society on a new basis, and as they gravitated toward philosophical materialism they concluded that politics could not be comprehended apart from society.

The conclusion that comprehensive "human emancipation" was within reach but required the abolition of class society precipitated their early theoretical turn toward communism. The resulting criticism of property led them to reject all "merely political" revolutions as too weak to organize the conscious satisfaction of human needs. Their replacement of Hegel's bureaucracy by the propertyless proletariat as bourgeois society's "universal class" derived from this early interest in social transformation. Driven by a radical democracy whose power rested on its commitment to democratize both society *and* the state, Marx and Engels's communism would receive its first systematic expression with the 1848 publication of *The Communist Manifesto*. The theory of the dictatorship of the proletariat expressed its political meaning in content if not yet in name.

"Real, Practical Emancipation"

Marx's first articles in the *Rheinische Zeitung* of 1842 were conventional Hegelian defenses of freedom of the press and plebian wood-gathering against both the arbitrariness of Prussian bureaucrats and the greed of local landowners. Censorship makes the search for the common good impossible, he announced, because it holds the truth hostage to the will of a single official who cannot help but be partial in his understanding. The rational comprehension of the public interest is paralyzed in such conditions and in time the state is bound to become as powerful and destructive a source of disorder as the civil society whose incoherence Hegel had hoped it could overcome. Accidental social "position" will come to replace "character" or "science" in applying the law, and bureaucratic regulations will become the weapon of "one party against another" instead of serving as "a law of the state promulgated for its citizens."[1] Operating well within the boundaries of middle-class radicalism, the young Marx began moving toward a break with "purely political" matters almost as soon as he came in contact with the Prussian state.

No matter how abstract they sounded, his articles were bound to attract the attention of the censors. The authorities' hostile reaction to commentaries which Marx had naively assumed were "correct" simply because they told the truth forced him to confront the possibility that the bureaucracy might not be the objective guardian of the public good he had hoped. It soon became clear that the state's partiality enabled the powerful to strengthen themselves even further by transforming their feudal privileges into modern rights. The customary practices of the poor had never been recognized in legislation and thus appeared as accidental and revocable concessions instead of legally sanctioned and enforceable rights.[2] By the fall of 1842 Marx was opposing private property to the informal and time-honored customs of the poor and was beginning to suggest that there might be a contradiction between the rights of the propertied few and the interests of the propertyless many.[3] His democratic orientation forced him to the limits of Hegel's theory of the state almost as soon as he turned his attention to the real world.

Like Marx, Engels turned away from Hegel because of his early confrontation with real social conditions. He identified the "thirst for profit" as a major obstacle to democracy at the very beginning of his journalistic career, and some of the articles on England which he submitted to the *Rheinische Zeitung* exposed the differences between the formal promises of political democracy and the realities of social privilege.[4] "Is the much-vaunted English freedom anything but the purely formal right to act or not to act, as one sees fit, within the existing legal limits?" he asked. "Is not the House of Commons a corporation alien to the people, elected by means of wholesale bribery? Does not Parliament continually trample underfoot the will of the people? Has public opinion on general questions the slightest influence on the government?"[5] He described Chartism as the country's most democratic force precisely because it was the political representative of the working class and would therefore be driven to extend freedom and equality into society.[6]

Even as Engels showed an appreciation for the political influence of social classes sooner than Marx, both men's early orientation toward social matters was leading them away from Hegel's claim that a study of the state is the path to the comprehension of human freedom. Their independent observations of the actual workings of Prussian officialdom and of English politics led them to conclude that the state's partisanship rendered obsolete Hegel's hope that freedom would be guaranteed by an objective and public-spirited bureaucracy. Their growing suspicion that the state did not work as Hegel had said it did led them to reevaluate the relationship between it and civil society and to reformulate the political theory with which they were familiar.

Hegel thought that the modern network of market relations served to strengthen the private and acquisitive nature of what nineteenth-century thinkers were fond of calling "civil society." It had been dominated by the state in ancient Israel and Greece, where a variety of political restrictions had protected the slave owners from the potentially dangerous consequences of too much social inequality. Society had been tied up with the state in feudalism as well, for social estates had direct political consequences and private rights had been fused with a public power whose express purpose was to defend the aristocracy's privileges.

For Hegel the emergence of separate social and political spheres was one of the French Revolution's distinctive contributions to modern life. It made possible the recovery of an autonomous political realm because it distinguished private rights and a public sphere which were juridically, if not socially, separate. The unitary sovereign public authority which had emerged would be able to organize a society whose foundation in competitive private acquisitiveness always threatened to dissolve into a Hobbesian universal chaos. Hegel's statism, which most German political theorists of the period shared, was a response to the anarchy of the marketplace and represented his attempt to solve the nineteenth century's "social question."

Marx shared Hegel's desire to mitigate civil society's chaotic destructiveness; his crucial step was to wonder whether the state could do the job which

Hegel had assigned it. His confrontation with the Prussian bureaucracy had raised the possibility that the state was a false universal and that it was the network of material interests centered in property which shaped politics rather than the other way around. The differentiation of the state from society and the development of distinct public and private spheres had led Hegel to regard the state as the arena of man's freedom. Marx's developing materialism led him to examine the abstract equality of the modern state in light of actual social conditions and find it illusory.

His thinking was based on Hegel's analysis of the way religion, craft, residence, property, and the like had been emptied of formal political meaning and become characteristics of private individuals. In place of the formal particularism and open discrimination of feudalism, the modern state had developed on the basis of what appeared to be common to all members of society. The acquisitive civil society of the market, whose principle is "*enjoyment* and the *capacity to enjoy*," became the home of the "bourgeois" as the state became the home of the "*citoyen.*"[7] But the bourgeois claim that one's private desires have no direct political bearing can never be anything more than an abstraction. Driving them out of the public sphere may free the state from society, but it simultaneously liberates society from the state. If public affairs are no longer formally determined by religion or property, then by the same token religion and property are free to develop independently of political restrictions. Their hold over man is not weakened by their formal separation from politics; quite to the contrary, emptying them of formal political content has strengthened them. "The emancipation of the state from religion is not the emancipation of the real man from religion," observed Marx as he explained that the American separation of church from state was the indispensable condition for the citizenry's substantive and unprecedented subordination to religion.[8] Since property, religion, and other "private" matters are now responsible to nothing outside the mechanism of the market and the conscience of the individual, modern life opposes the imaginary universality of the citizen in the state to the real individuality of the individual in civil society. Formal political equality may have been a step forward compared to feudal irrationality and prejudice, but in market conditions it both masks and is denied by real social inequality. The gap between its promise and social reality is reflected in modern religious life, for if "it is an historical advance which has transformed the *political estates* into *social estates*, so that, just as the Christians are equal in heaven, but unequal on earth, so the individual members of the nation are *equal* in the heaven of their political world, but unequal in the earthly existence of *society.*"[9] The real domination of bourgeois society over its state works through and because of its formal separation from modern politics.

Classical liberalism's "rights of man" were the pure ideological expression of the market's domination, and Marx's important criticism of the limits of political emancipation developed as a direct attack on rights-based conceptions of democracy. Man in civil society is private, self-regarding, egoistic man; his rights guarantee his ability to pursue his self-interest apart from, and in opposition to, all the other members of civil society, now considered only as potential enemies. Rights presuppose conflict and antagonism; they assume that the selfish and acquisitive individual needs protection from other, equally predatory individuals; they define the limits of cooperation because they are based upon competition, and their superficial universality masks society's real antagonism. Such rights receive their fullest expression in bourgeois conceptions of "liberty," whose foundation is the antisocial loneliness of the market. "The right of man to liberty is based not on the association of man with man, but on the separation of man from man. It is the *right* of this separation, the right of the *restricted* individual, withdrawn into himself."[10] The independence and domination of bourgeois society mean that "the *state* can free itself from a restriction without man being *really* free from this restriction, that the state can be a free *state* without man being a *free man*."[11] "Political emancipation" can do no more than remove the formal limits to civil society's egoism, and its "liberty" can do no more than guarantee to each individual the right to pursue his own self-interest in equal and "fair" competition with other individuals. It helps dissolve civil society into a mass of independent and antagonistic atoms who have no relationship with one another apart from their mutual pursuit of self-interest and whose unending competition is loosely regulated by the law and the market. "Political emancipation is the reduction of man, on the one hand, to a member of civil society, to an *egoistic, independent* individual and, on the other hand, to a *citoyen*, a juridical person."[12] The man of civil society is immediate, concrete, real; the citizen of the state is formal, abstract, allegorical. Formal equality in market conditions ensures an inequality founded on private self-advancement. "Hence man was not freed from religion, he received religious freedom. He was not freed from property, he received freedom of property. He was not freed from the egoism of business, he received freedom to engage in business."[13] The "rights of man" culminate in an individually held private property and express the irreducibly antagonistic character of modern social life:

> The practical application of man's right to liberty is man's right to *private property*.
> The right of man to private property is, therefore, the right to enjoy one's property and to dispose of it at one's discretion, without regard to other men, independently of society, the right of self-interest. This individual liberty and its application form the real basis of civil society. It makes every man see in other men not the *realization* of his own freedom, but the *barrier* to it.[14]

Marx had been forced to reevaluate Hegel's theory of the state in light of the real relationship between Rhenish landlords and Prussian censors. Engels, living in England and contributing articles about politics and economics to the German democratic press, came to similar conclusions about the limits of "merely political" emancipation. As great a step forward as formal political democracy was, more was needed. If "the origin of social reforms, in France, is a political one," then "it is found, that democracy cannot give real equality, and therefore the communist scheme is called to its aid."[15] He soon came to the familiar position that only the abolition of private property could give substance to the "political" revolution's pretensions about equality and democracy, a view whose wide currency on the Left helps explain why Engels came to it independently of and simultaneously with Marx. "Real" liberty and "real" equality demand social and political transformations so extensive as to be incompatible with the foundations of contemporary society:

> The French Revolution was the rise of democracy in Europe. Democracy is, as I take all forms of government to be, a contradiction in itself, an untruth, nothing but hypocrisy (ideology, as we Germans call it), at the bottom. Political liberty is sham-liberty, the worst possible slavery; the appearance of liberty and therefore the reality of servitude. Political equality is the same; therefore democracy, as well as every other form of government, must ultimately break to pieces; hypocrisy cannot subsist, the contradiction hidden in it must come out; we must either have a regular slavery—that is, an undisguised despotism, or real liberty and real equality—that is, Communism. Both these consequences were brought out in the French Revolution; Napoleon established the first, and Babeuf the second.[16]

Engels's further reports described how egoism corrupted democracy, how venality, hucksterism, and greed negated the pretensions of "free" English elections, how property ruled the country, converted all the formal freedoms of the political sphere into weapons of the rich, and sullied the democracy of even the House of Commons.[17] At the same time, this scion of a conservative Barmen factory owner reported that everything alive and decent in English public life drew its strength from the working class, whose democratic character he now described as a direct function of its property-lessness.[18] The French Revolution's political form had taken shape in opposition to the monarchy and feudalism, but the working-class democracy of which Engels was beginning to speak would have the "middle class and property" as its antitheses. His criticism of political democracy, reached independently of Marx and articulated just before their first collaboration in *The Holy Family* of 1844, was the same as that of his future partner: it did not go far enough and strengthened the very market conditions whose abolition was now the point. What Engels was now calling "socialism" is what Marx had been calling "human emancipation," and both formulations anticipated a political theory which could help provide solutions to social questions:

> But democracy by itself is not capable of curing political ills. Democratic equality is a chimera, the fight of the poor against the rich cannot be fought out on a basis of democracy or even of politics as a whole. This step is thus only a transition, the last purely political remedy which has still to be tried and from which a new element is bound to develop at once, a principle transcending everything of a political nature.
> This principle is the principle of socialism.[19]

"The revolution will be social, not political," announced Engels as he echoed Marx's abandonment of Hegel.[20] It would be considerably broader and deeper than the relatively limited earlier upheavals, for "the only true revolution is a social revolution, to which political and philosophical revolution must lead."[21] Working independently of each other, both men concluded that what they had been calling the "communist revolution" would be unique in its comprehensiveness. Such a view was common enough on the European Left, but it was important that in repudiating both the inflated claims of "merely political" revolutions and the statism of the Hegelians and the revolutionary Jacobins, Marx and Engels also avoided the temptation to reject politics altogether. Driven forward by their separate goals of "human emancipation" and "social revolution," they knew that more was required than changes in politics or religiosity. "*Political* emancipation is, of course, a big step forward. True, it is not the final form of human emancipation in general, but it is the final form of human emancipation *within* the hitherto existing world order. It goes without saying that we are speaking here of real, practical emancipation.[22] As important as it was, political democracy had failed to eliminate inequality because it had not touched the social foundations of the market. Private property was the heart of the problem, and it was now up to Marx and Engels to identify the social force capable of abolishing it and bring "the hitherto existing world order" to a close.

Property and the Proletariat

Neither their criticisms of "merely political" revolutions nor their attacks on private property distinguished Marx and Engels from their contemporaries. It was their identification of the proletariat as the agent of social transformation which marked their communism. Having discovered that Hegel's bureaucracy could not be the "universal class," Marx observed that earlier revolutions had been led by a section of the population whose social position made it a general standard against which all other situations could be measured. The bourgeoisie had led the struggle against feudalism because its demands had incorporated the minimal conditions within which the other antifeudal classes could be emancipated. In a similar vein, Hegel's faith in the bureaucracy expressed his hope that its nonclass objectivity would make possible the preservation of the status quo. But the need to break with the entire existing order of private property signified to Marx that the emancipatory class of capitalist society will be able to lead because of its *differences* with the foundations of this society. The proletariat represented the *negation* of the status quo, and what made it so different from the rest of official society had suddenly become critical:

> In the formation of a class with *radical* chains, a class of civil society which is not a class of civil society, an estate which is the dissolution of all estates, a sphere which has a universal character by its universal suffering and claims no *particular right* because no *particular wrong* but *wrong generally* is perpetrated against it; which can no longer invoke a *historical* but only a *human* title; which does not stand in any one-sided antithesis to the consequences but in an all-round antithesis to the premises of the German state; a sphere, finally, which cannot emancipate itself without emancipating itself from all other spheres of society and thereby emancipating all other spheres of society, which, in a word, is the *complete loss* of man and hence can win itself only through the *complete rewinning of man*. This entire dissolution of society as a particular estate is the *proletariat.*[23]

The decisive material root of contemporary society is private property, and its propertylessness is what made the proletariat Marx's revolutionary class. "By proclaiming the *dissolution of the hitherto existing world order* the proletariat merely states the *secret of its own existence*, for it is in fact the dissolution of that world order. By demanding the *negation of private property*, the proletariat merely raises to the rank of a *principle* of *society* what society has made the principle of the *proletariat*, what, without its own cooperation, is already incorporated in it as the negative result of society."[24] The proletariat's ability to represent the majority is a function not of its size but of its objective social position, a position defined above all by its lack of property in the means of production.

Marx and Engels decisively changed European socialism's orientation toward the modern working class. Earlier leftists had tended to see it as the hardest working, most numerous, or most exploited part of the laboring population. For Marx and Engels it was special because it had no stake in and thus no reason to preserve the existing world order. It was cut off from the very civil society which its labor made possible. The bourgeoisie had been able to represent the general interest in its own struggles against the medieval aristocracy, but its continuing attachment to property now made it an obstacle to further social change. Bourgeois political revolutions cannot help but "leave the pillars of the house standing" even if they had once been important steps on the road to "human emancipation."

If the proletarian is "the man who, being without capital and rent, lives purely by labor," then capital is "private property in the products of other men's labor."[25] The proletarian must work because he does not own and thus has no control over what he produces, and this is the "general wrong" which civil society perpetrates against him. It is a "social" wrong because it results from a definite system of social production, and it can be overcome only by a change in that system. Marx's understanding of private property would evolve as he devoted more attention to economic matters, but for the moment he had identified the abolition of private property as the first step in the "complete rewinning of man." The social revolution's generality and depth can begin to reintegrate human affairs; "the emancipation of the workers contains universal human emancipation—and it contains this, because the whole of human servitude is involved in the relation of the worker to production, and all relations of servitude are but modifications and consequences of this relation."[26] Human emancipation requires the abolition of private property in the means of production. Freedom demands communism.

Classes and Society

The uniquely radical character of the social revolution whose outlines Marx had begun to sketch came from its break with a history which had moved within the boundaries of private property for a long time. A propertyless proletariat now lived at the heart of modern life, and only it could undertake the social appropriation of modern productive forces and precipitate a break with existing notions of justice, freedom, and equality.[27] As characteristic of the bourgeois order as conceptions of honor and loyalty had been to feudalism, they expressed the entirely legal "right" of the propertied to appropriate the products of others' labor. Bourgeois "freedom" had now become the issue. Indeed, "communists will certainly carry out 'robbery' of what the bourgeois regards as 'personal,' " for an attack on bourgeois property necessitates a corresponding attack on the political conceptions which accompany and reinforce it.[28] "The modern state, the rule of the bourgeoisie, is based on *freedom of labor*. . . . [F]reedom of labor is free competition of the workers among themselves. . . . Labor is free in all civilized countries; it is not a matter of freeing labor but of abolishing it."[29] Human emancipation requires a break with the entire body of existing conceptions of justice, freedom, and equality.

The social appropriation and use of the forces of production will finally make possible the satisfaction of man's needs and establish the material condition of "real" equality. "Voluntarily productive activity is the highest enjoyment known to us," said the young Engels in a presentiment of his and Marx's mature theory, "and its conscious organization and regulation are conditions of human freedom."[30] It was their orientation toward the social satisfaction of human needs which made their communism so intrinsically revolutionary. It "differs from all previous movements in that it overthrows the basis of all earlier relations of production and intercourse, and for the first time consciously treats all naturally evolved premises as the creations of hitherto existing men, strips them of their natural character and subjugates them to the power of united individuals."[31]

Capitalism's free market acts to divide people on the basis of the needs they share. Abolishing its property and freedom means that, "since production is no longer in the hands of private producers but in those of the community and its administrative bodies, it is a trifling matter *to regulate production according to need*."[32] This viewpoint would reappear later on, but for the moment the abolition of property gave an entirely new content to equality, understood now as more than formal equality before the law or equality of opportunity because it spoke to the one thing which all people, *as people*, share:

> But one of the most vital principles of communism, a principle which distinguishes it from all reactionary socialism, is its empirical view, based on a knowledge of man's nature, that differences of *brain* and of intellectual ability do not imply any differences in the nature of the *stomach* and of physical *needs*, therefore the false tenet, based upon existing circumstances, "to each according to his abilities" must be changed, insofar as it relates to enjoyment in the narrowest sense, into the tenet, "to each according to his need"; in other words, a *different form* of activity, of labor, does not justify *inequality*, confers no privileges in respect of possession and enjoyment.[33]

If communism can unite people on the basis of their needs, its abolition of property will make possible the development of man's productive forces because their social nature will be frankly recognized as a condition of emancipation. The conscious social satisfaction of needs will replace the solitary pursuit of self-interest as the motivation for productive activity, the individual's ties with others will become truly cooperative and fully moral in nature, and social antagonism will end as scarcity yields to abundance and classes disappear. People will no longer experience each other as obstacles and problems because their all-round satisfaction will give a fully human purpose to what had been blind and unconscious social activity. This is what

Engels had in mind when he said that to organize communist equality is "to do away with all class antagonisms."[34]

The proletariat is now the universal class because, in moving against bourgeois private property, it will be compelled to move against the division of society into classes *as such* with all that this implies. "The positive transcendence of *private property*, as the appropriation of *human* life, is therefore the positive transcendence of all estrangement—that is to say, the return of man from religion, family, state, etc., to his *human*, i.e., *social*, existence."[35] The criticism of Hegel's state had become the criticism of the bourgeoisie's society, "merely political" democracy had been broadened to social democracy, and superficial political revolution had yielded to radical social transformation. This is what Marx's Tenth Thesis on Feuerbach meant when it observed that "the standpoint of the old materialism is '*civil*' society; the standpoint of the new is *human* society, or associated humanity."[36] A classless society is the only environment in which the real human emancipation of which he and Engels had been speaking can be grounded, and the emancipation of the proletariat begins the most radical, profound, and difficult revolution in human history:

> The condition for the emancipation of the working class is the abolition of all classes, just as the condition for the emancipation of the third estate, of the bourgeois order, was the abolition of all estates and all orders. The working class, in the course of its development, will substitute for the old civil society an association which will exclude classes and their antagonism, and there will be no more political power properly so-called, since political power is precisely the official expression of antagonism in civil society.[37]

Marx and Engels were certainly not the first to commit themselves to the fight for a social democracy understood as a classless society. As ancient a root of plebian protest as were such protests themselves, it had stood at the center of such diverse rebellions as those of the Anabaptists and Thomas Munzer in Germany, the Levellers and Diggers in England, and Babeuf and Hébert in France. By the middle of the nineteenth century it had become a distinctive feature of the modern working class and was shared to some extent by other elements of the laboring poor as well. It differentiated proletarian and petty-bourgeois conceptions of democracy from those of the bourgeoisie proper because it signaled a willingness to interfere with existing property relations. It stood to reason that the more Marx and Engels developed their commitment to social equality defined as the full and conscious satisfaction of human needs, the more attention they would pay to the propertyless workers.

It was just as clear that the proletarian goal of social equality contained within it the commitment to a classless society. Bourgeois and petty bourgeois ideologists could go no further than to speak of equality before the law and of opportunity, the rights of man, freedom, justice, and the like because their attachment to property limited them to proposing adjustments in the existing social structure. Marx and Engels's orientation toward social equality was so threatening because it was a demand for the abolition of classes *as such*, not just for the adjustment of relations between them. There was no way the structure of any class society could be reconciled with the social equality of which they were beginning to speak.

To say that the "ultimate result" of the communist movement is the abolition of classes is to summarize the Marxist theory of social revolution and to distinguish it from both the bourgeoisie's interest in preserving the existing class structure and from the petty bourgeoisie's desire to adjust it. Marx and Engels had come to understand the role of the proletariat through their criticism of Hegel's statism and their resulting turn toward a theory of social transformation. But the criticism of "merely political" revolutions did not lead to the abandonment of all political activity, and the seizure of political power by the organized working class would emerge as the immediate goal of the communist and labor movements. It would make possible the transformation of society as a whole, the abolition of classes and their consequent antagonism, and ultimately the overcoming of politics altogether. The use of proletarian state power "against" the class state's social foundations stands in an indissoluble and contradictory relationship to the goal of social transformation, and we will be able to understand the complex relationship between politics and economics in Marxist revolutionary theory only if we keep the ultimate goals and the historical uniqueness of the proletarian revolution at the center of our understanding. Just as the preservation of its private property conditioned the democratic content of the bourgeoisie's liberalism and the petty bourgeoisie's democracy, so the social transformations which the proletariat would be compelled to initiate would demand an unprecedentedly powerful and radical class democracy of its own. Marxism's political theory is coherent only if it is evaluated from the standpoint of a society without classes and the equality of human needs.

NOTES

1. Karl Marx, "Comments on the Latest Prussian Censorship Instructions," Karl Marx and Frederick Engels, *Collected Works* (New York: Progress Publishers, 1975–   ), 1:109, 120, 131. Unless otherwise noted, all references from Marx and Engels will be to the *Collected Works*.

2. Karl Marx, "Debates on the Law on Thefts of Wood," 1:230, 272.

3. *Ibid.*, 230–32.

4. Frederick Engels, "An Outing to Bremerhaven," 2:112.
5. Engels, "The Internal Crisis," 2:371.
6. Engels, "The Position of the Political Parties," 2:375.
7. Marx, "Contribution to the Critique of Hegel's Philosophy of Law," 3:81.
8. "On the Jewish Question," 3:160.
9. Marx, "Contribution to the Critique of Hegel's Philosophy of Law," 3:79.
10. "On the Jewish Question," 3:163.
11. *Ibid.*, 152.
12. *Ibid.*, 168.
13. *Ibid.*, 167.
14. *Ibid.*, 162–63.
15. Engels, "Progress of Social Reform on the Continent," 3:397.
16. *Ibid.*, 393.
17. "The Condition of England," 3:497, 504ff.
18. *Ibid.*, 487.
19. *Ibid.*, 513.
20. "The Internal Crisis," 2:374.
21. "The Condition of England," 3:469.
22. Marx, "On the Jewish Question," 3:155.
23. "Contribution to the Critique of Hegel's Philosophy of Law. Introduction," 3:186.
24. *Ibid.*
25. Marx, "Economic and Philosophic Manuscripts of 1844," 3:241, 246.
26. *Ibid.*, 280.
27. Marx and Engels, "The German Ideology," 5:438–39.
28. *Ibid.*, 208.
29. *Ibid.*, 205.
30. Engels, "The Condition of the Working Class in England," 4:415.
31. "The German Ideology," 5:81.
32. Engels, "Speeches at Elberfeld," 4:246.
33. "The German Ideology," 5:527.
34. "The Condition of the Working Class in England," 4:581–82.
35. "Contribution to the Critique of Hegel's Philosophy of Law. Introduction," 3:297.
36. "Theses on Feuerbach," 5:8.
37. Marx, "The Poverty of Philosophy," 6:212.

Chapter 2

"Immediate Aim"

Marx and Engels's theoretical turn toward communism had been precipitated by their criticism of private property, the abolition of which they now considered necessary for "human emancipation." With no stake in the existing order, the propertyless proletariat was the only class capable of leading a social transformation of unparalleled scope and complexity. It was precisely the comprehensiveness of the workers' social revolution which led to the seemingly paradoxical emphasis on political affairs which came to characterize modern communism. Marx and Engels's assertion that the social revolution's first step would have to be the seizure of state power is what distinguished their work from that of their more mechanically nonpolitical radical contemporaries. George Plekhanov and Lenin continued Marx and Engels's struggle for the leading role of politics during the formative years of Russian Social-Democracy and developed a democratic theory which would be built on, rather than stand against, a powerful and active proletarian state. A comprehensive theory of politics in the service of social revolution yielded a conception of democracy which was considerably broader than the bourgeoisie's self-interested emphasis on "merely political" rights, freedom, and privacy.

"The Active, Conscious and Official Expression"

Marx and Engels had become communists as they had become materialists, and their discovery that the state was shaped by civil society had led them to conclude that a "merely political" revolution would be too weak to uproot the economic foundations of strife and antagonism in modern life. Marx called their approach a "radical" one because it drove them to "get to the root of things" and develop an integrated theory of social and political revolution. Concentrating on economic transformation in the absence of politics might have led them to little more than a narrow and eclectic reformism, but the Jacobin tendency to think of emancipation in exclusively political terms would come to rest in an acceptance of the status quo as well. The problem was that "the mightier the state, and the *more political* therefore a country is, the less it is inclined to grasp the *general* principle of *social* maladies and to seek their bases in the *principle of the state*, hence in the *present structure* of society, the active, conscious and official expression of which is the state."[1] It would be necessary to overturn existing property relations, but it remained to establish the role of political affairs in a proletarian revolution whose *raison d'être* was social transformation.

Throughout their careers Marx and Engels were animated by the classical view that politics is the broadest plane on which public affairs are conducted and is simultaneously the most concentrated expression of social life. It was the breadth of the political struggle which, when applied to social transformation, gave their politics a striking power and transformative force which had been lacking in the odd assortment of socialist sects which flourished for a time before the Revolution of 1848 swept them away. Paradoxically, it was the social root of the proletariat's demands which prompted them to assign a central role to politics in the communist revolution. The young Engels had seen that the English workers themselves regarded politics as an agent of social transformation and observed:

> Therein lies the difference between Chartist democracy and all previous political bourgeois democracy. Chartism is of an essentially social nature, a class movement. The "Six Points" which for the Radical bourgeois are the beginning and end of the matter, which are meant, at the utmost, to call forth certain further reforms of the Constitution, are for the proletarian a rare means to further ends. "Political power our means, social happiness our end", is now the clearly formulated war-cry of the Chartists.[2]

Marx and Engels's early development was driven by more than their rejection of Hegel's idealism. A variety of nonpolitical socialist doctrines had sprung up as critics of capitalism began to pay attention to economic matters, and their early work was directed as much against the followers of Owen,

Fourier, Saint-Simon, the "true socialists," and the "Young Hegelians" as against the hyperpolitics of the Jacobins and the Blanquists. By rejecting the extremes of a total abstention from political activity and an exclusive reliance on it, they developed Marx's early claim that politics is the "only" path by which philosophy can become truth by linking it to the fundamental struggle against the division of society into classes.[3] Overcoming the antagonisms of class society requires a revolution whose thoroughness moves it inexorably in the direction of politics:

> Out of this very contradiction between the particular and the common interests, the common interest assumes an independent form as the *state*, which is divorced from the real individual and collective interests, and at the same time as an illusory community, always based, however, on the real ties existing in every family agglomeration and tribal conglomeration—such as flesh and blood, language, division of labor on a larger scale, and other interests—and especially, as we shall show later, on the classes, already implied by the division of labor, which in every such mass of men separate out, and one of which dominates all the others. It follows from all this that all struggles within the state, the struggle between democracy, aristocracy and monarchy, the struggle for the franchise, etc., etc., are merely the illusory form—altogether the general interest is the illusory form of common interests—in which the real struggles of the different classes are fought out among one another. . . . Further, it follows that every class which is aiming at domination, even when its domination, as is the case with the proletariat, leads to the abolition of the old form of society in its entirety and of domination in general, must first conquer political power in order to represent its interest as the general interest, which in the first moment it is forced to do.[4]

The bourgeoisie had been the first modern class whose material interests were sufficiently comprehensive and complex to require a modern political apparatus for their protection.[5] Its roots might lie in the property relations of civil society, but when it acted *as a class* it did so in the political arena. Only there could it give its particular class rule a general expression through legislation and law. Its development from the welter of medieval estates called the modern state into being because it needed to defend its home market against foreign rivals and its property against domestic enemies. The first class in modern history to organize itself on a national level, the bourgeoisie developed the nation-state as its characteristic instrument of political organization and domination:

> By the mere fact that it is a *class* and no longer an *estate*, the bourgeoisie is forced to organize itself no longer locally, but nationally, and to give a general form to its average interests. Through the emancipation of private property

from the community, the state has become a separate entity, alongside and outside civil society; but it is nothing more than the form of organization which the bourgeois are compelled to adopt, both for internal and external purposes, for the mutual guarantee of their property and interests. The independence of the state is only found nowadays in those countries where the estates have not yet completely developed into classes, where the estates, done away with in more advanced countries, will play a part and there exists a mixture, where consequently no section of the population can achieve dominance over the others. . . . Since the state is the form in which the individuals of a ruling class assert their common interests, and in which the whole civil society of an epoch is epitomized, it follows that all common institutions are set up with the help of the state and are given a political form.[6]

It is precisely because it must rule *as a class* that the bourgeoisie's political activity tends to be so general and comprehensive. This is what distinguishes it from the other property-owning strata engendered by the market relations of capitalist society. The petty bourgeoisie, for example, springs up in conditions of local trade and relatively restricted conditions of production and exchange. This is why it generally goes no further than to demand local self-government and economic decentralization. For the most part it is content to try to live in peace alongside other groupings and its spokesmen tend to develop political conceptions of shared power and local autonomy. But the bourgeoisie proper develops in conditions of general international trade and needs a political apparatus to organize and protect its conditions of appropriation in an unstable and competitive civil society. Its activity is shaped by the market relations which simultaneously sustain and threaten it, and the state reflects its need to forcibly establish and maintain its exclusive class political domination:

> In short, if the petty bourgeois can content himself with opposing to the nobility and the bureaucracy his inert weight, with securing for himself influence on the official power through his *vis inertiae*, the bourgeois cannot do this. He must make his class dominant, his interests crucial, in legislation, administration, justice, taxation and foreign policy. The bourgeoisie must develop itself to the full, daily expand its capital, daily reduce the production costs of its commodities, daily expand its trade connections and markets, daily improve its communications, *in order not to be ruined*. The competition on the world market compels it to do so. And to be able to develop freely and to the full, what it requires is precisely political dominance, the subordination of all other interests to its own.[7]

Marx and Engels's early orientation toward politics informed their work throughout their lives and underlay much of their ongoing struggles with the likes of Proudhon, Bakunin, and Lassalle. Similarly, the early years of Russian Social-Democracy were marked by its intense theoretical struggle against a variety of nonpolitical radicalisms. Populism, the most influential of these trends, was based on the economic grievances and political disorgaanization of the enormous peasantry, and it fell to George Plekhanov to reaffirm the orthodox Marxist position that the social character of the revolution's ultimate goals could be immediately expressed only in political terms. His successful and largely theoretical struggle for a political socialism was instrumental in establishing Marxism as the dominant trend on the Russian Left.

Like Marx, Engels, and Plekhanov, Lenin was driven to assert the centrality of politics against early tendencies to deny its importance altogether. Like them, he anticipated that the workers' social struggle would be expressed politically because the autocracy's expected assaults would leave them no choice but to defend the interests of the entire laboring population as they defended their own. The workers' political movement might be self-interested in the short run but would have to take all other classes and strata of the population into account. "Social-Democracy," Lenin said, "leads the struggle of the working class, not only for better terms for the sale of labor-power, but for the abolition of the social system that compels the propertyless to sell themselves to the rich. Social-Democracy represents the working class, not in its relation to a given group of employers alone, but in its relation to all classes of modern society and to the state as an organized political force."[8]

The fight Lenin was waging within the embryonic Russian communist movement was not for politics as such; it was for revolutionary Social-Democratic politics, and this struggle is what generated his orthodox orientation toward the capture and use of state power for the purpose of social transformation. His classic definition of proletarian class-consciousness is noteworthy because of its complexity and sweep. The breadth and depth of the social revolution against property requires an extraordinarily comprehensive understanding which lies at the heart of Marxism's very classical understanding of politics:

> Working-class consciousness cannot be genuine political consciousness unless the workers are trained to respond to *all* cases of tyranny, violence, and abuse, no matter *what* class is affected—unless they are trained, moreover, to respond from a Social-Democratic point of view and no other. The consciousness of the working masses cannot be genuine class-consciousness, unless the workers learn, from concrete, and above all from topical, political facts and events to observe *every* other social class in *all* the manifestations of its intellectual, ethical, and political life, unless they learn to apply in practice the materialist analysis and the materialist estimate of *all* aspects of the life and activity of

all classes, strata, and groups of the population. Those who concentrate the attention, observation, and consciousness of the working class exclusively, or even mainly, upon itself are not Social-Democrats, for the self-knowledge of the working class is indissolubly bound up, not only with a fully clear theoretical understanding—or rather not so much with the theoretical, as with the practical, understanding—of the relationships between *all* the various classes of modern society, acquired through the experience of political life.[9]

It was Lenin's fusion of different aspects of the workers' movement into a comprehensive revolutionary theory which brought the issue of political power to the center of the stage. Only as it raises general issues and openly contests for leadership of the entire social order can the proletariat become a class "for itself."[10] It becomes a class as, and to the extent that, it becomes what *The Communist Manifesto* called a "political party" able to concentrate and express its social goals in political terms. Politics does not leave out, but makes possible, the resolution of the workers' social struggle because it shapes the general environment within which other problems can be addressed:

We are all agreed that our task is that of the organization of the proletarian class struggle. But what is this class struggle? When the workers of a single factory or of a single branch of industry engage in struggle against their employer or employers, is this class struggle? No, this is only a weak embryo of it. The struggle of the workers becomes a class struggle only when all the foremost representatives of the entire working class of the whole country are conscious of themselves as a single working class and launch a struggle that is directed, not against individual employers, but against the *entire class* of capitalists and against the government that supports that class. Only when the individual worker realizes that he is a member of the entire working class, only when he recognizes the fact that his petty day-to-day struggle against individual employers and individual government figures is a struggle against the entire bourgeoisie and the entire government, does his struggle become a political struggle. "Every class struggle is a political struggle"—these famous words of Marx are not to be understood to mean that any struggle of workers against employers must *always* be a political struggle. They must be understood to mean that the struggle of the workers against the capitalists inevitably *becomes* a political struggle *insofar as* it becomes a *class* struggle.[11]

There is nothing inherent in its social position which pushes the proletariat toward politics; it is the bourgeois state which does so by continually intervening on the side of capital. This forces the workers to combat the bourgeoisie on an increasingly broad and comprehensive plane until they are raising the most general social and political matters.[12] Like that of any class, the proletarian movement arises from the economic structure of civil society, but it speaks *as a class* when it speaks politically, and it speaks politically when it speaks for all the downtrodden. "The political movement of the working class will inevitably lead the workers to realize that their only salvation lies in socialism," Lenin declared. "On the other hand, socialism will become a force only when it becomes the aim of the *political* movement of the working *class*."[13] The bourgeoisie can be defeated economically only if it is first defeated politically, and this is why Marx and Engels made it clear that "the immediate aim of the Communists is the same as that of all the other proletarian parties: formation of the proletariat into a class, overthrow of the bourgeois supremacy, conquest of political power by the proletariat."[14] As important as it was to insist on the political character of the workers' "immediate aim," however, it was no less essential to be clear that political power was not an end in itself.

The Leading Role of Politics

Marx and Engels made it clear that *The Communist Manifesto*'s call for the abolition of existing property relations was not unique to the proletariat—after all, the bourgeoisie had demanded the same thing in its struggle against the feudal aristocracy. It was the demand for the abolition of *all* private property which set the proletarian revolution apart from its predecessors. The workers' initial demand for the abolition of specifically bourgeois property seemed simple. "But modern bourgeois property is the final and most complete expression of the system of producing and appropriating products, that is based on class antagonisms, on the exploitation of the many by the few. In this sense, the theory of the communists may be summed up in the single sentence: Abolition of private property."[15] The proletariat is the only class whose revolution must move beyond the replacement of one form of private property by another more highly developed form:

> All the preceding classes that got the upper hand, sought to fortify their already acquired status by subjecting society at large to their conditions of appropriation. The proletarians cannot become masters of the productive forces of society, except by abolishing their own previous mode of appropriation, and thereby also every other previous mode of appropriation. They have nothing of their own to fortify; their mission is to destroy all previous securities for, and insurance of, individual property.
>
> All previous historical movements were movements of minorities, or in the interest of minorities. The proletarian revolution is the self-conscious, independent movement of the immense majority, in the interest of the immense minority.

The proletariat, the lowest stratum of our present society, cannot stir, cannot raise itself up, without the whole superincumbent strata of official society being sprung into the air.[16]

Marx and Engels insisted that politics must be primary in the proletarian revolution because they defined its uniquely radical and democratic character as its inability to compromise with anything connected to private property. This is what distinguished it from its predecessors, which had broken out after the more or less finished forms of the bourgeois order had slowly grown within the structures of feudal society. Bourgeois property and bourgeois production had largely supplanted feudal property and feudal production prior to the outbreak of the "open" revolutionary assault on the feudal state. The basic task of the bourgeois revolution thus reduced itself to breaking the political supremacy of the aristocracy, a supremacy which had already been undermined by the lengthy crisis of feudal economy. Since the basic structures of bourgeois social relations were largely in place before political power passed to the bourgeoisie itself, the "open" political revolution did little more than adjust an obsolete superstructure to an already-transformed base. This is why Marx, Engels, and Lenin consistently described bourgeois revolutions as the last in a series of political transformations which replaced one form of private property in the means of production with another, more highly developed, form. Just as slave property had to be sacrificed in order to guarantee feudal property, so feudal property had yielded to bourgeois property. The very real incompatibility between them notwithstanding, their common root in private ownership explains why feudalism grew out of slavery and why capitalism had its material and social roots in the feudal order.

But it is because the finished forms of the socialist order are *absent* from bourgeois society and *cannot* be generated within the boundaries of private property that the tasks and historical rhythm of the socialist revolution differ so markedly from those of its predecessors. The social relations of a classless society can develop only as part of the abolition of private ownership of the means of production; they cannot and do not grow spontaneously within bourgeois society. The bourgeoisie's seizure of political power ended the transformation of feudalism and marked its ascendancy to the position of sole ruling class, but its proletarian counterpart is the indispensable precondition of a socialist revolution which begins *before the social and material conditions for its completion are in place*. This is why Marx and Engels knew that the workers' revolution would become more radical even after its apparent "victory":

... the first step in the revolution by the working class, is to raise the proletariat to the position of ruling class, to win the battle of democracy.

The working class will use its political supremacy to wrest, by degrees, all capital from the bourgeoisie, to centralize all instruments of production in the hands of the State, i.e., of the proletariat organized as the ruling class; and to increase the total of productive forces as rapidly as possible.

Of course, in the beginning, this cannot be effected except by means of despotic inroads on the rights of property, and on the conditions of bourgeois production; by means of measures, therefore, which appear economically insufficient and untenable, but which, in the course of the movement, outstrip themselves, necessitate further inroads upon the old social order, and are unavoidable as a means of entirely revolutionizing the mode of production.[17]

Marx and Engels offer different accounts of the bourgeois and the proletarian revolutions, and these differences have very important implications. Capitalism developed as the result of a long and "natural" transformation of feudalism, but a radical break in continuity separates it from communism. The leading role of politics distinguishes Marxism's theory of socialist revolution from its description of the bourgeoisie's rise to supremacy.[18] Since it was already rooted in a definite system of social production and appropriation, the bourgeoisie developed a set of theories which gave as much play as possible to the operations of the market and assigned to the political sphere the task of safeguarding the integrity of civil society. This tendency was reinforced by the aristocracy's use of its political power to obstruct the continued development of a market whose unfettered operations exposed it to ruin. This is why bourgeois political theory developed on the basis of a mistrust and suspicion of the effect that politics in general, and the state in particular, had on society; it was largely to free the private calculations of the market from public "interference" that such revolutions had been fought in the first place. That theories of weak government accompanied most of them does not negate the often-dramatic interventions of the state in shaping capitalist relations of production.

The transition from private to public ownership of the means of production reverses the established relationship between political power and social structure. Because socialist relations of production cannot and do not develop spontaneously within the boundaries of capitalism, private ownership must be broken before social transformation can begin. Bourgeois conceptions of revolution and democracy developed as rights-based theories of weak government, suspicion of politics, and the conviction that the operations of the market were the surest guarantees of democracy, freedom, and equality. Marxist democratic theory, on the other hand, reserves a central role to a powerful and transformative political apparatus whose mission is to lead the attack on private property and the social relations which accompany it. The leading role assigned to an active political sphere means that the proletarian revolution begins with the seizure of political power precisely because it aims at the "abolition of the bourgeois relations of production, an abolition that can be effected only by a revolution."[19] The "ultimate results" of the workers' revolution are social in character but its "immediate goal" is a political one. This is what Marx was getting at when he tried to specify the role of political power in the work of constructing a new society. "Revolution in general—the *overthrow* of the existing power and *dissolution* of the old relationships—is a *political* act. But *socialism* cannot be realized without *revolution*. It needs this *political* act insofar as it needs *destruction* and *dissolution*. But where its *organizing activity* begins, where its *proper object*, its *soul*, comes to the fore—there socialism throws off the *political* cloak."[20] He would come to modify his suggestion that the political content of the revolution is exclusively expressed as the "destruction and dissolution" of the old, but for the moment it stood to reason that the historical uniqueness of the proletarian revolution would precipitate radically new ways of thinking:

> But whatever form they may have taken, one fact is common to all past ages, *viz.*, the exploitation of one part of society by another. No wonder, then, that the social consciousness of past ages, despite all the multiplicity and variety it displays, moves within certain common forms, or general ideas, which cannot completely vanish except with the total disappearance of class antagonisms.
>
> The communist revolution is the most radical rupture with traditional property relations; no wonder that its development involves the most radical rupture with traditional ideas.[21]

Nowhere would this expectation be revealed more dramatically than in the relationship between politics and society on the one hand and between the state and democracy on the other.

State and Society Redux

In a sense Marx, Engels, and Lenin had come full circle and ended up back with Hegel, for the abolition of classes is also the abolition of politics and the reabsorption of the state by society. Overcoming the antagonisms which accompany private property and necessitate the state makes possible the conscious reunion of the individual with his fellows and with the collectivity of which he is a part. Even if the proletarian revolution moves through politics and seems to have been made possible by state power, its ultimate aim is to abolish both by making them unnecessary, since "previous revolutions within the framework of division of labor were bound to lead to new political institutions; it follows then that the communist revolution, which removes the division of labor, ultimately abolishes political institutions" as well.[22] This use of state power "against" the state is only one of many deeply contradictory aspects of the theory of the dictatorship of the proletariat which would mark the later history of the Russian Revolution. Marx and Engels shared the socialist Left's hostility toward the state; they disagreed with most of their contemporaries in their assertion that it would disappear only if the workers held political power and used it in the construction of a new society. Just as the proletariat's class struggle must end in its own disappearance, so a socialist state's ultimate purpose is to make its own continued existence unnecessary. This contradictory view shaped Marx and Engels's understanding of the content and the difficulties of proletarian democracy:

> When, in the course of development, class distinctions have disappeared, and all production has been concentrated in the hands of a vast association of the whole nation, the public power will lose its political character. Political power, properly so called, is merely the organized power of one class for oppressing another. If the proletariat during its contest with the bourgeoisie is compelled, by the force of circumstances, to organize itself as a class, if, by means of a revolution, it makes itself the ruling class, and, as such, sweeps away by force the old conditions of production, then it will, along with these conditions, have swept away the conditions for the existence of class antagonisms and of classes generally, and will thereby have abolished its own supremacy as a class.
>
> In place of the old bourgeois society, with its classes and class antagonisms, we shall have an association, in which the free development of each is the condition for the free development of all.[23]

Marx and Engels's early investigations had shown that the division of society into classes depended upon the formal liberty and equality of the marketplace. This had led them to their criticisms of "merely political" democracy in social conditions which made it an instrument of inequality and misery. They were not the first commentators to note this, of course, but they were uniquely able to move past the Left's familiar denunciations of formal equality's shortcomings because they tied them to a theory of history and to their decisive orientation toward a free association of producers. "Gentlemen!" Marx exclaimed to the workers. "Do not be deluded by the abstract word Freedom! Whose freedom? Not the freedom of one individual in relation to another, but freedom of Capital to crush the worker. Why should you desire further to sanction unlimited competition with this idea of freedom, when the idea of freedom itself is only the product of a special condition based upon Free Competition?"[24] " 'Freedom' is a grand word," said Lenin in a different context, "but under the banner of freedom for industry the most predatory wars were waged, under the banner of freedom of labor, the working people were robbed."[25] If free competition is one of the secrets of the bourgeoisie's domination, it was fairly simple for him to conclude that the workers must abolish it, since "what distinguishes classes from one other is not legal privileges, but social conditions. . . . [C]onsequently, classes in modern society presuppose *legal equality*."[26]

When Marx, Engels, and Lenin asked the workers to answer the decisive and partisan question "for whom?" they knew that the proletarian understanding of "freedom" would be very different from that of the bourgeoisie. Their early struggles to understand the role of politics in the single class struggle of the workers were expressed as a fight for a politically revolutionary socialism whose goal was the democratization of the entire society. The integrative role of politics in fusing together different elements of the class struggle, the organization of this "single class struggle of the proletariat" around the winning of political power, the projected use of this power in the attack on bourgeois social relations and in the construction of communism *de novo*—these central elements of mature Marxism's political theory posed social transformation as the motivation for political revolution. Lenin summarized his, Marx's, and Engels's views with his customary clarity:

> The emancipation of the workers must be the act of the working class itself. All the other classes of present-day society stand for the preservation of the foundations of the existing economic system. The real emancipation of the working class requires a social revolution—which is being prepared by the entire development of capitalism—i.e., the abolition of private ownership of the means of production, their conversion into public property, and the replacement of capitalist production of commodities by the socialist organization of production of articles by society as a whole, with the object of securing full well-being and free, all-round, development for all its members.
>
> This proletarian revolution will completely abolish the division of society into classes and, consequently, all social and political inequality arising from that division.
>
> To effect this social revolution the proletariat must win political power, which will make it master of the situation and enable it to remove all obstacles along the road to its great goal. In this sense the dictatorship of the proletariat is an essential political condition of the social revolution.[27]

Most of the major elements of mature Marxism's political theory had taken shape by 1848 and found full expression in *The Communist Manifesto*. But it was one thing to convince the workers that they had to win political power and quite another to guarantee that they would know what to do with it once they had it. If the workers' state would be more powerful than its predecessors because it had a social project, it would also have to be more democratic as it made possible the self-emancipation of the "immense majority." If it had established the fundamental importance of the fight for a strengthened public power, the clear emphasis on politics seemed to raise more questions than it solved. What would this new workers' state look like? Would it be the old structure with a proletarian content? What would be the relationship of the proletarian state to the bourgeois state, of proletarian democracy to bourgeois democracy? These questions did not seem to be very important in the calm before the storms of 1848 and 1905 and their resolutions would wait until Marx, Engels, Lenin, and the proletarian movements they were beginning to lead had matured. Further clarification would come as it often does—with defeat.

NOTES

1. Karl Marx, "Critical Marginal Notes on the Article 'The King of Prussia and Social Reform. By a Prussian,' " Karl Marx and Frederick Engels, *Collected Works* (New York: Progress Publishers, 1975-), 3:199. Unless otherwise noted, all references from Marx and Engels will be to the *Collected Works*.

2. Frederick Engels, "The Condition of the Working Class in England," 4:524.

3. Marx, Letter to Arnold Ruge of March 13, 1843, 1:400.

4. Marx and Engels, "The German Ideology," 5:46–47.

5. *Ibid.*, 92, 357.

6. *Ibid.*, 90.

7. Engels, "The Constitutional Question in Germany," 6:90.

8. V. I. Lenin, "What Is to Be Done?" *Collected Works* (Moscow: Progress Publishers, 1960–72), 5:400. Unless otherwise noted, all subsequent references will be to this edition.

9. *Ibid.*, 412–13.

10. Lenin, "Draft and Explanation of a Programme for the Social-Democratic Party," 2:103–17.

11. Lenin, "Our Immediate Task," 4:215–16.

12. See Lenin, "To the Tsarist Government," 2:125; "The New Factory Law," 2:278; and "To the Rural Poor," 6:363.

13. "Frederick Engels," 2:22–23.

14. "The Communist Manifesto," 6:498.

15. *Ibid.*

16. *Ibid.*, 495.

17. *Ibid.*, 504.

18. Engels, "Principles of Communism," 6:345–46, 381.

19. "The Communist Manifesto," 6:514. See also Engels, "Draft of a Communist Confession of Faith, 6:102; Marx, "Amoralizing Criticism and Critical Morality," 6:319; Lenin, "Our Programme," 4:211, and "A Retrograde Trend in Russian Social-Democracy," 4:275–76.

20. "Critical Marginal Notes on the Article 'The King of Prussia and Social Reform. By a Prussian,' " 3:206. There is a voluminous secondary literature on this important matter, much of which misses the differences between Marx's accounts of the bourgeois and the proletarian revolutions. See Stanley Moore, "Marx and Lenin as Historical Materialists," *Philosophy and Public Affairs*, 4 (1975): 171–94 for one of the best known.

21. "The Communist Manifesto," 6:504.

22. "The German Ideology," 5:380.

23. "The Communist Manifesto," 6:505–6.

24. "Speech on the Question of Free Trade," 6:463–64.

25. "What Is to Be Done?" 5:355.

26. "Germs of Narodnik Project–Mongering," 2:463.

27. "Draft Programme of the Russian Social-Democratic Labor Party," 6:26–27.

Part II

Democracy and Dictatorship

Chapter 3

Learning from Defeat

By 1848 Marx and Engels had concluded that the proletariat would have to use its class political power to begin the transition to a classless society and a free association of producers. Launched by their turn toward social criticism, their communism remained heavily influenced by Hegel until the events of that year provided them with their first opportunity to participate in a real revolution.

In France, the events of 1848 posed the "property question" on a national level and pitted the workers against the capitalists in a particularly direct fashion. This forced the bourgeoisie to reveal its counterrevolutionary nature as soon as the February Revolution sent the genial Louis-Philippe, "King of the Bourse," to his comfortable English exile. After its bloody June defeat of the workers, it established a direct political dictatorship in the name of liberty, order, and property, shared power with no other class, and tried to organize its undivided rule through a classic "pure" republic. When its own cohesion began to unravel it abandoned the direct exercise of power and handed the state over to a new Bonaparte so its social roots could be protected. In Germany, where bourgeois property was comparatively safe, the liberals proved unable to lead even a mildly democratic struggle against feudalism and showed a marked tendency to compromise with the reaction from the very beginning of the revolution. Marx and Engels had noted theoretically that its connection to property compromised the bourgeoisie's democracy and had identified the propertyless proletariat as the most democratic element of the population at the beginning of their careers. The events of 1848–1851 provided dramatic and important confirmation of their views and suggested that future democratic revolutions would have to be anti-bourgeois in content.

The Russian Revolution of 1905 was similar in some important respects to those of 1848, and it broke out at a similar point in Lenin's development. Its content was "bourgeois" in the sense that its immediate task was to eliminate the vestiges of feudalism which distorted the development of Russian capitalism, but its participants were different from those of the classical democratic revolutions of the past. The years which separated 1848 from 1905 had witnessed the prodigious growth of Russia's productive forces, the development of a home market, the emergence of an active and combative labor movement, and the rapid differentiation of an impoverished peasantry. The threat to the Russian bourgeoisie from below was much stronger in 1905 than it had been in 1848 Germany, its drift toward counterrevolution much more pronounced than when Marx and Engels had attacked the German liberals for their vacillation and treachery. Like Marx and Engels, Lenin would distill important conclusions from the failed revolution of 1905 as he struggled to understand the relationship between political and social democracy. Like them, his new insights would lead him to a more developed theory of proletarian revolution, dictatorship, and democracy than had been possible earlier.

Property and Democracy

In France the antagonism between bourgeois and proletarian democracy became apparent as soon as the workers forced the Provisional Government to confront their social demands, the most prominent of which was expressed as the "right to work." The workers had won some mild concessions after February and the National Workshops and Luxembourg Commission embodied their hopes for social reorganization and a public commitment to full employment. This seemed to demand what the French called "a republic with social institutions," but the desire for some public limitations on property rights collided directly with the bourgeoisie's refusal to go further than a "pure" republic shorn of any social trappings. As Marx and Engels had anticipated theoretically, popular social democracy proved incompatible with bourgeois property.

The Provisional Government's attack on the National Workshops and the Luxembourg Commission began as soon as they were organized. The bourgeoisie knew a threat when it saw one because it understood that capitalism can "organize" work only through the labor market and the wage system. Its Provisional Government could not meet the workers' rather mild demands because they implied an unacceptable measure of public control over capital. Under the circumstances, social revolution could not be far behind. "Behind the right to work stands the power over capital," observed Marx; "behind the power over capital, the appropriation of the means of production, their subjection to the associated working class and, therefore, the abolition of wage labor, of capital and of their mutual relations. Behind the *'right to work'* stood the June insurrection."[1]

The workers' hopes that a social republic would emancipate all classes together died a violent death as the June massacres announced the bourgeoisie's intention to maintain the existing social order. February's "merely political" democratic revolution, which Marx and Engels had criticized theoretically because of its weakness, turned murderously energetic when it confronted the workers' desire to impose public controls on freedom of property in the name of social welfare. With the workers driven from the stage and the petty bourgeoisie vacillating, the "pure" bourgeois republic emerged as the political formation within which the industrial and financial wings of the bourgeoisie would try to rule the country together. The republic was the most natural and complete form of exclusive bourgeois rule, the only political framework within which its unified dictatorship could be organized.[2] The July Monarchy had seen a fraction of the bourgeoisie rule in the name of the king; a republic might enable a united class to rule in the name of the people.[3] Its content would be thoroughly dictatorial even if its form was republican, since "as the Party of Order they exercised more unrestricted and sterner domination over the other classes of society than ever previously under the Restoration or under the July Monarchy, a domination which, in general, was only possible under the form of the parliamentary republic, for only under this form could the two great divisions of the French bourgeoisie unite, and thus put the rule of their class instead of the rule of a privileged faction of it on the order of the day."[4]

It was Marx's understanding of dictatorship as the unshared rule of a single class which led him to characterize the parliamentary republic as one. The French bourgeoisie's dictatorship would certainly contain some democratic elements, for open debate among different fractions of the governing class would help the Party of Order organize its rule. But capitalism's economic processes continuously worked to undermine its political requirements, and it did not take very long for the republic to fall into paralysis because the market constantly tended to divide its dominant class. It was difficult for the bourgeoisie to rule directly because the complexities of national life often required protracted negotiations and the temporary ascendancy of this or that section of the class. The democratic republic existed as much to organize and contain the civil war within the bourgeoisie as to guarantee its conditions of appropriation but the social roots of this civil war ultimately proved stronger than the momentary political unity made possible by the June victory.

Less attached to political formalities than to its social roots, the bourgeoisie abandoned its republicanism and turned to the second Bonaparte when its economic and political divisions began to jeopardize its property. The republic may have been the most complete form of its political rule in theory, but this did not mean that the bourgeoisie was sufficiently developed to make use of it. In any event, it did not hesitate long before it handed power to a shameless adventurer who would save it from the consequences of its own incompetence in the short run, for

> the bourgeoisie confesses that its own interests dictate that it should be delivered from the danger of its *own rule*; that, in order to restore tranquility in the country, the bourgeois parliament must, first of all, be laid to rest; that, in order to preserve its social power intact, its political power must be broken; that the individual bourgeois can continue to exploit the other classes and to enjoy undisturbed property, family, religion and order only on condition that their class be condemned along with the other classes to similar political nullity; that, in order to save its purse, it must forfeit the crown, and the sword that is to safeguard it must at the same time be hung over its own head as a sword of Damocles.[5]

The June Days, the political paralysis which followed, and the bourgeoisie's resulting turn toward Bonapartism underlined Marx and Engels's view that the issue in France had moved past the formation of a liberal regime to the direct seizure of political power by the proletariat. The 1848 republic with social institutions "should" have succeeded the 1830 monarchy with republican institutions, but the bourgeoisie's open turn toward counterrevolution and reaction now raised the issue of social revolution. "February 25, 1848, had granted the republic to France," Marx observed. "June 25 thrust the *revolution* upon her. And revolution, after June, meant: *overthrow of bourgeois society*, whereas before February it had meant: *overthrow of the form of government*."[6] Its June defeat taught the proletariat that it could not lead the transformation of society unless it held exclusive political power. Its earlier fight for the "right to work" had been overtaken by one which expressed its interests more directly:

> The Paris proletariat was *forced* into the June insurrection by the bourgeoisie. This sufficed to mark its doom. Its immediate, avowed needs did not drive it to engage in a fight for the forcible overthrow of the bourgeoisie, nor was it equal to this task. The *Moniteur* had to inform it officially that the time was past when the republic saw any occasion to bow and scrape to its illusions, and

only its defeat convinced it of the truth that the slightest improvement in its position remains a *utopia* within the bourgeois republic, a utopia that becomes a crime as soon as it wants to become a reality. In place of its demands, exuberant in form, but petty and even bourgeois still in content, the concession of which it wanted to wring from the February republic, there appeared the bold slogan of revolutionary struggle: *Overthrow of the bourgeoisie! Dictatorship of the working class!*[7]

If this "dictatorship of the working class" was the indispensable condition for the overthrow of bourgeois society in France, what would happen in backward Germany? The bourgeoisie's hostility to feudalism and absolutism had thrust it into a temporary union with the proletariat, peasantry, and petty bourgeoisie—the three working classes which together comprised "the people." Its slogans of "freedom" and "liberty" would allow it to debate its affairs openly, assemble freely, and organize itself politically. But even this comparatively mild democracy held potential dangers. Germany's general backwardness and her undeveloped class structure meant that its weakened bourgeoisie was even more likely to betray its democratic pretensions than was the case in France.

The German bourgeoisie had come to lead the March events not, as it desired, through an accommodation with the crown, but as the result of a popular insurrection which it did not want and which it dared not lead. But the crown had long been only the "fig-leaf" behind which it had been ruling for some time. The development of capitalist relations of production had rendered the monarchy obsolete, and the bourgeoisie was now compelled by its material interests and the momentum of events to come out of hiding and try to rule directly. Like its French cousin, it proved unequal to the task. It had to confront the popular movement which had elevated it to power and it was soon evident that, unlike its revolutionary English and French predecessors, it could not speak for the population as a whole. It had no inclination to extend the same political freedoms to "the people" that it was demanding for itself because the workers, peasants, and petty bourgeoisie were exhibiting an alarming tendency to use these very liberties to restrict its freedom of property. Trapped between the demands of a popular movement which was pushing it toward a confrontation with the crown and its own basis in private property, it tried to extract concessions from the monarchy by threatening it with an insurrection and to hold the popular movement in check by warning it about the government's violence. In the long run it was unable to steer a middle ground because it could not have it both ways. Faced with a choice between its material interests and its "principles," it embraced the former and threw in its lot with the monarchy.

The German revolution may have been "bourgeois" in the sense that its historical mission was to eliminate the remnants of feudalism, but Marx now concluded that its general-democratic content could be safeguarded only by a more radical revolutionary process than that of the classical bourgeois revolutions of the past. The same German backwardness which had precipitated the revolution in the first place conspired to narrow the range of its possible outcomes; it meant that "a purely *bourgeois revolution* in the form of a *constitutional monarchy* is impossible in Germany, and that only a feudal absolutist counterrevolution or a *social republican revolution* is possible.[8] The French bourgeoisie had imposed its dictatorship through a "pure republic," and the workers had responded with the slogan of proletarian dictatorship. In Germany the workers were the most democratic and "radical" element of the population, and their revolution could not come to rest in a "mere" political democracy. "Can the petty bourgeoisie and, the more so, the proletarians, find a better political form for representing their interests than the democratic republic?" asked Marx. "Are not precisely these classes the most radical, the most democratic, of society as a whole? Is it not precisely the proletariat that is the specifically *red* class?"[9] The political sovereignty of the people would require a popular democratic government with a social agenda.[10]

The revolutions of 1848 did not develop into the continental upheaval which Marx and Engels hoped for, but they did confirm their view that the bourgeoisie was no longer able to accomplish the general-democratic tasks of "its" revolution. Some other class would have to step forward to assume leadership of the struggle for democracy. Nowhere was this more clear than in the countryside.

The French bourgeoisie of 1789 had liberated its peasant allies from the burden of their feudal obligations. It had done so in its own interests but the Great Revolution's general–democratic character was revealed in the fact that it "never left its allies, the peasants, in the lurch. It knew that the abolition of feudalism in the countryside and the creation of a free, land-owning peasant class was the basis of its rule." But its German cousins were not so farsighted in 1848, and the peasants would have to look elsewhere for land and liberty. "The German bourgeoisie of 1848 unhesitatingly betrays the peasants, who are its *natural allies*, flesh of its own flesh, and without whom it cannot stand up to the autocracy."[11] Both the liberals and the democracy they hoped to organize would be irrevocably damaged by this abandonment.

If the proletariat and the peasantry were natural allies in the fight for bourgeois democracy in Germany, this was no less true of the workers' directly socialist fight for the overthrow of French capitalism. The Great Revolution had abolished feudalism but had done little more than replace the peasantry's old problems with new ones. The development of bourgeois society had set in motion the market forces which worked to impoverish many rural smallholders. This created the conditions for a popular political alliance against all exploitation, for the peasants' "differs only in *form* from the exploitation of the industrial proletariat. The exploiter is the same: *capital*. The individual capitalists exploit the individual peasants through *mortgages* and *usury*; the capitalist class exploits the peasant class through the *state taxes*. The peasant's title to property is the talisman by which capital holds him hitherto under its spell, the pretext under which it sets him against the industrial proletariat. Only the fall of capital can raise the peasant; only an anti-capitalist, a proletarian government can break his economic misery, his social degradation. The *constitutional republic* is the dictatorship of his united exploiters; *the social-democratic, the Red* republic, is the dictatorship of his allies."[12] Marx and Engels were looking for signs of a popular alliance between the workers and the peasants which could be the core of both an anti-feudal "people's" movement in Germany and a direct proletarian revolution in France.

Its guarantee of the peasantry's smallholding had enabled the French bourgeoisie to crush feudalism, prevent its return and conquer most of Europe. But by 1848 emancipation from poverty and misery required radical anticapitalist social measures. Ruined by the very freedom for which it had fought earlier, the French peasantry retained its capacity for revolutionary activity because bourgeois society could not offer it the secure future it craved. It had two faces, two histories, and two futures, and the workers could win the decisive struggle for its allegiance only if they could understand its dilemma and support its democratic aspirations. It was absolutely clear that the bourgeoisie could do neither:

> The Bonaparte dynasty represents not the revolutionary, but the conservative peasant, not the peasant that strikes out beyond the conditions of his social existence, the smallholding, but rather the peasant who wants to consolidate this holding, not the country folk who, linked up with the towns, want to overthrow the old order through their own energies, but on the contrary those who, in stupefied seclusion within this old order, want to see themselves and their smallholdings saved and favored by the ghost of the empire. It represents not the enlightenment, but the superstition of the peasant; not his judgement, but his prejudice; not his future, but his past; not his modern Cévennes, but his modern Vendée.[13]

Bourgeois property necessitated popular democratic dictatorships in France and Germany, and this meant that the workers would have to compromise with allies whose demands did not go as far as theirs. The bulk of the petty bourgeoisie was interested in democratizing social and political life but Marx and Engels expected it to try to come to power with as little disruption of the existing social order as possible. Its vulnerable position led it to demand various measures to protect its small property and small production from the bigger concentrations of capital which constituted the most immediate threat to its prized—and largely imaginary—independence. Free credit, legal protection against monopolies, economic decentralization, reformed political institutions, and social peace defined its democracy. To some extent these positions brought it close to the workers, but the proletariat's social demands went considerably farther than its horizons because the workers had no property to defend. The proletariat would have to be careful to maintain its independence from a petty-bourgeois "general democratic" movement which was both an indispensable ally and a potentially mortal threat:

> But these demands can in no wise suffice for the party of the proletariat. While the democratic petty bourgeoisie wish to bring the revolution to a conclusion as quickly as possible, . . . it is our interest and our task to make the revolution permanent, until all more or less possessing classes have been forced out of their position of dominance, the proletariat has conquered state power, and the association of proletarians, not only in one country but in all the dominant countries of the world, has advanced so far that competition among the proletarians in these countries has ceased and that at least the decisive productive forces are concentrated in the hands of the proletarians. For us the issue cannot be the alteration of private property but only its annihilation, not the smoothing over of class antagonisms but the abolition of classes, not the improvement of existing society but the foundation of a new one.[14]

Eighteen forty-eight confirmed Marx and Engels's theoretical expectation that property would compel the bourgeoisie, and tempt much of the petty bourgeoisie, to compromise with reaction and betray democracy. When they called the proletarian revolution a democratic one, they expressed their understanding that it could take shape as only a "people's" movement of the workers and their laboring allies, who together constituted the vast majority of the population. They could have meant little else in the middle of the nineteenth century. But things did not work out as they had hoped. The political alliances they had outlined could not be maintained because economic affairs revived and counterrevolution triumphed across Europe. Instead of signaling the death knell of capitalism, 1848 marked the beginning of its great nineteenth-century expansion. But temporary defeat did not prevent the theory of proletarian leadership of the democratic and socialist revolutions from becoming a central element of modern communism. "*Revolt against bourgeois dictatorship, need for a change in society, adherence to democratic-republican institutions as organs of their movement, grouping around the proletariat as the power*—these are the common characteristics of the *so-called party of social-democracy, the party of the Red republic,*" said Marx.[15] The need for this "change in society" would shape a proletarian state whose democratic and dictatorial content would be shaped by its motion toward the "ultimate result" of the workers' movement:

> [T]he *proletariat* increasingly organizes itself around *revolutionary socialism,* around *Communism,* for which the bourgeoisie itself has invented the name of *Blanqui.* This Socialism is the *declaration of the permanence of the revolution,* the *class dictatorship* of the proletariat as the necessary transit point to the *abolition of class distinctions generally,* to the abolition of all the relations of production on which they rest, to the abolition of all the social relations that correspond to these relations of production, to the revolutionizing of all the ideas that result from these social relations.[16]

Although the tasks of this "class dictatorship of the proletariat" were defined in negative terms for the moment, Marx had clearly signaled his view that it was an essential element in the transition to a classless society. Having established its revolutionary content, it remained for him to specify how such a state could issue from the existing political order.

"Breaking" the State

As divided as it was, the French bourgeoisie knew how to deal with the workers when it had to and the June Days had provided eloquent proof of its ability to unite when faced with a threat from below. But its less developed German counterparts were unable to confront the developing reaction with anything more than hot air, and Marx and Engels's denunciations of the Frankfurt "talking-shop" expressed their concern that even the relatively mild German revolution would be unable to defend itself. "Every provisional political set-up following a revolution requires a dictatorship, and an energetic dictatorship at that," said Marx, and Engels agreed that all modern revolutions since 1789 had needed "revolutionary dictatorships" to defend themselves from inevitable attempts at restoration.[17] But the German revolution was particularly vulnerable because of the way it had developed. The liberals had tried to insinuate democratic reforms behind the backs of the crown and the people, to trick both in order to carve out an area in which they could maneuver without having to answer to either. They sought to negotiate an end to absolutism and preached moderation because they wanted no more than to reform the existing political structure. Their understandable fear of the popular movement made them incapable of resisting a reaction which began to take shape as soon as the democratic revolution had apparently succeeded.

An institution's structure is a function of its class content, and it was clear to Marx that there could be no reforms which would benefit "the people" unless the existing political apparatus was broken up and replaced by a different one. The Frankfurt liberals would have to abolish the administrative, judicial, and military organs of state, purge the government, and arm the population if they wanted to guarantee popular supervision of a new democratic government.[18] But their desire to safeguard their property led them to try to preserve the coercive structure of the existing state for possible future use against their present allies, and this proved their undoing. "From the very beginning we blamed Camphausen for not having acted in a dictatorial manner, for not having immediately smashed up and removed the remnants of the old institutions," said Marx of the most prominent German liberal.[19] The bourgeoisie was more afraid of the people than of the reaction, and its unwillingness to organize an armed popular dictatorship to defend even the mild democracy it had won pushed it inexorably toward the accelerating counterrevolution.

"He let the old Prussian laws dealing with political crimes and the old courts continue to function," Marx continued about Camphausen. "Under his government the old bureaucracy and the old army gained time to recover from their fright and to reconstitute themselves completely. All the leading personalities of the old regime were left untouched in their positions."[20] There is no way a serious revolution can be started, much less consummated, under such conditions. Here again the revolutionary French bourgeoisie had understood things far better than the weak-kneed Germans, for "the French *Convention* is and remains the beacon for all revolutionary epochs. It inaugurated the revolution by means of a decree *dismissing all officials*."[21] This was not the case in the German bourgeoisie's 1848 play at revolution. "What caused the defeat of the *March* revolution?" asked Marx rhetorically. He supplied his own very important answer:

> It reformed only the highest political summit, it left all the groundwork of this summit intact—the old bureaucracy, the old army, the old boards of prosecuting magistrates, the old judiciary which had grown gray in the service of absolutism.[22]

Neither the French nor the German bourgeoisies of 1848 had the slightest interest in social reconstruction and this is why they bitterly resisted any fundamental changes in the organization of state power. "The *existence* of the state power is embodied precisely in its *officials*, the army, the administration and the courts" and the Frankfurt liberals should have learned from the Convention by dismissing all government employees.[23] The preservation of democracy demanded the complete recasting of political power. This lay behind Marx's famous observation that the proletarian revolution differed from its predecessors in its attitude toward the state; "all revolutions perfected this machine instead of breaking it. The parties that contended in turn for domination regarded the possession of this huge state edifice as the principal spoils of the victor."[24] No popular revolution could be defended or deepened with a political apparatus whose very *raison d'être* was to repress the population's productive majority. "Breaking" the existing state was now an explicit prerequisite to the full democratic organization and use of popular political power in the service of social transformation.

The revolutionary quality of the new state would be guaranteed by "the people" as a whole, and the need to arm the laboring population figured prominently in Marx and Engels's accounts of 1848. All important issues in politics are ultimately decided by force, they repeatedly observed.[25] The Frankfurt liberals would not represent the interests of "the people" just because they had promised to, or even because they imagined that their interests coincided with those of the population as a whole. Their property would always drive them toward the crown, and only the armed workers could provide the counterweight to reaction. These "positive" and "negative" tasks of the revolution, the need to organize a democratic political structure so as to suppress counterrevolution, were mutually dependent elements of Marx and Engels's assessment of 1848. They stood behind Marx's declaration that "there is only *one means* by which the death agonies of the old society and the bloody birth throes of the new society can be shortened, simplified and concentrated—and that is by *revolutionary terror*."[26] The lessons of the French Revolution were not lost on him as he paid homage to the Hungarians, described this "terror," and summarized an issue of general-theoretical importance:

> Mass uprising, national manufacture of arms, issue of banknotes, short shrift for anyone hindering the revolutionary movement, revolution in permanence—in short, all the main features of the glorious year 1793 are found again in the Hungary which Kossuth has armed, organized and inspired with enthusiasm.[27]

Marx and Engels had developed a communist analysis before the revolutions of 1848 broke out and their analyses of the French and the German events of that year revealed a deeply democratic point of view. They had already gone much further than ensuring the political and civil liberties associated with the rise of capitalism in western Europe, and by 1848 they were substantially more than the radical guardians of bourgeois democracy's left wing. A proletarian social revolution which now appeared to be a very real possibility informed all their work. It expressed the communist potential of what remained of the petty bourgeoisie's revolutionary democracy. "Behind the abolition of taxation lies the abolition of the state," they observed. "The abolition of the state has meaning with the Communists, only as the necessary consequence of the abolition of classes, with which the need for the organized might of one class to keep the others down automatically disappears."[28]

Indeed, it was the revolutionary quality of their democracy which led them to define it in dictatorial terms. Stamped by the conditions of its birth in the struggle for a free market and the elimination of feudal privilege, bourgeois democratic theory understands "dictatorship" as limitations on freedom and rights, one-man rule, and the like. But the core of Marxist political theory lies in its claim that the state—any state—is an instrument of *class* domination. No matter what its form, every state is a dictatorship in content. Except in the rarest of circumstances, one class monopolizes the instruments of coercion and uses them to shape society in accordance with its conditions of appropriation. The workers' state derived its democratic character from the objective necessity that it defend the interests of the vast majority of the population whose social position and relationship to the means of production forced it to work for a living. It would have to repress a small minority made powerful beyond its numbers by its property and its consequent political strength. The uniqueness of the workers' state did not consist in its class character or in its coerciveness, for that was something it shared with every state. It was unique in the democratic character of its coerciveness.

All political formations may be "dictatorships" on this reading, but Marx and Engels's popular dictatorship in Germany and proletarian dictatorship in France were linked to the bourgeoisie's now-general fear of and hostility to democracy. There is a real break in historical continuity between proletarian revolutions against private property and all their historical antecedents. The workers' radicalism had brought democracy to the edge of a qualitatively new meaning. "The social revolution of the nineteenth century cannot draw its poetry from the past, but only from the future," Marx said. "It cannot begin with itself before it has stripped off all superstitions about the past. Earlier revolutions required recollections of past world history in order to dull themselves on their own content. In order to arrive at its own content, the revolution of the nineteenth century must let the dead bury their dead. There the words went beyond the content; here the content goes beyond the words."[29]

But he and Engels were wrong about the possibilities for both French socialism and German democracy, and they came to realize it soon after Louis Bonaparte's election. Germany's general social and political backwardness submerged the proletarian current of the democratic revolution beneath the confused strivings of the propertied classes, and the independent interests of the workers were not a factor in the events of the day to nearly the same extent that they had been in the ascending period of the French movement. Even if the course of the revolution did not live up to Marx and Engels's expectations, it encouraged important clarifications of the relationship between democracy and dictatorship, between workers and peasants, between politics and society. The lessons they learned would serve them well in the future and would be of enormous value to Lenin as he struggled to understand Russia's 1848.

Class and Democracy in 1905

If the workers had been weaker than Marx and Engels had hoped in France and Germany, the proletarian wing of the 1905 Russian Revolution was stronger and the independent class interests of the workers more clearly articulated than had been possible in 1848. It was as clear to Lenin as it was to almost all Social-Democrats that no sustained progress was possible in any sphere of national life unless the surviving remnants of feudal social relations and the powerful autocracy which defended them were overthrown.[30] The class content of the coming revolution would be eminently "bourgeois" but Lenin was as convinced as Marx and Engels had been that the bourgeoisie would be incapable of leading "its" democratic revolution. Lenin expected it to ape its German counterpart, try to negotiate with the government, use the crown and the people against each other, and introduce meaningless reforms so it could steal toward power. Bourgeois democracy demanded the overthrow of the autocracy and the elimination of feudalism, but this would require a revolution which the bourgeoisie did not want, would try to derail, and would ultimately work to defeat.

Lenin turned out to be more accurate in 1905 than Marx and Engels had been in 1848. The driving force of the democratic revolution was provided by the workers and peasants. Its main achievements—the granting of a constitution, convocation of the State Duma, establishment of some formal political liberties, and formation of some new political parties—were all bourgeois in content in that they did not interfere with existing property relations even as they seemed to strike at the autocracy. But they had been made possible only by the independent activity of the popular movement in direct confrontation with the state. They proved abortive and came to nothing in the end because the workers were not yet strong or organized enough to take the lead of the movement themselves and because the bourgeoisie proved incapable of even helping to consolidate a revolution made for it by others.

The 1848 German revolution had broken out where important remnants of feudalism obstructed further social development and where the bourgeoisie was incapable of determined or consistent democratic leadership. In France, the struggle for political democracy had spilled over to the abolition of private property. Both revolutions had failed, but the Russian Revolution of 1905 preserved elements of each. The conditions of Russian industrialization presented the complex phenomenon of the simultaneous development of a bourgeois-democratic and a proletarian-socialist revolution which Lenin tried to understand in both their differences and their connections. He took this to mean that the revolution of 1905 could not succeed as a bourgeois accommodation with tsarism under the leadership of the liberal Cadets. It could succeed as only a bourgeois-democratic revolution under the leadership of the proletariat. It was here that the differences between the two main tendencies in Russian Social-Democracy proved so important.

The Mensheviks agreed with Lenin that the democratic and the socialist revolutions were not and could not be the same and that the motive forces, historic possibilities, and sociopolitical programs accompanying each would have to differ. They considered Russian capitalism too immature for a proletarian revolution in the foreseeable future and insisted that a definite interval would separate the antifeudal democratic and the anticapitalist socialist revolutions. They tended to deny the possibility of independent proletarian political struggle in the short term and generally concluded that the workers would have to follow the political lead of the bourgeois liberals and the petty-bourgeois democrats. For the most part they thought that the Russian bourgeoisie could lead the Russian bourgeois revolution.

For the Bolsheviks only the workers could lead the democratic revolution all the way to the overthrow of the autocracy and they could do so only if they remained independent of the bourgeoisie's siren calls. Their natural allies were the democratic peasants rather than the liberals. This position was expressed in Lenin's complicated formulation of a "democratic dictatorship of the proletariat and the peasantry," the Russian counterpart to the "people's dictatorship" of which Marx and Engels had talked in 1848. While he remained careful to distinguish this radical democratic alliance from the fully socialist dictatorship of the proletariat, his early investigation of Russian capitalism had indicated that a socialist revolution was developing before the bourgeois revolution had been completed. The complete overthrow of the autocracy was the first condition for the success of democracy, but the independent activity of the workers and peasants was forcing the bourgeoisie to renounce "its" revolution. "The bourgeois mind can conceive *only* of incomplete democratic revolutions (for at bottom the interests of the bourgeoisie require incomplete revolutions)," Lenin observed. "The bourgeois mind shuns all non-parliamentary forms of struggle, all open mass actions, any revolution in the direct sense of the term. The bourgeois instinctively hastens to declare, proclaim and accept all sham parliamentarism as real parliamentarism in order to put a stop to the "dizzying whirlwind" (which may be dangerous not only for the heads of many weak-kneed bourgeois, but also for their pockets)."[31] Only the revolutionary-democratic dictatorship of the workers and peasants could break feudalism and absolutism in Russia. This perspective encouraged Lenin to reaffirm Marxism's revolutionary core as he applied the lessons of 1848 to the reality of 1905:

> Comrade Tserteli referred to the history of Europe. "The year '48," he said, "not only taught us that the conditions for socialism were not yet ripe, but also that it is impossible to fight for freedom without some sort of alliance with bourgeois democracy." Comrade Tserteli's argument is revisionism of the worst sort. On the contrary, both the revolution of 1848 and subsequent historical experience have taught international Social-Democracy the very opposite, namely, that bourgeois democracy takes its stand more and more against the proletariat, that the fight for freedom is waged consistently only when it is led by the proletariat. The year 1848 does not teach us to make alliance with bourgeois democrats, but rather the need to free the least developed sections of the masses from the illusion of bourgeois democracy, which is incapable of fighting even for democracy.[32]

If the bourgeoisie would not fight for the full measure of social democracy and political freedom, the workers were ready to take up the struggle against the autocracy—indeed, they were already doing so. The massive political strikes of the fall of 1905 proved that their revolutionary-democratic movement was spontaneously taking on a political character and was heading toward a direct confrontation with the regime. The working class had become such a potent force in Russian political life that every oppositional tendency, not to mention the autocracy itself, was striving to control it and turn it to its own purposes.

Not only did the Social-Democrats have to deal with liberals, populists, Mensheviks, and the police; their task was further complicated by the appearance of an ideological trend within Social-Democracy itself which denied the possibility of a systematic political campaign for democracy. Agreeing with the Mensheviks that the gradual development of the productive forces would spontaneously produce revolutionary consciousness in the working class, the "economists" denied the need for political action and recommended that the workers confine themselves to economic matters. The political needs of the labor and democratic movements would be handled by the liberal intelligentsia until the workers were sufficiently mature to wage the struggle on their own—and the "economists" agreed with the Mensheviks that this might take a long time.

Lenin's rejoinder was a simple one, and it reasserted both the revolutionary core of Marxism and the centrality of politics in it. The growth of a powerful working-class movement demanded consistent political leadership by the Social-Democrats. The labor movement's spontaneous activity was outstripping the theoretical and organizational ability of the revolutionaries to influence it, and the resulting crisis was exclusively a crisis of leadership;

"the principal cause of the present crisis in Russian Social-Democracy is *the lag of the leaders . . .* behind *the spontaneous upsurge of the masses.*"[33] The workers and peasants were ready to undertake a direct and open political struggle for democracy and socialism. The only question was whether the communists were ready for them.

Given Social-Democracy's organizational backwardness, Lenin's fight for clarity was mostly conducted on the level of theory. He repeatedly pointed out that the liberal Cadets were seeking to confine the popular movement to the struggle for mild reforms without committing themselves to more fundamental political and social changes. Their call for a Constituent Assembly elected on the basis of universal, direct and equal suffrage by secret ballot summarized the political program of liberal bourgeois democracy in a time of social revolution. Lenin now called for a popular insurrection which would overthrow the autocracy and replace it with a fully democratic republic and considered this a precondition for any further democratic reforms. Democracy could be won only as the result of revolution. "If the tsarist government is not utterly defeated and replaced by a provisional revolutionary government," he warned, "every representative assembly, whatever title—'popular', 'constituent', etc.—may be conferred upon it, will in fact be an assembly of representatives of the big bourgeoisie convened for the purpose of bargaining with the tsar for a division of power."[34] No democracy would be possible unless the people seized state power.

It was the proletariat's social position which compelled it to seek alliances with the peasantry and win democracy directly rather than through the negotiations or piecemeal reforms favored by the propertied bourgeoisie. Any measure of democracy will strengthen the popular movement; the more rapid and consistent such democracy is, the better it will be for both the people and for democracy.[35] From this "the Bolsheviks deduce the *basic* tactics of the socialist proletariat in the bourgeois revolution—to carry with them the democratic petty bourgeoisie, especially the peasant petty bourgeoisie, draw them away from the liberals, paralyze the instability of the liberal bourgeoisie, and develop the struggle of the *masses* for the complete *abolition* of all traces of serfdom, including landed proprietorship."[36] Almost every class in Russia needs democracy for its own purposes, but the workers need more of it because their purposes are so comprehensive:

> The Social-Democratic Party, as the conscious exponent of the working-class movement, aims at the complete liberation of the toiling masses from every form of oppression and exploitation. The achievement of this objective—the abolition of private property in the means of production and the creation of the socialist society—calls for a very high development of the productive forces of capitalism and a high degree of organization of the working class. The full

development of the productive forces in modern bourgeois society, a broad, free, and open class struggle, and the political education, training, and rallying of the masses of the proletariat are inconceivable without political freedom. Therefore it has always been the aim of the class-conscious proletariat to wage a determined struggle for complete political freedom and the democratic revolution.[37]

It was important that the socialist workers support the petty-bourgeois democrats when they acted in a revolutionary fashion against the regime, but it was equally important that they remain independent of the "general democratic movement." The common struggle of the workers and some elements of the bourgeoisie should not blind the proletariat to the fundamental antagonism between its long-term interests and those of all propertied classes, Lenin warned, arguing that it was precisely the bourgeois character of the developing revolution, the disintegration of the peasantry, and the appearance of a bewildering variety of democratic trends which made the independence of the revolutionary socialist workers from bourgeois and petty-bourgeois democracy more essential than ever.[38] If the workers support the revolutionary democrats against the autocracy, they do so only to the extent that such elements are directly engaged in the revolutionary overthrow of tsarism and not because they have any faith in their long-run consistency or reliability. Such support "is necessarily in the interests of achieving the independent social-revolutionary aims of the proletariat" and that is the only reason to offer it.[39]

The bourgeoisie tends to voice its opposition to absolutism in the form of liberalism, but it expresses its suspicion of popular democracy in the same way. Because their democracy is narrower than that of the workers, the liberals will try to prevent the appearance of a fully independent working-class political party and can be expected to argue that class-conscious proletarian politics will aid the counterrevolution by dividing the democratic opposition. Like Marx and Engels, Lenin repeatedly warned the workers that merging their democratic demands with those of the bourgeoisie would guarantee both their own defeat and the failure of a democracy which could be won only as a consequence of the revolutionary overthrow of the autocracy.[40] If the bourgeoisie turns its back on "its" revolution because of its fear of the independent workers, so much the better for democracy:

[T]he Russian revolution will begin to assume its real sweep, and will really assume the widest revolutionary sweep possible in the epoch of bourgeois-democratic revolutions, only when the bourgeoisie recoils from it and when the masses of the peasantry come out as active revolutionaries side by side with the proletariat. To be consistently carried through to the end, our democratic revolution must rely on forces capable of paralyzing the inevitable inconsistency of the bourgeoisie. . . .

> *The proletariat must carry the democratic revolution to completion, allying to itself the mass of the peasantry, in order to crush the autocracy's resistance by force and paralyze the bourgeoisie's instability. The proletariat must accomplish the socialist revolution, allying to itself the mass of the semi-proletarian elements of the population, so as to crush the bourgeoisie's resistance by force and paralyze the instability of the peasantry and the petty bourgeoisie.* Such are the tasks of the proletariat.[41]

More than simply irrelevant to the success of the democratic revolution, the bourgeoisie has become an active antagonist to its completion. Unable to support the social measures which are necessary for success in the struggle against landed property and the autocracy, its democracy's active hostility is now a condition for the successful completion of a democratic revolution which cannot move forward except in oppostion to everything the bourgeoisie stands for.

Dictatorship and Revolution

The European revolutions of 1848 had failed partly because the bourgeoisie had been unwilling to consider any substantive social changes and because the workers had not been strong enough to force the issue. That dynamic was repeated in the Russian Revolution of 1905. The spontaneous motion of the Russian workers and peasants was to deepen the democratic content of the bourgeois revolution, while the bourgeoisie sought to limit its force and keep intact as much of the old political order as might be necessary for the protection of its property. As Marx and Engels had earlier, Lenin considered its drive to preserve the monarchy, bureaucracy, army, and police as the decisive sign of its generally counterrevolutionary and antidemocratic politics. It was now a quality of the bourgeoisie *as such*. Its spokesmen "always regard the abolition of the old regime as utopian because it wants to use these organs against the proletariat and against the revolutionary peasantry."[42] The need to break the existing state and construct a new one had been elevated from an observation to a general theoretical principle and the demand that the population be armed was inextricably linked to it:

> Everywhere, in all countries, the standing army is used not so much against the external enemy as against the internal enemy. Everywhere the standing army has become the weapon of reaction, the servant of capital in its struggle against labor, the executioner of the people's liberty. Let us not, therefore, stop short

at mere partial demands in our great liberating revolution. Let us tear the evil up by the roots. Let us do away with the standing army altogether. Let the army merge with the armed people. Let the soldiers bring to the people their military knowledge. Let the barracks disappear to be replaced by free military schools. No power on earth will dare to encroach upon free Russia, if the bulwark of her liberty is an armed people which has destroyed the military caste, which has made all soldiers citizens and all citizens capable of bearing arms, soldiers. . . . So long as there are oppressed and exploited people in the world, we must strive, not for disarmament, but for the arming of the whole people. It alone will fully safeguard liberty. It alone will completely overthrow reaction. Only when this change has been effected will the millions of toilers, and not a mere handful of exploiters, enjoy real liberty.[43]

By the summer of 1906 it was clear that the basic content of the democratic revolution—transfering land to the peasantry and winning complete political liberty—required the forcible destruction of the autocracy. Even the political general strike, the great discovery of 1905, was no longer sufficient; "only the complete and decisive victory of an uprising can make it fully possible to establish genuine self-government."[44] Lenin's "democratic dictatorship of the proletariat and the peasantry" described a proletarian-led democratic revolution in a society whose economic conditions were not sufficiently developed to begin the transition to socialism. He insisted that "the task facing our revolution *now* is not that of effecting the socialist revolution but that of removing the political obstacles to the development of the existing, capitalist, mode of production."[45] The Bolsheviks' "minimum program" for the democratic revolution called for a republic, arming the people, separating church and state, full democratic liberties, and "decisive economic reforms," the most important of which was the transfer of the land to the peasantry. None of these measures could be carried out without the revolutionary, democratic, and dictatorial use of a state power whose core would be the popular alliance of the workers and peasants.

Lenin's call for a republic was for "not only and not so much a form of government as the sum-total of democratic changes envisaged in our minimum program" which would establish the revolutionary government's legitimacy through a popular insurrection rather than on its status as the legal outgrowth of the previous regime.[46] A radical break with the existing political order was required if a legitimate and democratic state was to be constructed. Just as Marx had characterized terror as the plebian way of dealing with counterrevolution in France and had advocated it for a time in 1848, so Lenin was now convinced that only a popularly based democratic dictatorship could forcibly uproot the autocracy and defend democracy from counterrevolution. "If . . . the autocratic government is really overthrown, it will have to be replaced by another. This other can be only a provisional revolutionary government. It can base itself for support only on the revolutionary people—on the proletariat and the peasantry. It can be only a dictatorship, that is, not an organization of 'order', but an organization of war."[47] "Winning the battle of democracy" now had a social side and required a dictatorship which could be consolidated only in a democratic and revolutionary fashion:

> We all talk of achieving the republic. To achieve it in reality, we must "strike together" at the autocracy—"we" being the revolutionary people, the proletariat and the peasantry. But that is not all. It is not enough even to "strike the finishing blow together" at the autocracy, that is, completely to overthrow the autocratic government. We shall also have to "repulse together" the inevitable attempts to restore the deposed autocracy. In a revolutionary epoch this "repulsing together" is, in effect, the revolutionary-democratic dictatorship of the proletariat and the peasantry, the participation of the proletariat in the revolutionary government.[48]

When Lenin characterized Russia's republic as a democratic dictatorship and identified its leading elements as the workers and peasants, he did not mean to deny its bourgeois character. He intended to describe the politics of a period in which the bourgeoisie no longer represented freedom but the proletariat was not yet ready to lead the democratic revolution. 1905 was the Russian equivalent of 1848. His emphasis on direct popular revolutionary activity took him beyond any form of parliamentarism even while he was calling for a republic. Russia's democracy would be a popular dictatorship because its insurrectionary character would break the bourgeois limits of democracy even as its immediate purpose was to facilitate the most rapid possible development of capitalism:

> ... the only force capable of gaining "a decisive victory over tsarism" is the *people*, i.e., the proletariat and the peasantry, if we take the main, big forces, and distribute the rural and urban petty bourgeoisie (also part of "the people") between the two. "The revolution's decisive victory over tsarism" means the establishment of the *revolutionary-democratic dictatorship of the proletariat and the peasantry.* . . . No other force is capable of gaining a decisive victory over tsarism.
>
> And such a victory will be precisely a dictatorship, i.e., it must invariably rely on military force, on the arming of *the masses, on an insurrection, and not on institutions of one kind or another established in a "lawful" or "peaceful"* way. It can be only a dictatorship, for realization of the changes urgently and absolutely indispensable to the proletariat and the peasantry will evoke desperate resistance from the landlords, the big bourgeoisie, and tsarism. Without a dictatorship it is impossible to break down that resistance and repel

counter-revolutionary attempts. But of course it will be a democratic, not a socialist dictatorship, it will be unable (without a series of intermediary stages of revolutionary development) to affect the foundations of capitalism. At best, it may bring about a radical redistribution of landed property in favor of the peasantry, establish consistent and full democracy, including the formation of a republic, eradicate all the oppressive features of Asiatic bondage, not only in rural but also in factory life, lay the foundations for a thorough improvement in the conditions of the owners and for a rise in their standard of living, and—last but not least—carry the revolutionary conflagration into Europe. Such a victory will not yet by any means transform our bourgeois revolution into a socialist revolution; the democratic revolution will not immediately overstep the bounds of bourgeois social and economic relationships; nevertheless, the significance of such a victory for the future development of Russia and of the whole world will be immense.[49]

Russia's democratic republic would be a dictatorship because it would be openly founded on popular force and be organized to accomplish the purposes of a particular social class. Lenin's thinking in 1905 was substantially the same as that of Marx and Engels in 1848. Dictatorship was not the arbitrary or coercive rule of a single individual; "dictatorship means unlimited power based on force, and not on law. In civil war, any victorious power can only be a dictatorship. The point is, however, that there is the dictatorship of the minority over the majority, the dictatorship of a handful of police officials over the people; and there is the dictatorship of the over-whelming majority of the people over a handful of tyrants, robbers and usurpers of people's power."[50] Lenin was not advocating a lawless regime; when he based a revolutionary state on force instead of law, he was doing nothing more than developing and refining Marx's insight that the workers would have to forcibly break the bourgeoisie's state structure if they were to build their own. If all states are dictatorships and differ only in their class content, then this revolutionary-democratic dictatorship of the workers and peasants would have a substantially broader social base than any bourgeois dictatorship—and would be more democratic as a result. It would not be the fully socialist "dictatorship of the proletariat" but Lenin had identified the participants, specified the methods, and described the goals of a class dictatorship which alone could guide Russia's democratic revolution.

This revolutionary understanding of democracy is what enabled Lenin to consider institutions like the peasant committees to be democratic. They had issued from the powerful wave of spontaneous peasant attacks on feudal property, were instruments in the direct expropriation of the landlords, and were the insurrectionary foundation of rural democracy.[51] The same thinking underlay his orientation toward the "soviets," another spontaneous product of the enormous revolutionary wave that swept over Russia in the fall of

1905. The political strikes, often organized around demands for freedom of speech and assembly, open elections, the eight-hour day, and the like, produced democratically elected councils which were initially organized for the attainment of specific goals. As the revolution developed they began to provide a measure of coordination to locally based struggles against particular employers and government officials. This tendency toward increasingly general political combat encouraged the proliferation of soviets all across the country and their democratic quality was intimately related to their insurrectionary character.

Throughout the Revolution of 1905 Lenin held to his view that the revolutionary-democratic dictatorship of the workers and peasants would succeed only if it culminated in an armed insurrection and the formation of a Provisional Revolutionary Government. The forcible destruction of the autocracy was a condition for the attack on the landowners. The leading role of politics in the workers' revolution, stated theoretically by Marx and Engels in an earlier period, was confirmed by the press of events. Proletarian and bourgeois democratic trends were developing together in 1905, and the conflict between them was rooted in their antagonistic class contents rather than in the proclivities of this or that leader. Unable to express themselves through existing political institutions, the workers had discovered their own organs in the soviets. Whether they assisted in arming strikers and their supporters, collecting strike funds, assisting the unemployed, or getting out a newspaper, the soviets helped organize the workers' economic struggle against the employers and their political struggle against the regime. In some cases they began to act like a parallel government, issuing decrees granting freedom of the press and popular access to government buildings while organizing workers' militias to impose popular supervision on the police. As the strike wave crested in October 1905, they tended to establish relations with other factory soviets, trade unions, peasant committees, student organizations, and—very importantly—the soviets which were developing in the armed forces. The result of this drive toward coordination, which quickly assumed a distinctly revolutionary character, was the creation of the St. Petersburg Soviet of Workers' Deputies, the "soviet of soviets." This raised the possibility that the soviets could serve as the nucleus of the revolutionary-democratic dictatorship of the proletariat and the peasantry. "I may be wrong, but I believe," said Lenin from his Swiss exile in November, "that politically the Soviet of Workers' Deputies should be regarded as the embryo of a *provisional revolutionary government*. I think the Soviet should proclaim itself the provisional revolutionary government of the whole of Russia as early as possible, or should *set up* a provisional revolutionary government (which would amount to the same thing, only in another form)."[52]

The open, broad, and non-Party character of the soviets offended the sectarianism of many Bolsheviks, but Lenin regarded this as the source of their strength. Perhaps they could organize the revolutionary alliance of democratic and socialist workers, peasants, soldiers, sailors, and intellectuals which could overthrow the autocracy and make possible the convocation of a nationwide Constituent Assembly which would carry through the democratic revolution. His crucial 1917 insight—that the soviets were inherently revolutionary organs of working-class power whose very existence was a direct challenge to the landlord and bourgeois state—was based on his 1905 observations of their behavior.

But the soviets, peasant and worker committees, trade unions, and other organizations were crushed by December. Their political demands had been confined for the most part to calls for a democratic republic because their leaders tended to think in terms of convening a Constituent Assembly rather than seeing the soviets as the basis of a new proletarian state.[53] Lenin too had initially regarded them as instruments of an insurrection which could organize a provisional revolutionary government and facilitate the final victory of the democratic revolution. If they could organize the workers' overthrow of the government, it was theoretically possible that they could also serve as organs of an entirely new political apparatus. But Lenin was almost alone here. Whatever their role and their future, the soviets clearly demanded attention and he was one of the few socialist theoreticians who would try to understand their role even after the victorious reaction had broken them up.

Past and Future

The revolutions of 1848 and 1905 broke out at similar points in Marx's, Engels's and Lenin's theoretical and political development and affected all three men in similar ways. Both occurred unexpectedly, furnished opportunities to clarify and develop preliminary observations, and ended an early period of largely theoretical development. Theory was tested and extended in a period of highly concentrated political activity.

If there was one theme which underlay their work, it was the proposition that democracy can be won only by a proletarian-led armed population which would use political power to break the existing political structure and create new state organs of popular sovereignty. Every revolution requires a class dictatorship for its consolidation, defense, and further advance. The class content of the revolution shapes the character of the dictatorship, understood now as direct class rule based on force. Whether in Germany or Russia's "bourgeois" revolution or in France's "proletarian" one, the majority could not organize its political power if the repressive and bureaucratic structures of the existing state remained in place. Reaction ultimately triumphed in 1848 and 1905 because the need to "break" this apparatus was not yet sufficiently clear on a theoretical level and because the popular movements were not yet sufficiently powerful to accomplish the task even if it had been. Nevertheless, the refined Marxist theory of the state which emerged from the failures of both revolutions was as connected to the "ultimate results" of a classless society as the earlier version had been.[54]

By the time the revolutions were defeated, Marx, Engels, and Lenin had come to a richer understanding of revolutionary democracy because real life had shown how political and social transformation depended on each other. They firmly believed that a legitimate democratic government could issue only from the popular overthrow of the old regime and not from the previous organization of state power. Its role as an instrument of further political and social transformation connected democracy to revolution and explained each in light of the other. The prolonged reaction which followed the collapse of the upsurges of 1848 and 1905 provided them with the chance to learn what could be learned from failure. What they made of this opportunity proved as important as anything else in the further development of both their theoretical understanding and their practical politics.

NOTES

1. Karl Marx, "The Class Struggles in France 1848–1850," Karl Marx and Frederick Engels, *Collected Works* (New York: Progress Publishers, 1975–), 10:78. Unless otherwise noted, all references to Marx and Engels will be to the *Collected Works*.

2. *Ibid.*, 76.

3. Marx, "The Eighteenth Brumaire of Louis Bonaparte," 11:110.

4. *Ibid.*, 129.

5. *Ibid.*, 143.

6. "The Class Struggles in France 1848–1850," 10:71.

7. *Ibid.*, 69.

8. Marx, "The Bourgeoisie and the Counter-Revolution," 8:178.

9. "The *Kolnische Zeitung* on the Elections," 8:289.

10. See Hal Draper, *Karl Marx's Theory of Revolution, The "Dictatorship of the Proletariat"* (New York: Monthly Review Press, 1986), 3:61–67, and Alan Gilbert, *Marx's Politics: Communists and Citizens* (New Brunswick: Rutgers University Press, 1981).

11. Marx, "The Bill Proposing the Abolition of Feudal Obligations," 7:295.

12. Marx, "The Class Struggles in France 1848–1850," 10:118.

13. Marx, "The Eighteenth Brumaire of Louis Bonaparte," 11:188.

14. Marx and Engels, "Address of the Central Authority to the League," 10:281.

15. "The Class Struggles in France 1848–1850," 10:125.

16. *Ibid.*, 127.

17. Marx, "The Crisis and the Counter-Revolution," 7:431; Frederick Engels, "The Agreement Session of July 4," 7:205.

18. Engels, "The Agreement Session of July 4," 7:200–7.

19. "The Crisis and the Counter-Revolution," 7:431.

20. "The Bourgeoisie and the Counter-Revolution," 8:157.

21. *Ibid.*, 197.

22. Marx, "Speech at the First Trial of the Neue Rheinische Zeitung," 8:316–17.

23. Marx, "Lassalle," 8:464.

24. "The Eighteenth Brumaire of Louis Bonaparte," 11:186.

25. See, for example, Engels, "Huser," 7:20–23, and Marx, "The Democratic Party," 7:27–29.

26. "The Victory of the Counter-Revolution in Vienna," 7:506.

27. "The Magyar Struggle," 8:227–28.

28. Marx and Engels, "Review of *Le Socialisme et l'impôt*, par Emile de Girardin," 10:333. See also letter from Engels to Marx, 21 August 1851, 38:434–35.

29. "The Eighteenth Brumaire of Louis Bonaparte," 11:106.

30. Lenin, "The Working Class and Revolution," *Collected Works* (Moscow: Progress Publishers, 1960–72), 9:207. Unless otherwise noted, all subsequent references will be to this edition.

31. "The Victory of the Cadets and the Tasks of the Workers' Party," 10:255–56.

32. "Speech on the Report on the Activities of the Duma Group," 12:448–49.

33. "Speech on the Activities of the Duma Group," 12:396.

34. "The Democratic Tasks of the Revolutionary Proletariat," 8:517. See also "Three Constitutions or Three Systems of Government," 8:557–59.

35. Lenin, "Two Tactics of Social-Democracy in the Democratic Revolution," 9:48–53.

36. "The Bolsheviks and the Petty Bourgeoisie," 12:182.

37. "The Democratic Tasks of the Revolutionary Proletariat," 8:511.

38. "From Narodism to Marxism," 8:83; "Two Tactics of Social-Democracy in the Democratic Revolution," 9:48.

39. "Working Class and Bourgeois Democracy," 8:82.

40. "From Narodism to Marxism," 8:89.

41. "Two Tactics of Social-Democracy in the Democratic Revolution," 9:100.

42. "The Cadet Duma Grants Money to the Pogrom-Mongers' Government,"

11:63. See also "The Armed Forces and the Revolution," 11:64, and "The Dissolution of the Duma and the Tasks of the Proletariat," 11:115.

43. "The Armed Forces and the Revolution," 11:56–57.

44. "In the Wake of the Monarchist Bourgeoisie, or In the Wake of the Revolutionary Proletariat and Peasantry?" 9:221. See also "While the Proletariat is Doing the Fighting the Bourgeoisie is Stealing Towards Power," 9:184.

45. "The Proletariat and the Peasantry," 8:232.

46. "The Revolutionary-Democratic Dictatorship of the Proletariat and the Peasantry," 8:299.

47. "Report on the Question of Participation of the Social-Democrats in a Provisional Revolutionary Government," 8:385.

48. "On the Provisional Revolutionary Government," 8:464–65.

49. "Two Tactics of Social-Democracy in the Democratic Revolution," 9:56–57.

50. "The Victory of the Cadets and the Tasks of the Workers' Party," 10:216

51. "Revision of the Agrarian Programme of the Workers' Party," 10:192–93.

52. "Our Tasks and the Soviet of Workers' Deputies," 10:21.

53. Oskar Anweiler, *The Soviets: The Russian Workers', Peasants', and Soldiers' Councils, 1905–1921*, trans. Ruth Hein (New York: Pantheon, 1974).

54. Marx and Engels, "Statement," 10:387–88.

Chapter 4

Clarifications and Refinements

Economic recovery and political reaction combined to defeat the revolutionary movements of 1848 and 1905. The rudimentary organizations which had appeared were easily crushed, and it soon became clear that the bourgeoisie's abandonment of democracy did not guarantee that "the people" would be able to defend it. Indeed, the politics of both periods were shaped by the fact that neither the workers nor the peasants were strong enough to lead a revolution whose democratic content now depended on its ability to interfere with existing property relations and political structures.

Their expectations frustrated, many revolutionaries retreated into the abstract theorizing and complicated intrigues of disappointed *émigrés*. Marx, Engels, and Lenin devoted themselves to journalism, education, and propaganda until the revival of the workers' movements made possible the organization of the International Workingman's Association in 1864 and the heightened activity of a rejuvenated Bolshevik Party in 1911. Both organizations issued from the gradual development of a strictly proletarian political current and its separation from the "general-democratic" movements of 1848 and 1905. The idea that state power in the hands of the working class could be the decisive engine of social revolution had demarcated proletarian-socialist from other democratic tendencies for some time, and the political conclusions which they drew from defeat would enable Marx, Engels, and

Lenin to take the full measure of the structures which the insurrectionary workers would spontaneously discover for themselves in 1871 and 1917.

Problems of Popular Democracy

In France and Germany the counterrevolution triumphed as the propertied classes, terrified of the consequences of their own victory, fled into the arms of the same monarchist-feudal reaction which they had momentarily helped overthrow. Whether French or German, liberal or Bonapartist, Orleanist or Legitimist, the bourgeoisie had prevailed largely because it had been able to use a state power whose basic structure had been preserved through all the dramatic events of 1848. Its hostility to democracy came as no particular surprise to Marx or Engels, but its refusal to countenance any restrictions on its use of property or changes in the structure of its state led both men to warn the workers about the petty-bourgeois democrats. Unable to go any farther than proposing changes in the existing political regime yet capable of some revolutionary initiative against the remnants of feudalism, they had proven unable to break with capitalism on their own. Taken by itself, their "pure" democracy had turned out to be little more than an ideological stalking-horse for the bourgeoisie's liberalism because they were unable to make a clean break with the existing political structure or to endorse serious public restrictions on property. The workers had shown considerable independent activity across Europe during the revolution *because* of their propertylessness, however, and the appearance of a distinct proletarian tendency encouraged Marx and Engels to describe a policy toward the democrats which would assist Lenin during the spring and summer of 1917. Where directly socialist measures were out of the question they urged the workers to organize themselves independently of their unstable democratic allies if they were to avoid falling under the bourgeoisie's domination. The workers

> must compel the democrats to carry out their present terrorist phrases. They must work to prevent the direct revolutionary excitement from being suppressed again immediately after the victory. On the contrary, they must keep it alive as long as possible. Far from opposing so-called excesses, instances of popular revenge against hated individuals or public buildings that are associated only with hateful recollections, such instances must not only be tolerated but the lead in them must be taken.[1]

Their immediate task was to push the democrats further than they would ordinarily go, and this would require the workers to "immediately establish their own revolutionary workers' governments" alongside the official structures, "whether in the form of municipal committees and municipal councils or in the form of workers' clubs or workers' committees." An armed "proletarian guard" would replace the traditional civic militia which the bourgeoisie had used in 1848. Everything depended on the workers' ability to organize themselves independently of the existing political institutions and authorities.[2] If 1848 proved anything to Marx and Engels, it was that democracy depended on the workers' ability to break with the entire structure of the bourgeois state. The political independence of the socialist workers from the petty-bourgeois democrats was now the first condition for a successful democratic movement.

Marx's analysis of events in Italy was based on this perspective while it simultaneously insisted on the importance of social matters. If state power remained at the center of his and Engels's thinking, it is essential to remember *why* it was so important. Mazzini was interested in a unified Italian bourgeois republic and thus represented part of the general-democratic movement, but his hostility to any social change doomed his narrow political project. "He has," said Marx, "figured as the chief of the Republican formalists of Europe. Exclusively bent on the political forms of the state, they have had no eye for the organization of society on which the political superstructure rests."[3] Louis-Bonaparte's intrigues aimed at unifying Italy through a counter-revolutionary alliance between his imperial interests and those of the Piedmont dynasty. Marx hoped that the revolutionary Italian democrats would organize the peasantry, intelligentsia, and working class and initiate a national uprising which would unite "the people" around a social program and thus assist the European revolutionary movement as a whole.[4] In contrast to Mazzini's narrowness, Marx thought that "Garibaldi's plan, whether successful or not, is the only one that, under present circumstances, holds out any chance of rescuing Italy, not only from its old tyrants and divisions, but also from the clutches of the new French protectorate."[5] Only Italy's "popular dictator" understood the connection between national unification and the social welfare of the people, and this accounted for both his success and Marx's support.[6]

The American Civil War presented similar problems. Lincoln's initial goal had been to preserve the Union, but the Confederacy's evident desire to extend slavery to the territories had transformed the terms of a struggle which could now be won only by organizing and unleashing the full measure of Northern democratic energy. Lincoln would have to proclaim the abolition of slavery as his goal and transform what had been a war for defense of the union into a revolutionary interference with existing property relations. The slavers may have indignantly proclaimed that American "liberty" depended on the preservation of slavery, but the Northern workers and farmers knew full well that their own freedom required the revolutionary-democratic expropriation of property in human beings and the social transformation of the South.[7]

But a familiar pattern reasserted itself as the Union leadership shrank back from what was required to win, and the South stood on the verge of military victory because the North was afraid of its consequences. Indolence and indifference characterized the Union war effort, Engels complained to Marx; there was no aggressiveness, resilience, or talent among the army officers or the political leaders.[8] Radical measures like the Homestead Act and the organization of Negro units in the Army would doubtless strengthen democracy, but it was the slavers who were able to muster popular enthusiasm during the early months of the war.[9] The defeatism which swept over the North in the fall of 1862 provoked a revealing outburst from Engels:

> That a people placed in a great historical dilemma, and one in which its very existence is at stake to boot, should turn reactionary *en masse* and vote for abject surrender after 18 months' fighting, is really beyond my comprehension. Desirable though it may be, on the one hand, that the bourgeois republic should be utterly discredited in America too, so that in future it may never be preached ON ITS OWN MERITS, but only as a means towards, and a form of transition to, social revolution, it is, nevertheless, annoying that a rotten oligarchy, with a population only half as large, should evince such strength as the great, fat, helpless democracy.[10]

The revolutionary character of Marx and Engels's democracy had always issued from a social core which tended to push it beyond the exclusively political formulations of the Jacobin left. They were certainly interested in democratic political institutions and in popular government, but their politics remained informed by their radical commitment to social revolution. The fight for a democratic state derived its meaning from the fight for a democratic society, and Marx's revealing criticisms of the cooperative movement provided another example of his approach. Cooperation was doubtless a more advanced form of social labor than the "pauperizing and despotic" subordination of individual labor to capital, but without a thoroughgoing political change it could be nothing more than an interesting experiment in bourgeois society. No small-scale efforts at regeneration could be anything more than a palliative reform in the absence of the general transformation which was the exclusive preserve of politics:

> Restricted, however, to the dwarfish forms into which individual wages slaves can elaborate it by their private efforts, the co-operative system will never transform capitalist society. To convert social production into one large and

harmonious system of free and co-operative labor, *general social changes* are wanted, *changes of the general conditions of society*, never to be realized save by the transfer of the organized forces of society, viz., the state power, from capitalists and landlords to the producers themselves.[11]

No important social changes are possible unless the class content and the formal structure of the existing state are broken. Marx and Engels continued to insist on the leading role of politics as they carried on the theoretical struggle against a new variety of the same antipolitical radicalism they had combated earlier. Their criticism of Bakunin's calls for the "equalization of classes" and the abolition of inheritance were made in the name of the workers' general political struggle. Inheritance does not cause the transfer of wealth from the direct producers to the idle owners of capital, said Marx. Exploitation is the inevitable result of private property in the means of production, and simply announcing its abolition will not touch the economic foundations of class society.[12] Bakunin's slogans expressed the crude egalitarianism of a petty-bourgeois democracy which sought to harmonize the interests of all classes, and Marx repeated his earlier suggestion that full equality could come only with the abolition of classes.[13] No partial reform could eliminate poverty and misery as long as the social foundations of bourgeois rule were left untouched.[14] Now as before he insisted that these foundations could be uprooted only by a proletariat in possession of state power.

The comprehensiveness of the political struggle remained at the heart of his thinking; the emancipation of labor was ultimately a social problem, but only the conquest of state power could provide the workers with the weapon they could use to transform bourgeois social relations on the most general level. It was Marx's fusion of the political and social aspects of the workers' movement which stood behind his insistence that the International recognize that "to conquer political power has therefore become the great duty of the working classes."[15] The economic subjection of labor to capital may be the fundamental cause of servitude in all its forms, but erecting a proletarian state is the indispensable first step toward the emancipation of the working class.[16] Once again Marx had given expression to the distinctive element of his socialism, and he identified it unambiguously in his famous 1852 letter to Joseph Weydemeyer:

Now as for myself, I do not claim to have discovered either the existence of classes in modern society or the struggle between them. Long before me, bourgeois historians had described the historical development of this struggle between the classes, as had bourgeois economists their economic anatomy. My own contribution was 1. to show that the *existence of classes* is merely bound up with *certain historical phases in the development of production*; 2. that the class struggle necessarily leads to the *dictatorship of the proletariat*; 3. that this dictatorship itself constitutes no more than a transition to the *abolition of all classes* and to a *classless society.*[17]

The comprehensive guidance of a workers' state, which Marx now called simply the "dictatorship of the proletariat," is the entire transition to a classless society. Politics will lead economics throughout this period, and the social foundations of communism will require the active intervention of a proletarian state based on continuous mass revolutionary democracy exercised from below. Whatever form this class state would assume—and Marx knew very little about this except that it would look very different from any bourgeois structure—its contribution to the revolutionary process and to democracy could be gauged solely by the extent to which it contributed to the development of a classless society. Marx's words to Weydemeyer tied together the political and economic aspects of the proletarian revolution as he understood it as surely as they expressed his revolutionary fusion of dictatorship and democracy.

Proletarians and Peasants

Like the events of 1848, the Russian Revolution of 1905 had been generated by complex and contradictory forces. Lenin knew that it was important to understand what had produced it, why it had accomplished so much, and why it had ultimately failed. His own orientation toward the "ultimate goal" of a classless society was as central to his effort as it had been in Marx's words to Weydemeyer. The 1905 "bourgeois" revolution's motive force had come from the workers and peasants. The mass political strikes, huge demonstrations, and armed insurrections had been taken with the workers in the lead; the impact of a distinctly proletarian current in the democratic movement was more developed in 1905 than in 1848, the role of the workers more pronounced than earlier. This shaped Lenin's observation that "all that the liberation movement in Russia has won up to now was won entirely and exclusively by the revolutionary struggle of the masses headed by the proletariat."[18] Proletarian methods of combat had driven a bourgeois revolution much more directly than ever before. The soviets and the peasant committees, the most important and democratic mass organizations created by the revolutionary movement, had appeared because popular demands could no longer be articulated within the boundaries of the existing political structure. Their very existence posed a direct challenge to the existing state and was fundamentally incompatible with it.

The soviets were particularly important, for their working-class composition and revolutionary orientation had encouraged Lenin to think that they might serve as the "embryos" of a new revolutionary power which would issue from the overthrow of the autocracy. The German workers had not had enough time to develop such institutions in the relatively backward social conditions of the 1848 revolution, and the liberals had been able to seduce the democrats with the "constitutional illusion" that democracy could be won without changing existing institutions or compromising private property. But Russia's 1905 revolution had moved forward because the people had directly seized and briefly exercised political liberty and power. For Lenin, the soviets' legitimacy stemmed from their origin in this direct popular activity exercised without regard to and in defiance of existing laws and regulations. The same had been true of other institutions like the Peasant Committees, and if the revolution's course had confirmed the proletariat's leading role, it was also true that the Russia of 1905 was an overwhelmingly agrarian society and that much of the struggle to uproot patriarchal social relations would be waged in the countryside. This generated powerful tendencies to subordinate the proletariat's interests to those of the bourgeoisie through the medium of the peasant democrats and made the socialist workers' orientation toward bourgeois democracy and the bourgeois state more important than ever. For the next twelve years the Bolsheviks would work to pose a proletarian-socialist alternative to the bourgeoisie's liberalism and the petty bourgeoisie's democracy. The outcome of this struggle depended on Lenin's ability to accurately assess the economic and political motion of the enormous peasantry.

His entire analysis rested on his position that the democratic revolution in Russia was not and could not be a bourgeois revolution pure and simple. He now characterized it as a "bourgeois peasant" revolution in an effort to identify all the rural laborers as the driving force in the assault on the old order. Their demand for land placed them in revolutionary opposition to the existing social and political system, and their direct occupations and expropriations had dealt a serious blow to the autocracy and the landlords in 1905. Since 1899 Lenin had believed that the immediate cause of Russia's backwardness was the survival of large noble estates, peasant smallholdings, *corvée* labor, and a host of other feudal labor services in the countryside. The democratic revolution could not proceed without the abolition of the entire rural system, and the immediate transfer of land to the peasants was at the center of his agrarian program.[19] The demand for the complete abolition of the landed estates distinguished proletarian democracy from that of the liberal bourgeoisie and from Stolypin's newly reformist government, chastened by the firestorm which had swept over the countryside in 1905. "The standpoint of the police official and of the Russian liberal," said Lenin by way of summary, "is: how to provide the muzhik with an allotment? The standpoint of the class-conscious worker is: how to free the muzhik from feudal landlordism? How to break up the feudal latifundia?"[20]

Represented by the democratic slogans of the Socialist-Revolutionaries, most peasants shared the workers' desire to expropriate the landlords and distribute land to the rural laborers. But Socialist-Revolutionary calls for the transfer of land to village communes based on the "labor principle" of equalized land tenure were not socialist proposals. As he had during the revolution, Lenin supported the Socialist-Revolutionaries when they acted like revolutionary democrats, but he disputed their socialist pretensions because they wanted to protect private trade, commodity production, capital in agriculture, and wage labor. He continued to insist that the proletariat and the peasantry were two distinct classes, that the peasantry's perspectives could not rise any further than those of the petty bourgeoisie until the democratic revolution had been won, and that its democratic demands could not be part of the socialist revolution until the proletariat stepped forward to provide the leadership which could help the poorest peasants understand the need to abolish all private property. The disintegration of the peasantry would create a distinct class of rural proletarians who could adopt such a perspective, but both the existing agrarian system and the autocratic state would have to be broken before that could happen.[21] "The peasantry cannot carry out an agrarian revolution without abolishing the old regime, the standing army and the bureaucracy, because all these are the most reliable mainstays of landlordism, bound to it by thousands of ties. That is why the idea of achieving a peasant revolution by democratizing only the local institutions without completely breaking up the central institutions is scientifically unsound."[22] The direct struggle for socialism in agriculture would be made possible by the workers' prior seizure of political power. The question of state power was as central to the revolution in the countryside as it was elsewhere.

The victory of this bourgeois peasant revolution would be the "revolutionary-democratic dictatorship of the proletariat and the peasantry." The democratic revolution was now defined in more radical terms than traditional bourgeois revolutions and depended on an alliance between the peasants and the workers. Democracy in Russia could be carried to completion only if a popular worker-peasant revolution from below carried out an assault on the entire economic and political structure of landlordism, an assault which Lenin fully expected the liberal bourgeoisie to resist. Marx and Engels had discovered the need to break up the existing state apparatus during the revolution of 1848, and Lenin had applied their analysis to the Russian events of 1905. It remained for him to link his economic and political assessments of Russia's new sort of bourgeois revolution.

Prussia or America?

The key to Lenin's revolutionary democracy was his judgment that the upheaval of 1905, far from solving Russia's crisis, had merely expressed it in a particularly concentrated way. The 1861 emancipation of the serfs had been a "feudal" reform which had actually strengthened the existing order in the countryside and left the laboring population as dependent on the landlords as it had been earlier. As long as the agrarian system and the monarchy remained intact, no reform could lead to anything more than a slightly less deformed capitalism. Overthrowing the autocracy and expropriating the landlords were the two indispensable yet necessary revolutionary conditions of even the mildest sort of democratic movement.

Lenin was certain that Russia's immediate future was a capitalist one. But the lateness of the hour meant that its capitalism could come in a variety of forms depending on which class held political power. The autocracy recognized the future as clearly as anyone else and Stolypin was trying to generate a "Prussian" solution to Russia's agrarian problem before it was too late. His strategy, which the crown would follow until it was swept away in 1917, aimed at developing a prosperous landed peasantry, eliminating the village communes, and reforming the big latifundia so market forces would gradually replace feudal forms of exploitation and transform the landlords into Junkers. The power of the autocracy and the privileges of the nobility would be preserved even as bourgeois relations of production developed *à la Prusse*.

Lenin's alternative to Stolypin was the "American" path of a rapid and thorough democratization of the economy and polity. It foresaw the elimination of the latifundia, nationalization of agriculture and equalization of landholdings, democratization of the political system, and evolution of an agrarian economy of small peasant farmers. The "Prussian" and "American" paths were equally "bourgeois" in content, and it was Lenin's preference for the latter which defined his strategy of seeking agreement with the peasant democrats. His center of gravity lay in the familiar claim that the bourgeoisie would not be able to lead the democratic revolution in Russia and that only an alliance between the workers and peasants could sweep away the old system and make possible the rapid development of capitalism. The "American path" would assume the state form of the "revolutionary-democratic dictatorship of the workers and peasants":

> To facilitate the development of the productive forces (this highest criterion of social progress) we must support not bourgeois evolution of the landlord type, but bourgeois evolution of the peasant type. The former implies the utmost preservation of bondage and serfdom (remodelled on bourgeois lines), the least

possible development of the productive forces, and the retarded development of capitalism; it implies infinitely greater misery and suffering, exploitation and oppression for the broad mass of the peasantry and, consequently, also for the proletariat. The second type involves the most rapid development of the productive forces and the best possible (under commodity production) conditions of existence for the mass of the peasantry. The tactics of Social-Democracy are determined not by the task of supporting the liberal bourgeoisie, as the opportunists think, but by the task of supporting the fighting peasantry.[23]

The agrarian problem was "the central issue in our 1905 Revolution," and Stolypin's attempt to encourage a Prussian solution to it is what lay behind Lenin's well-known contention that Russia suffered from both the presence and the incompleteness of capitalism. The thirty thousand biggest landowners owned as much land as ten million peasant households, and until that was changed the suffocating poverty of the peasantry, the primitive state of agriculture, the inadequacy of the home market, the dependence of the smallholders, and the survival of various forms of labor-service could only worsen. The issue was as clear now as it had been before 1905. Democracy could come to Russia only as a result of a revolution and a dictatorship. The immediate issue was

> whether landed proprietorship would remain intact—in which case the poverty-stricken, wretched, starving, browbeaten and downtrodden peasantry would for many years to come *inevitably* remain as the bulk of the population—or whether the bulk of the population would succeed in winning for themselves more or less human conditions, conditions even slightly resembling the civil liberties of the European countries. This, however, *would not be accomplished* unless landed proprietorship and the landowner monarchy inseparably bound up with it were abolished by a revolution.[24]

The political dimensions of this situation were molded by its economics. The 1861 Reform had begun the evolution of the feudal monarchy into a bourgeois monarchy.[25] This gradual transformation tended to generate two kinds of bourgeois politics.

The bourgeois liberals had become the monarchy's most important allies. Mildly reformist in orientation, they tried to contain social unrest and encourage gradual political evolution so they could jockey between the autocracy and the popular movement. Mimicking their German counterparts of 1848, the Cadets defended liberty but were afraid of democracy, sought a constitutional monarchy but were willing to preserve important feudal privileges. In all cases they sought to avoid a situation where they would have to openly confront a powerful popular movement, and Lenin expected them to defend "liberty" in words while they opposed democracy in deeds.

Unlike the bourgeois liberals, the peasant democrats stood for the democratization of Russia's political and social systems and, *given an independent working-class political movement*, could play an important part in a democratic revolution to rid the country of the autocracy and the landlords. Supporters of the "American" path, the Socialist Revolutionaries spoke for the smaller proprietors who stood to benefit from the complete elimination of medievalism. They often imagined themselves to be socialists, however, and when Lenin called them peasant democrats he did so not to insult them but to remind the peasants that no redivision of the land or political changes in the state would remove the pressure of capital on their small property and small production. His constant warnings about liberal treachery flowed from his view that Social-Democracy's most important task was to win the allegiance of the peasant democrats, and he pictured the Cadets as defenders of feudal reaction because he was so intent on weaning the democrats from their influence. He considered this to be the crucial political problem facing the workers and it would take a dozen years of class struggle, war, and revolution to solve it. For the moment two avenues of capitalist development remained open, and everything would depend on forging a revolutionary alliance between working-class democracy and peasant democracy. It would not be easy, for "the representatives of the democratic tendency, while marching toward their goal, continually waver and are subject to the influences of liberalism. To prevent these waverings and to end this subjection is one of the most important tasks of Marxism in Russia."[26] The trick was to find a political formula which would express the revolutionary alliance between the socialist workers and the democratic peasants and give Russian substance to the observation Marx had made half a century earlier that "THE WHOLE THING IN GERMANY will depend on whether it is possible TO BACK THE PROLETARIAN REVOLUTION BY SOME SECOND EDITION OF THE PEASANTS' WAR. In which case the affair should go swimmingly."[27]

Revolutionary Dictatorship

The "revolutionary-democratic dictatorship of the proletariat and the peasantry" was Lenin's description of the "American" path's state structure. It expressed his fusion of social and political matters, for the destruction of landlordism in agriculture and of the autocracy in politics could not proceed apart from one another and together constituted the democratic revolution.[28] It named the proletariat and the peasantry as the insurrectionary leaders of the "bourgeois" revolution and called for strong measures to limit bourgeois freedom and bourgeois property in the name of democracy. His understanding of the political requirements of Russia's social revolution shaped Lenin's strategy until he developed a new assessment in April 1917:

> . . . the concept of bourgeois revolution is not a sufficient definition of the forces which may achieve victory in such a revolution. Bourgeois revolutions are possible, and have occurred, in which the commercial, or commercial and industrial, bourgeoisie played the part of the chief motive force. The victory of such revolutions was possible as the victory of the appropriate section of the bourgeoisie over its adversaries (such as the privileged nobility or the absolute monarchy). In Russia things are different. The victory of the bourgeois revolution is impossible in our country *as the victory of the bourgeoisie*. This sounds paradoxical, but it is a fact. The preponderance of the peasant population, its terrible oppression by the semi-feudal big landowning system, the strength and class-consciousness of the proletariat already organized in a socialist party—all these circumstances impart to our bourgeois revolution a *specific* character. This peculiarity does not eliminate the bourgeois character of the revolution. . . . It only determines the counter-revolutionary character of our bourgeoisie and the necessity of a dictatorship of the proletariat and the peasantry for victory in *such* a revolution. For a "coalition of the proletariat and the peasantry," winning *victory* in a bourgeois revolution, happens to be nothing else than the revolutionary-democratic dictatorship of the proletariat and the peasantry.[29]

Lenin's analysis of 1905 paralleled that of Marx and Engels in 1848. Both identified the peasantry as the decisive ally of the proletariat in a society where the relations of production were not yet sufficiently developed to permit the direct struggle for communism. Marx's "red republic" of 1848 found its equivalent in Lenin's 1905 hybrid dictatorship of the country's two revolutionary classes. Only such a state could consummate the bourgeois revolution; the present struggle in Russia, Lenin emphasized repeatedly, was between two different kinds of capitalism, two paths to its possible development, and two forms of bourgeois-democratic institutions and state structures. The "American path" could be won only through the revolutionary-democratic dictatorship of the proletariat and the peasantry.

The new regime would be a dictatorship because it would issue directly from an insurrection of a laboring population which would have broken the existing organization of state power. It would constitute a radical break with all earlier political structures because it would rest on the direct initiative of the most revolutionary sections of the people and would be legitimated by its democratic character rather than by its formal legality. Revolutions are never legal; the workers had organized soviets because the events of 1905 had forced them to confiscate governmental funds, appeal to the population to stop paying taxes, seize printing presses, arrest individual police officers, and the like. They "were undoubtedly the embryos of a new, people's, or, if you will, revolutionary government. In their social and political character, they were the rudiments of the dictatorship of the revolutionary elements of the people," the workers and peasants.[30] "Authority—unlimited, outside the law, and based on force in the most direct sense of the word—is dictatorship," Lenin said once again. He urged his readers to remember "the difference between dictatorship *over* the people and dictatorship *of* the revolutionary people," for entirely different state structures would be required for each.[31] A dictatorship of the majority would be a democratic dictatorship, and the soviets were perfectly structured to exercise it:

> As the dictatorship of a minority, the old regime was able to maintain itself solely with the aid of police devices, solely by preventing the masses of the people from taking part in the government and from supervising the government. The old authority persistently distrusted the masses, feared the light, maintained itself by deception. As the dictatorship of the overwhelming majority, the new authority maintained itself and could maintain itself solely because it enjoyed the confidence of the vast masses, solely because it, in the freest, widest and most resolute manner, enlisted all the masses in the task of government. It concealed nothing, it had no secrets, no regulations, no formalities. It said, in effect: Are you a working man? Do you want to fight to rid Russia of the gang of police bullies? You are our comrade. Elect your deputy. Elect him at once, immediately, whichever way you think best. We will willingly and gladly accept him as a full member of our Soviet of Workers' Deputies, Peasant Committee, Soviet of Soldiers' Deputies, and so forth. It was an authority open to all, it carried out all its functions before the eyes of the masses, was accessible to the masses, sprang directly from the masses, and was a direct and immediate instrument of the popular masses, of their will. Such was the new authority, or, to be exact, its embryo, for the victory of the old authority trampled down the shoots of this young plant very soon.[32]

Lenin's notion that the two classes which comprised "the masses" could exercise a joint revolutionary-democratic dictatorship reflected the peculiarities of Russian social development even as it seemed to collide with Marx's view that only one class can exercise state power. The Russian proletariat was numerically small in a society dominated by a huge peasantry but was politically the country's most advanced class. The joint dictatorship of which Lenin spoke was a developed version of Marx and Engels's analyses of 1848. While it could not undertake directly socialist measures, it could carry the democratic revolution to its end and at some point might have to go over to actively obstructing bourgeois institutions. It was a contradictory hybrid and reflected Lenin's view that the peasantry would power the democratic revolution even if the workers would lead it. The same problems would reappear a dozen years later and challenge his political analysis of the period between 1917's two revolutions. In the meantime, the "three pillars" of a democratic republic, the confiscation of the landlords' estates, and the eight-hour day constituted the principal democratic slogans of the Bolsheviks until April 1917. They summarized the unfulfilled demands of 1905, represented the socialist workers' alliance with the democratic peasantry, and signified the revolution's willingness to interfere with existing property relations in the name of social and political democracy. They became the practical slogans of the democratic revolution over the course of a dozen years of intensifying crisis, world war, and social collapse.

Imperialism and Democracy

The necessity to break with Bismarck proved as important to Marx and Engels's analysis of the Franco-Prussian War as it was to Lenin's discussion of Russian agriculture. Their initial view was that France had begun an aggressive war of conquest and that Louis Bonaparte's defeat might remove the "incubus" of the Second Empire from French life and thus permit the working class to reorganize and reassert itself. But twenty years of corruption had made it impossible for France to wage war against inferior German forces, and within two months the cream of its army had been defeated and its emperor taken prisoner at Sedan.[33] The proclamation of a conservative bourgeois republic in Paris and Bismarck's decision to continue the war forced a change in Marx and Engels's views. A German war of national defense had degenerated into a war of military conquest and territorial annexation made most obvious when the Prussians announced their intention to seize Alsace and Lorraine.[34]

Germany's defeat was now necessary if the war was to come to a democratic conclusion, but the French Government of National Defense had quickly agreed to Bismarck's demand for a huge indemnity, surrender of the Paris fortifications, and disarmament of the army and the partisans. As they had looked to the English workers to defend the independence of the Irish and to the Northern workers to defeat slavery in the United States, Marx and Engels now looked to the German workers to insist on a nonannexationist and honorable peace with the French Republic:

> The German working class has resolutely supported this war, which it was not in their power to prevent, as a war for German independence and the liberation of France and Europe from that pestilential incubus, the Second Empire. It was the German workmen who, together with the rural laborers, furnished the sinews and muscles of heroic hosts, leaving behind their half-starved families. Decimated by the battles abroad, they will be once more

decimated by misery at home. In their turn they are now coming forward to ask for "guarantees"—guarantees that their immense sacrifices will not have been brought in vain, that they have conquered liberty, that the victory over the imperialist armies will not, as in 1815, be turned into the defeat of the German people; and, as the first of these guarantees, they claim an *honorable peace for France, and the recognition of the French Republic.*[35]

Like the Americans, the French would have to conduct a revolutionary popular war if they hoped to defeat the Germans. But the Orleanist bourgeoisie which led the Republic was unable to do what was necessary to defend the country. They would not organize or arm the population—especially the workers of Paris—and, since they were more frightened of "their" working class than of the German invaders, their military defeat was as guaranteed as was their continued economic survival. Just as the false Bonaparte had rescued them from social revolution in 1851 and appropriated political power as his reward, so Bismarck saved them from the proletariat as he humiliated them on the battlefield and despoiled them of two provinces and a great deal of money. The French military command, adamantly opposed to relieving the German siege of the capital by arming Paris, did not hesitate to communicate its concern that the people might use their arms to defend the city against Prussian armies today and against French property tomorrow. French negotiators had assured the Germans that disarming the Parisians would be the Republic's first priority after the conclusion of a peace treaty, and this led Marx to repeat his 1848 warning that, while the republicans had control of the "talking ministries," the Orleanists held the important posts of the police and the army.[36] The question of which class exercised political power in an unreconstructed state apparatus was still at the heart of his thinking on the eve of an event which would dramatically enrich it.

It was because the situation was so full of danger, and because even a counterrevolutionary bourgeois republic would be better than the Empire, that Marx warned that "the French working class moves, therefore, under circumstances of extreme difficulty. Any attempt at upsetting the new government in the present crisis, when the enemy is almost knocking at the doors of Paris, would be a desperate folly."[37] The immediate need was to consolidate whatever measure of liberty had been made possible by Bonaparte's defeat. It would fall to the workers of every country to defend the republic, and the more militant they were in doing so the closer would come the day of their own emancipation. The demands for a nonannexationist peace, the democratic unification of Germany, and the defense of the French Republic would be as incendiary in 1870 as similar demands would be forty-seven years later.

The general-democratic struggles which Marx and Engels described were "bourgeois" in class content even if they could be led by only the workers. Their analyses of the American Civil War, the "national question," and the Franco-Prussian War illustrated their view that some potential for democratic politics remained even within bourgeois society. Marx's *Capital* described a competitive nineteenth-century system which required formal equality before the law and a developed structure of bourgeois liberty. But Lenin's 1916 analysis of imperialism argued that monopoly had supplanted competition in economics and that outright reaction had replaced liberalism as the bourgeoisie's characteristic political stance. Imperialism had so intensified capitalism's basic trends that the entire bourgeoisie was now distinctly counterrevolutionary and antidemocratic in all areas of an increasingly violent and retrograde political environment. Militarism and bureaucracy had come to dominate the national life of all advanced capitalist countries without exception.

It was precisely because he defined imperialism's economic content as monopoly that Lenin thought of its political content as reaction. During its competitive stage, capitalism had been economically progressive and politically democratic in relation to the feudalism from which it had grown. But imperialism marked the definitive limit of bourgeois democracy's progressive potential because of its new and defining economic feature—the replacement of free competition by monopoly and the accompanying domination of a financial oligarchy. Shaped by the economy's tendency to decay and stagnation, imperialism's political tendency toward war and domination constantly negated freedom and compromised democracy. The petty-bourgeois "anti-imperialism," which developed at the beginning of the twentieth century, turned out to be the last faint vestige of bourgeois democracy.[38] A radically democratic anti-feudal revolution was still the path to socialism in a country like Russia, but the advent of imperialism meant that the path could be shortened considerably. Free competition no longer defined capitalist economics, and bourgeois democracy no longer characterized its politics. Any fight for democracy was bound to become linked to the fight for socialism in a much more direct fashion than had been the case when Marx and Engels had been active.

The weakness of the bourgeoisie's commitment to democracy had long been a central tenet of Marxist orthodoxy, but Lenin's new analysis suggested that the bourgeoisie as a whole was lost to democracy. No general-democratic problem could be solved within the boundaries of the "old" bourgeois-democratic revolution. They had all become part of the "new" proletarian-socialist revolution. If the bourgeoisie could not lead its own admittedly mild revolution when Marx and Engels had been active, the advent of imperialism sealed its implacable hostility to new democratic revolutions which would have to be more radical than their predecessors. The problems which the century's general-democratic movements had addressed could now be solved only with a revolutionary break with the entire structure of capitalism as such.[39] Capitalism had utterly exhausted whatever demo-cratic potential it had retained from its earlier competitive period. Its parasiti-cal, decadent, and predatory final stage posed the issue of its unreserved hostility to democracy so sharply that it could only be resolved through a revolutionary break with private property as such.

The "three pillars" of 1905 remained the centerpiece of Lenin's ap-proach to the democratic revolution throughout this period. A democratic republic, the confiscation of the landlords' estates, and an eight-hour day might not be socialism yet, but they certainly went beyond anything the bourgeoisie was capable of offering and entailed a much more dramatic break with its politics than had been possible earlier. Socialism is about class war and not class peace, Lenin insisted; it requires an orientation toward the immediate goal of state power, not defending the interests of the workers in bourgeois society or discovering ways in which they can share the fruits of imperialist exploitation. Its first task is organizing a new state to uproot private property rather than electing a few deputies to parliament and asking for a few crumbs from the imperialist bourgeoisie's "feast." World War I had become a problem for most European socialist leaders because it tended to narrow the possibilities for reform. Lenin was alone among almost all of them because he understood the revolutionary possibilities opened up by the carnage. His famous claim that "imperialism is the eve of the socialist revolution" expressed his view that the advent of monopoly capital had created a qualitatively new revolutionary situation. The "American" democ-racy he had been describing would still aim at the complete elimination of the remnants of Russian feudalism, but the historic change in his thinking was that imperialism—now described as "reaction up and down the line"—linked the struggle for democracy much more tightly than before to the possibility of socialism. The unaccomplished goals of 1905 remained at the heart of his thinking and were still summarized as the "three pillars." But World War I had intensified everything and democracy now required that the workers "convert the imperialist war into a civil war":

> Civil war, for which revolutionary Social-Democracy today calls, is an armed struggle of the proletariat against the bourgeoisie, for the expropriation of the capitalist class in the advanced capitalist countries, and for a democratic revolution in Russia (a democratic republic, an eight-hour working day, the confiscation of the landowners' estates), for a republic to be formed in the backward monarchist countries, etc.[40]

The increasing connections between the struggles for democracy and for socialism had been prefigured in 1905, and Lenin delivered a prophetic lecture about its meaning on the twelfth anniversary of Bloody Sunday. The events of 1905 had been bourgeois-democratic in their social content but proletarian in both the vanguard role of the urban workers and in their method of struggle—particularly the discovery of the political general strike and the soviets. The immediate aim of the revolution had been the bourgeois "three pillars," but its unprecedentedly militant character had been a direct function of the proletariat's leading role. The wide activity of the peasant masses was 1905's other important feature, but the revolutionaries had been too trusting of the liberals and too poorly organized to lead the workers effectively. By 1916 Lenin was as convinced that a new and more powerful 1905 was maturing as Marx and Engels had become during the 1870s. Having discovered theoretically and observed in practice how important it was to maintain socialism's criticism of the bourgeois state, all three men watched for signs of increased activity as the workers' movement slowly revived. Little did they suspect how quickly the proletarian contours of modern revolution and modern democracy would reveal themselves.

NOTES

1. Karl Marx and Frederick Engels, "Address of the Central Authority to the League," Karl Marx and Frederick Engels, *Collected Works* (New York: Progress Publishers, 1975–), 10:282. Unless otherwise noted, all references to Marx and Engels will be to the *Collected Works*.

2. *Ibid.*, 283.

3. "Mazzini and Napoleon," 15:485.

4. Marx, "On Italian Unity," 16:148–53.

5. "Interesting from Sicily—Garibaldi's Quarrel with La Fanna—A letter from Garibaldi," 17:422.

6. Engels, "Garibaldi's Movements," 17:449–52; Garibaldi's Progress," 17:471–75; Marx, "Affairs in Prussia—Prussia, France, and Italy," 17:488–92.

7. Marx, "The London *Times* on the Orleanist Princes in America," 19:27–31.

8. See Engels letters to Marx, 12 May 1862, 41:364; 30 July 1862, 41:386–88; 9 September 1862, 41:414–15; 5 November 1862, 41:422–23; and Marx letter to Engels, 10 September 1862, 41:415–17.

9. "A Criticism of American Affairs," 19:226–29.

10. Engels, letter to Marx, 15 November 1862, 41:428.

11. Marx, "Instructions for the Delegates of the Provisional General Council. The Different Questions," 20:190.

12. Marx, "Report of the General Council on the Right of Inheritance," 21:65–67.

13. "The General Council of the International Working Men's Association to the

Central Bureau of the International Alliance of Socialist Democracy," 21:45–46.

14. "Inaugural Address of the International Working Man's Association," 20:9.

15. *Ibid.*, 12.

16. "Provisional Rules of the Association," 20:14.

17. 39:62–63.

18. "Revolution and Counter-Revolution," *Collected Works* (Moscow: Progress Publishers, 1960–72), 13:116. Unless otherwise noted, all subsequent references will be to this edition.

19. "The Agrarian Programme of Social-Democracy in the First Russian Revolution 1905–1907," 13:227.

20. *Ibid.*, 230.

21. "How the Socialist-Revolutionaries Sum Up the Revolution and How the Revolution Has Summed Them Up," 15:330–44.

22. "The Agrarian Programme of Social-Democracy," 13:349.

23. "The Agrarian Programme of Social-Democracy in the First Russian Revolution 1905–1907," 13:243–44.

24. "Stolypin and the Revolution," 17:248.

25. "Apropos of an Anniversary," 17:114.

26. *Ibid.*, 118.

27. Marx, letter to Engels, 16 April, 1856, 40:41.

28. "Some Sources of the Present Ideological Discord," 16:87–88.

29. "The Assessment of the Russian Revolution," 15:56–57.

30. "The Victory of the Cadets and the Tasks of the Workers' Party," 10:243. For a somewhat different interpretation, see Hal Draper, *The "Dictatorship of the Proletariat" From Marx to Lenin* (New York: Monthly Review Press, 1987), 89–93.

31. "The Victory of the Cadets and the Tasks of the Workers' Party," 10:244.

32. *Ibid.*, 245.

33. Engels, "Notes on the War—XII," 22:70; "Notes on the War—XIV," 22:77; "The Rise and Fall of Armies," 22:98–99.

34. Engels, "How to Fight the Prussians," 22:104.

35. Marx, "Second Address on the Franco-Prussian War," 22:267–68.

36. Boris Nocolaievsky and Otto Maenchen-Helfen, *Karl Marx: Man and Fighter* (Hammondsworth: Penguin, 1976), 347–54.

37. "Second Address on the Franco-Prussian War," 22:269.

38. "Imperialism, the Highest Stage of Capitalism," 22:287.

39. Neil Harding, *Lenin's Political Thought, Theory and Practice in the Socialist Revolution* (New York: St. Martin's Press, 1981), 2: chaps. 3–6.

40. "Conference of the RSDLP Groups Abroad," 21:160.

Chapter 5

The Commune State

By 1848 the proletarian seizure and use of state power in the cause of social revolution had emerged as the political core of Marx and Engels's communism. The revolutions which broke out in that year demonstrated that the state's form was a function of its class content and that organizing the workers' public power could not proceed unless the existing bourgeois machine was broken. The appearance of the Soviets in 1905 raised this issue in a similarly concrete fashion for Lenin, but the defeat of both revolutions seemed to make irrelevant all but the most speculative discussion about what a new state might look like and what it might do. In the aftermath of defeat and withdrawal all three men concentrated their efforts on the struggle for as radical a democracy as existing economic and political conditions would permit.

The unexpected Paris Commune of 1871 and the spontaneous February Revolution of 1917 forced yet another modification of their theoretical understanding of the revolutionary state. At all times they understood how important it was to extract what was of general theoretical significance from both developments. Marx and Engels came to regard the Commune as the first proletarian dictatorship, and Lenin's use of its lessons to chart the passage from a bourgeois to a soviet republic marked a decisive turning point in the development of Marxist political theory and practice. Their unequivocal characterization of the dictatorship of the proletariat as the "commune state" helped all three men inform their theoretical understanding with the practical experiences of the revolutionary proletariat, and the result was a dramatic and productive enrichment of their political thought.

"At Last Discovered"

The September 2, 1870 German victory at Sedan and capture of Louis Bonaparte provoked massive working-class demonstrations in Paris two days later which overthrew the Empire and organized a temporary "Government of National Defense." A bourgeois-monarchist formation dominated by many of the same Orleanists and conservative republicans who had held power earlier, its formal mandate was limited to negotiating an armistice with the Prussians. Bismarck's intention to seize Alsace and Lorraine provoked its grandiose declaration that it would not yield "a centimeter of French territory," upon receipt of which the Germans promptly resumed their march on Paris. It was soon clear that this "government of national defense" would be no more capable of waging the popular war for which Marx and Engels had been calling than its discredited predecessor—precisely *because* it was a continuation of the Empire in everything but name. By the end of January 1871 the city was surrounded and the new government, housed symbolically at Versailles, capitulated without a fight. Bismarck now insisted that a National Assembly be elected with a legal mandate to do no more than negotiate a final peace treaty. Protected by the Prussian bayonets which had brought it into being, its monarchist majority ratified final peace terms after choosing Adolphe Thiers, a veteran Orleanist intriguer, to form its Executive.

Thiers' first task was to discipline Paris, and he borrowed a page from his predecessors by initiating a series of provocations similar to those which had driven the workers to their doomed insurrection in June 1848. The wartime moratorium on debts was ended, the pay of the National Guard was cut, working-class newspapers were suspended, and—most important— the National Assembly unilaterally announced its intention to continue governing the country from Versailles in open violation of its charge. The final insult came when the Executive tried to arrest the city's leaders and disarm the National Guard by organizing a secret raid to seize the two hundred cannons which public subscription had provided for the defense of the capital from the Prussians.

The Paris Commune was formed in the aftermath of the spontaneous public reaction to Versailles's attempt to steal the cannons. The workers held political power for the first time and Marx's seminal account of its brief history summarized what they did with it. For him its essence lay in the positive steps it took to break the bourgeois state, and it provided dramatic support for his long-held view that "the working class cannot lay hold of the ready-made State machinery, and wield it for its own purposes."[1] The Commune's deepest meaning lay in its destruction of the state's bureaucratic and coercive essence, defined as the standing army, police, bureaucracy, clergy, and judicature. Every commentary which Marx offered made two fundamental points: the objective press of events made a thoroughgoing attack on the state an indispensable requirement for the organization and exercise of working-class political power, and revolutionary democracy was the weapon which the workers would have to use to transform the state from an enemy to an instrument of human emancipation.

From the beginning Marx was convinced that the Commune involved much more than national defense or Thiers's attempt to repackage the old wine of the Empire in a new Orleanist bottle. Temporarily blocked by the class paralysis which had precipitated Louis Napoleon's new Bonapartism, the proletarian revolution could now finish what it had begun in 1848. The Commune *was* the "social revolution," and it began to organize a workers' state as it began to break the bourgeois one.[2] In so doing it began to prepare the transition to the communism whose outlines Marx had discerned in earlier revolutions:

> The direct antithesis to the Empire was the Commune. The cry of "Social Republic," with which the revolution of February was ushered in by the French proletariat, did but express a vague aspiration after a Republic that was not only to supersede the monarchical form of class-rule, but class-rule itself. The Commune was the perfect form of that Republic.[3]

Just as *The Communist Manifesto* had suggested that the workers' effort to abolish bourgeois property would inevitably be broadened into a drive to abolish all property, so the Commune expressed their movement's thrust to destroy the bourgeois state, lay the foundations of an embryonic proletarian structure, and ultimately overcome the state as such. Marx had no doubt that it issued from a "proletarian revolution"[4] and that "the majority of its members were naturally working men, or acknowledged representatives of the working class."[5] Its politics would have to lead its economics for some time, since

> [I]ts true secret was this. It was essentially a working-class government, the produce of the struggle of the producing against the expropriating class, the political form at last discovered under which to work out the economical emancipation of Labor.[6]

If the Commune was the "political form" of the social revolution, the workers would have to be armed. Engels had said repeatedly that the Prussians could be defeated only if the government organized a popular revolutionary war, and Marx had observed in a letter written before the proclamation of the Commune that, "however the war may end, it has given the French proletariat practice in arms, and that is the best guarantee of the future."[7] The bourgeoisie's Government of National Defense knew full well that in order to defend Paris against an expected Prussian siege it had to arm the city. "But Paris armed was the Revolution armed. A victory by Paris over the Prussian aggressor would have been a victory of the French workman over the French capitalist and his State parasites. In this conflict between national duty and class interest, the Government of National Defense did not hesitate one moment to turn into a Government of National Defection."[8]

Thiers's attack on the National Guard had been directed against the armed citizenry, the majority of whom were workers whose very organization constituted a threat to the bourgeois social order. "This fact was now to be transformed into an institution. The first decision of the Commune, therefore, was the suppression of the standing army, and the substitution for it of the armed people."[9] It was clear that replacing the army and the police, the "physical force elements of the old Government," would not eliminate repression in the short run.[10] Certain coercive functions were still necessary but they would now be discharged by representatives of the laboring majority, the "responsible and at all times revocable agents" of the Commune. This meant that these functions would be performed far more democratically than ever before, and this changed everything.[11] Since public officials were elected and easily recallable, paid workingman's wages, and directly accountable to the population, the "physical force elements" of the new state were no longer "political" in the old sense of the term. Their close connection to the people began to overcome the separation between state and society which had contributed to the development of a separate, artificial, and alien sphere of politics. Paradoxically, the Commune was so democratic *because* it was a such a powerful proletarian structure—because it was a dictatorship. Revolutionary dictatorial democracy was the workers' only weapon—but it was their decisive one.

The Commune Marx described was not just another working-class insurrection. The proletarian seizure of political power had begun to transform all the terms of traditional public discourse. Democracy and dictatorship had a qualitatively different meaning and had qualitatively different effects when organized by the productive majority than when they had been weapons of capital. When used by the insurrectionary workers, they became powerful levers with which the repressive bourgeois state could be transformed into its opposite.

Formed "of the municipal councilors, chosen by universal suffrage in the various wards of the town, responsible and revocable at short terms," the Commune was still an indirect democracy but organized such close and continuous supervision of its leaders that the representative principle, while not abolished, was changed beyond recognition.[12] The merger of legislative and executive functions was decisive; when Marx described the Commune as "a working, not a parliamentary, body, executive and legislative at the same time," he was speaking of a political formation whose democratic character rested not on its formal division of power but in its dependence on the continuous popular supervision of political life.[13] "The judicial functionaries were to be divested of that sham independence which had long served to mask their abject subserviency to all succeeding governments to which, in turn, they had taken, and broken, the oaths of allegiance. Like the rest of public servants, magistrates and judges were to be elective, responsible, and revocable."[14] Its power a direct function of its necessarily close connection to the population, the Commune's democracy was different from and more comprehensive than any bourgeois state's democracy, resting as it did on a weak and internally divided public sector's formal separation from an unequal social order.

The Commune's final step against the bourgeois state was its attack on the "parson power." All churches were disestablished and disendowed, religion made a private affair, and the formal influence of the church over education and science ended. At first blush this seems little more than the formal separation of church and state accomplished in earlier bourgeois revolutions, but driving religion out of public affairs—and especially out of education—had been so high on the agenda of the French Left for so long that it had effectively become part of the social revolution.

For Marx the Commune's democratic legitimacy lay in its insurrectionary root rather than in its connection to any prior structure of state power. It was the instrument of the entry of "the people" into active political life. Nowhere was this more evident than in the possibilities the proletariat held out to the peasantry and the petty bourgeoisie.

The wealth and power of the large landed proprietors constantly reminded the peasantry that its small property remained vulnerable a century after the Great Revolution had abolished feudalism. The high taxes which supported Bonaparte's bureaucracy and foreign adventures were combined with the "tyranny" of the local police, the ignorance in which the priests kept rural children, and the debts which burdened small agriculture. The peasantry's objective interests lay with the workers even if the Commune was not able to extend its influence into the countryside.[15] The same was true of the urban petty bourgeoisie; weighed down by exorbitant taxes, ruined by the swindling extravagance of the Empire, and offended by the arbitrariness, irrationality, and obscurantism of the Church, it too stood to benefit from a Commune which would have organized a "democratic centralist" national state if it had had the time:[16]

> The rural communes of every district were to administer their common affairs by an assembly of delegates to the central town, and these district assemblies were again to send deputies to the National Delegation in Paris, each delegate to be at any time revocable and bound by the *mandat impératif* (formal instructions) of his constituents. The few but important functions which still would remain for a central government were not to be suppressed, as has been intentionally mis-stated, but, on the contrary, to be organized by the Communal constitution, and to become a reality by the destruction of the State power which claimed to be the embodiment of that unity independent of, and superior to, the nation itself, from which it was but a parasitic excrescence.[17]

Embodying neither the federalists' network of small communities nor the anarchists' instantaneous "abolition" of the state, the Commune "amputated" the purely repressive organs of the old order by democratizing them. Society could begin to exercise the legitimate functions which had been formerly exercised by the state. "The Communal Constitution would have restored to the local body all the forces hitherto absorbed by the State parasite feeding upon, and clogging the free movements of, society. By this one act it would have initiated the regeneration of France."[18] The very nature of these forces and functions was irrevocably changed because the "immense majority" now held political power; what had formerly been repressive and bureaucratic had now become part of the transition to a classless society. The changed political environment had changed everything.

Like the changes it imparted to democracy, dictatorship, representation, centralism, and the like, the Commune's revolutionary democracy gave to universal suffrage a qualitatively different meaning than it had had during the Empire. "Instead of deciding once in three or six years which member of the ruling class was to misrepresent the people in Parliament, universal suffrage was to serve the people, constituted in Communes, as individual suffrage serves every other employer in the search for workmen and managers in his business."[19] A revolutionary break with the existing order transformed universal suffrage into the impartial instrument bourgeois politics promised in theory but denied in practice. Its broad, radical, and democratic character served as yet another illustration that the Commune was "a thoroughly expansive political form, while all previous forms of government had been emphatically repressive."[20]

Marx was interested in the Commune's social measures for similar reasons. Unlike the English and French oligarchs who had gorged themselves on the expropriation of the church and the aristocracy, the Paris workers did not attack bourgeois property directly. On the face of it ending nightwork for journeyman bakers, abolishing employers' ability to reduce wages through fines, and turning over closed workshops and factories to associations of workers had little to do with socialism but did represent the sort of public supervision of private property in which Marx had been interested for some time as a transitional measure. The Commune was an implicitly anticapitalist, though it could not yet be a consciously socialist, regime. Like his analysis of its nascent political form, Marx's investigation of its social measures focused on their tendencies rather than on their limited accomplishments.

It is of more than passing importance that the only serious criticism which he or Engels ever directed at the Commune echoed the charge they had directed against the revolutionaries of 1848: it was too weak. Burdened by their illusions about the bourgeoisie's ability to tolerate democracy and naively wedded to liberal moral and legal formalities, its leaders hesitated to take the necessarily dictatorial measures against Thiers lest they be blamed for starting a civil war which the Commune's very existence proclaimed. Marx had reminded the workers many times of the need to take energetic, even terroristic, measures against the bourgeoisie; their "conscientious scruples" led him to say that "if they are defeated, only their 'good nature' will be to blame."[21] They had been generous with the Paris swells since the proclamation of the Republic, but generosity become a fault when the Commune's Central Committee failed to respond to Thiers's "burglarious attempt" to seize the cannons by immediately marching on Versailles and putting a quick end to his conspiracy and his government.[22] It wasted much valuable time electing the Communal leadership and gave its enemy another chance at the ballot box.[23] It consistently paid too much attention to liberalism's procedural formalities, too little to the need for repression, and failed democracy in the process. Engels summarized his views in his report to the International's General Council:

As long as the Central Committee of the National Guards had managed the affair, it had gone on well but after the elections there had been talk and no action. The time for action against Versailles had been when it was weak but that opportunity had been lost and now it seemed that Versailles was getting the upper hand and driving the Parisians . . . In June 1848 the fight had been over in four days but then the work-people had had no cannon. It would not be over so quick now . . . The work-people—200,000 men—(were) far better organized than at any other insurrection.[24]

The old society could not tolerate a state which drew the productive population into the administration of public affairs. If the Paris workers of 1871 did not understand this any better than their predecessors had in June

1848, the bourgeoisie certainly did. The brutality with which it destroyed the Commune testified to the depth of the democratic challenge which a workers' state had hurled at the entire bourgeois order:

> When the Paris Commune took the management of the revolution in its own hands; when plain working men for the first time dared to infringe upon the Governmental privilege of their "natural superiors," and, under circumstances of unexampled difficulty, performed their work modestly, conscientiously, and efficiently—performed it at salaries the highest of which barely amounted to one-fifth of what, according to high scientific authority, is the minimum required for a secretary to a certain metropolitan schoolboard—the old world writhed in convulsions of rage at the sight of the Red Flag, the symbol of the Republic of Labor, floating over the Hôtel de Ville.[25]

The Commune signified considerably more than the replacement of one set of state institutions by another. Marx and Engels were interested in how the workers had begun to structure the political power they had taken, and this is why they paid more attention to its historical tendencies than to its more limited accomplishments. They are often accused of magnifying its importance out of all proportion to its actual impact and of saddling their successors with the unnecessarily mechanical claim that any proletarian state would have to be modeled on the Commune. But for them the Commune's whole point lay in what it represented and what it had begun to do. Its very existence illustrated the central theoretical discovery they had made a quarter of a century earlier:

> The political rule of the producer cannot coexist with the perpetuation of his social slavery. The Commune was therefore to serve as a lever for uprooting the economical foundations upon which rests the existence of classes, and therefore of class rule. With labor emancipated, every man becomes a working man, and productive labor ceases to be a class attribute.[26]

Had the Commune been given more time, it might have developed the assault on the social order which Marx and Engels had been anticipating for years. But its violent suppression did not change the fact that democratizing state and society now defined each other even more directly than they had earlier precisely because they had become practical matters. The same was true of the relationship between revolutionary democracy and dictatorship. A strong workers' state would be forced to undertake extreme measures of self-defense which would have the unintended effect of radicalizing the revolution and simultaneously initiating its own disappearance. No one expected the process to be a simple or straightforward one. Lenin would later come to appreciate the full thrust of Marx's observation that it would be a lot easier to begin the revolution than to carry it through:

> The working class did not expect miracles from the Commune. They have no ready-made utopias to introduce *par décret du peuple*. They know that in order to work out their own emancipation, and with it that higher form to which present society is irresistibly tending by its own economical agencies, they will have to pass through long struggles, through a series of historic processes, transforming circumstances and men. They have no ideals to realize, but to set free elements of the new society with which old collapsing bourgeois society itself is pregnant.[27]

The actual course of events revealed that Marx and Engels were as hasty in their 1871 projections as they had been in 1848, but their observations of the Commune had begun to describe the transition between capitalism and communism. Its fate was shaped by the contradictions of a crisis which was pushing it forward and a history which was simultaneously dragging it back. The fusion of political and social revolution and of democracy and dictatorship had momentarily created an environment which was qualitatively different from anything which had preceded it. A deepening crisis drove the workers to use their political power to assault the social roots of their exploitation. Even as the past exacted its price on the Commune, Marx's central discovery that the seizure of state power would change everything was not lost on Lenin.

April and the Soviet Republic

Neither Marx nor Engels ever had the opportunity to bring the lessons of the Commune to bear on another revolutionary situation, but Lenin did and his assessment of 1871 shaped much of his analysis of the Russian Revolution. Just as the Franco-Prussian War had provoked an insurrection and the Paris Commune, so World War I precipitated the February Revolution and the reappearance of the soviets. The commemoration of "Bloody Sunday" and International Women's Day led to huge demonstrations in early 1917 which rapidly accelerated because of the unending carnage at the front, deep famine in the cities, unsatisfied peasant land hunger, intensified oppression in the factories, and continuing demands for democratic reforms from almost all sectors of society. Hundreds of thousands of workers struck their employers, soldiers and sailors mutinied against their officers, peasants seized the land, and soviets sprang up all over the country. When the St. Petersburg garrison refused to fire on huge crowds of demonstrators, first the tsar and then his hand-picked successor abdicated in favor of a Cadet-

Octobrist Provisional Government formed from the State Duma's Provisional Committee and supported by the newly organized Soviet of Workers' Deputies.

The Revolution of 1905 had generated Lenin's cumbersome formulation of the "revolutionary-democratic dictatorship of the proletariat and the peasantry" as the specific form of the bourgeois revolution in Russia. Its "three pillars" were the democratic republic, the confiscation and redistribution of the landlords' estates, and the eight-hour day. The right of secession for oppressed nationalities, universal suffrage, separation of church and state, and the like completed the architecture of the Bolsheviks' "minimum program" for the democratic revolution—an "American" pattern of bourgeois development which would stimulate as rapid a transition to socialism as circumstances would permit. This analysis had dominated Lenin's thinking before the February Revolution and, substantially modified, formed the bedrock of his strategic and tactical projections between it and October.

The February Revolution and the organization of a Provisional Government marked the bourgeoisie's accession to full political power but it was the spontaneous reappearance of the Soviets of Workers' Deputies which decisively shaped Lenin's thinking. News that the autocracy had collapsed prompted him to observe that "the only *guarantee* of freedom and of the complete destruction of tsarism lies in *arming the proletariat*, in strengthening, extending and developing the role, significance and power of the Soviet of Workers' Deputies."[28] Both the Paris Commune and the events of 1905 had taught him that there was only one mechanism through which the workers could bring their political power to bear:

> Guided by their class instinct, the workers have realized that in revolutionary times they need *not only* ordinary, but an entirely different organization. They have rightly taken the path indicated by the experience of our 1905 Revolution and of the 1871 Paris Commune; they have set up a *Soviet of Workers' Deputies*; they have begun to develop, expand and strengthen it by drawing in *soldiers'* deputies and, undoubtedly, deputies from rural *wage*-workers, and then (in one form or another) from the entire peasant poor.[29]

It was precisely this "entirely different" quality of the soviets which impressed Lenin. Even if the direct transition to socialism was not yet on the order of the day, their very existence stood as living proof that the bourgeois revolution could no longer be consummated within a bourgeois political structure. Lenin had anticipated a radical democratic revolution since 1905 and the overthrow of the tsar prompted him to predict that the people "will learn, and probably very soon, that there is bread and that it can be obtained, but only by methods that *do not respect the sanctity of capital and landown-*

ership."[30] The reappearance of the soviets provided continuity from the Commune through 1905 to 1917 and beyond. Inherently revolutionary organizations of popular power, they stood in immediate and direct contradiction to the bourgeoisie's Provisional Government because they represented strivings for a measure of social and political democracy which could no longer be contained within bourgeois limits.

When Lenin returned to Russia from Swiss exile and presented his "April Theses" to the Petrograd Bolsheviks, however, he was speaking to a party leadership whose thinking was very different from his. It tended to fall back on the earlier and familiar analysis and to place the February events at the beginning of the revolutionary-democratic dictatorship of the proletariat and the peasantry. Since the revolution's minimum program had not been fulfilled, it appeared that the democratic revolution was still in progress and that some sort of qualified Bolshevik support of the Provisional Government would be in order.[31]

Lenin responded to his comrades' caution by noting that the Provisional Government was as committed to Russian participation in the World War as the autocracy had been. No support of such a government is possible under these conditions, and the second thesis came to the obvious—and decisive—conclusion. "The specific feature of the present situation in Russia," it declared, "is that the country is *passing* from the first stage of the revolution—which, owing to the insufficient class-consciousness and organization of the proletariat, placed power in the hands of the bourgeoisie—to its *second* stage, which must place power in the hands of the proletariat and the poorest sections of the peasants."[32] Lenin's critical April claim was that the bourgeois revolution had been *completed* with the organization of the Provisional Government. It was in transition to its next stage, hampered only by the workers' all-too-familiar tendency to trust the bourgeoisie, yield power to its Provisional Government, and wait for it to institute the democratic reforms promised by its spokesmen.

It was understandable for the workers to be led astray by their democratic illusions, Lenin said, but it was quite impermissible for the Bolsheviks to pander to them. The party's central ideological task was to explain that "the Soviets of Workers' Deputies are the *only possible* form of revolutionary government, and that therefore our task is, as long as *this* government yields to the influence of the bourgeoisie, to present a patient, systematic, and persistent *explanation* of the errors of their tactics, an explanation especially adapted to the practical needs of the masses."[33] This committed him to the basic position he would hold until the October Revolution: organized independently and working through the soviets, the socialist proletariat must convince the peasant democrats to join it in the seizure of power. Whether or not the Bolsheviks were in a position to win a majority in the soviets, it was essential to separate the proletarian-communist elements of the revolutionary-democratic dictatorship of the workers and peasants from the petty-bourgeois democratic elements. The time had come to move past February and construct

> [n]ot a parliamentary republic—to return to a parliamentary republic from the Soviets of Workers' Deputies would be a retrograde step—but a republic of Soviets of Workers', Agricultural Laborers' and Peasants' Deputies throughout the country, from top to bottom.[34]

This "soviet republic" would be the state form of the proletarian dictatorship, but the "highly important" feature of the present situation was that the Petrograd Soviet, which momentarily represented the "democratic dictatorship of the workers and peasants" and was led by the petty-bourgeois democrats, was voluntarily handing over power to its bourgeois antagonist. The February Revolution had become immobilized in a "dual power" marked by the coexistence of a bourgeois Provisional Government which was too weak to disperse the workers and a broadly democratic Soviet of Workers' Deputies whose leaders were content to play the role of loyal opposition. The Provisional Government, whose only claim to legitimacy rested in its continuity with the pre-existing autocratic state from which it had arisen, had declared an amnesty for all political prisoners. The Soviet, drawn directly from the ranks of the revolutionary population, had issued its famous Order Number One to the army and announced "to the people of the whole world" its desire for peace without annexations or indemnities. For Lenin the resulting paralysis "has led to the *interlocking of two* dictatorships: the dictatorship of the bourgeoisie . . . and the dictatorship of the proletariat and the peasantry."[35] The revolutionary process had developed more rapidly than the "old" Bolsheviks had anticipated, and an unexpectedly complex and unstable situation had arisen:

> There is not the slightest doubt that such an "interlocking" cannot last long. Two powers *cannot coexist* in a state. One of them is bound to pass away; and the entire Russian bourgeoisie is already trying its hardest everywhere and in every way to keep out and weaken the Soviets, to reduce them to naught, and to establish the undivided power of the bourgeoisie.
>
> The dual power merely expresses a *transitional* phase in the revolution's development, when it has gone farther than the ordinary bourgeois-democratic revolution, *but has not yet reached* a "pure" dictatorship of the proletariat and the peasantry.[36]

The soviets represented the same kind of power and anticipated the disappearance of the state in exactly the same manner as had the Paris Commune. In both cases the momentum was provided by an insurrectionary popular democracy which could not be contained within the existing political boundaries. "This, and this *alone*, constitutes the *essence* of the Paris Commune as a special type of state," Lenin claimed. Just as Marx and Engels had made it clear that the workers need an entirely different state from that of the bourgeoisie, so he sought to impress on his colleagues that "inasmuch as these Soviets exist, *inasmuch as* they are a power, we have in Russia a state of the *type* of the Paris Commune."[37] But the soviets represented nothing more than an "incipient" power because their petty-bourgeois leadership was voluntarily surrendering power to the Provisional Government. The "basic question of every revolution" remained unresolved—which class will hold and use political power? The revolutionary-democratic dictatorship of the proletariat and peasantry was temporarily locked in an unstable alliance with the dictatorship of the bourgeoisie, but the hour was late. "There is no other way out. Either we go back to supreme rule by the capitalists, or forward towards real democracy, towards majority decisions. This dual power cannot last long."[38]

The full dimensions of the crisis were graphically revealed in April, when the Miliukov Note announced the Provisional Government's intention to continue the war in the face of overwhelming popular opposition and the Executive of the Petrograd Soviet declared itself "satisfied" with its explanation. Tens of thousands of workers and soldiers were prepared to overthrow the government on the spot and had substantial support for an insurrection in the Bolshevik Party. But the entrance of the Mensheviks and Socialist-Revolutionaries into the Provisional Government convinced Lenin that the bulk of the democratic petty bourgeoisie still trusted it, and he managed to convince his colleagues that the seizure of power was out of the question until this changed:

> The slogan "Down with the Provisional Government!" is an incorrect one at the present moment because, in the absence of a solid (i.e., a class-conscious and organized) majority of the people on the side of the revolutionary proletariat, such a slogan is either an empty phrase, or, objectively, amounts to attempts of an adventurist character.
> We shall favor the transfer of power to the proletarians and semi-proletarians only when the Soviets of Workers' and Peasants' Deputies adopt our policy and are willing to take the power into their own hands.[39]

Lenin's attitude toward the soviets was based on four mutually reinforcing perspectives. He thought that they symbolized the democratic dictatorship of the workers, soldiers, and peasants, provided the most important arena in which the struggle for the allegiance of the peasantry could be waged, might be able to organize a successful insurrection, and could be the embryonic form of a Russian Commune state. Taken together, these four strands of thinking placed the soviets at the center of his thinking about democracy and dictatorship. "We need a state," he had said from Switzerland, "but *not* the kind the bourgeoisie needs, with organs of government in the shape of a police force, an army and a bureaucracy (officialdom) separate from and opposed to the people." The workers will have to smash the existing state, and this means "*merging* the police force, the army and the bureaucracy with *the entire armed people.*"[40] "Democracy from below, democracy without an officialdom," would be a democracy "without a police, without a standing army; voluntary social duty by a *militia* formed from a universally armed people—this is a guarantee of freedom which no tsars, no swashbuckling generals, and no capitalists can take away."[41] This new state will be in progress toward its own dissolution in the same way that the Paris Commune had signaled the growing revolutionary fusion of state and society.

Their different attitudes toward the soviets were one of the most important watersheds dividing the liberal bourgeoisie, the democratic petty bourgeoisie, and the socialist proletariat. As in 1848, the Cadets wanted to preserve the parliamentary republic with its army and bureaucracy because they anticipated that they might have to turn against the popular movement which had momentarily brought them to power in the first place. The Mensheviks and SRs talked about democracy in exclusively parliamentary terms and seemed to regard the soviets as steppingstones to a more democratic bourgeois democracy. The workers' approach must be different, said Lenin. The Soviets were the expression of proletarian political power and could not work unless the people take state and economic matters into their own hands.[42] Their very existence expressed the most important difference between the "old" and the "new" type of state because they dispensed with the entire machinery of minority rule as they organized the power of the productive population. "The parliamentary bourgeois republic hampers and stifles the independent political life of the *masses,* their direct participation in the *democratic* organization of the life of the state from the bottom up. The opposite is the case with the Soviets," which Lenin was increasingly disposed to view as the foundation of a Commune state.[43] Such a state would simplify the suppression of the landowners and capitalists which is "the purpose and significance of the dictatorship of the proletariat," but its deeper significance lay in the effect it had on the specifically bourgeois features of the old state. It is not a matter of introducing socialism all at once, Lenin repeatedly cautioned his comrades; "the Soviets must take power not for the purpose of building an ordinary bourgeois republic, nor for the purpose of making a direct transition to socialism."[44] It is a matter of taking certain concrete steps which can assist in the transition. Chief among them was solving the "agrarian problem" once and for all.

Soviets and Rural "America"

The continued survival of the landed estates remained the most important unresolved general-democratic issue after the overthrow of the autocracy, and Lenin repeatedly said that the revolution's future depended entirely on an alliance between the workers and the peasants to uproot them. The February Revolution would be a democratic one only if it was the first step in setting Russia on the "American path." A democratized political structure would encourage the market to develop and the peasantry to divide along modern class lines, with the poorer peasants and the agricultural wage-workers increasingly sympathetic to socialism and the more prosperous peasants moving toward the bourgeoisie. The Provisional Government shared Lenin's awareness of the explosive character of the peasants' land hunger but was afraid to satisfy it out of fear that the army might disintegrate and more dangerous attacks on property might develop. Its spokesmen repeatedly proclaimed the government's interest in agrarian democracy but they tended to implore the peasants to delay any action until the matter could be "studied," call for negotiations and compromises all around, and insist that land reform be accomplished in an "orderly," legal and "responsible" manner. In substance their pronouncements differed little from those of the authorities and the liberal Cadets in 1905.

The Socialist-Revolutionaries were the heirs of the great tradition of Narodnik populism and formed the most important peasant party in 1917.[45] Rooted in traditional peasant democratism and egalitarianism, they advocated the expropriation and equal division of the feudal estates, a prohibition on buying or selling land, and a ban on employing wage labor in agriculture. But the enormous peasantry's rapid economic differentiation was stimulating the development of modern social classes in the countryside, and the autocracy's downfall precipitated the political split which Lenin had anticipated for years. The party's right wing slowly gravitated toward the more prosperous peasants, adopted the political perspective of the liberals, and generally supported the Provisional Government. It rejected "illegal" peasant land seizures and gradually abandoned most anticommercial elements of the party's original position. The Left SRs, whose more radical democracy reflected the views of the poorer peasants, continued to demand the nationalization and equal division of the land, the prohibition on buying and selling, and the outlawing of wage labor. They were crucial to the future, and it was their turn toward the Bolsheviks in the fall which sealed the Provisional Government's fate and made the October Revolution possible.

Lenin had called for the uncompensated expropriation of the landlords by revolutionary peasant committees in 1905 and he repeated his call in 1917 as the Provisional Government tried to organize "voluntary agreements" between the peasants and landlords to preserve the very estates whose abolition was the condition of rural democracy. "Can you call it 'democracy,' 'people's freedom,' when the peasants, who constitute the overwhelming *majority* of the population, have no right to adopt and carry out their own decision, but must wait for a '*voluntary agreement*' between the tillers of the land and the landowners?" he asked.[46] His insistence that peasant soviets and committees seize the land right away without waiting for permission from a promised Constituent Assembly took him well beyond the democrats' equal-distribution schemes. Even if direct expropriation was a step toward nationalization, however, a soviet-led agrarian revolution would result in nothing more than the American "free labor on free soil." Converting peasants into farmers renting land from the state would be agrarian democracy *à l'américaine* but was not yet socialism.

> Does that mean that the land will be handed over to all working people? No, it does not. Free labor on free soil means that all the old forms of land tenure will be abolished and there will be no other form of ownership than national ownership; everyone rents land from the state; there is a single state authority, that of all the workers and peasants; a peasant can rent land from it as a leaseholder; between the peasant and the state there are no middle-men; the terms on which land is rented are equal for all; that is free labor on free soil.[47]

The expropriated land would no longer be private property, but even a radical "American" solution of the agrarian problem would not eliminate the causes of rural poverty. "You cannot eat land," Lenin observed; "every seizure must be an organized seizure," but nationalization's ultimate purpose was "not to make property of the seized land, not to divide it up, but to use it in common, as the property of the whole people."[48] "Can the majority of the peasants in Russia demand and carry out the nationalization of the land?" he asked. "Certainly it can. Would this be a socialist revolution? It would not. It would *still* be a bourgeois revolution, for the nationalization of the land is a measure that is not incompatible with the existence of capitalism. It is, however, a *blow* to private ownership of the most important means of production. Such a blow would *strengthen* the proletarians and semi-proletarians far more than was the case during the revolutions of the seventeenth, eighteenth and nineteenth centuries."[49]

If nationalization belonged to the era of bourgeois revolutions, it could conceivably be accomplished by the bourgeois Provisional Government. Anything more, in theory at least, would require the passage of state power to the proletariat and the organization of its dictatorship. The central question of the Russian Revolution—"whether the working class is to lead the peasants forward, to socialism, or whether the liberal bourgeoisie are to drag them back, to conciliation with capitalism"—was about to be answered as the alliance between the workers and the "semi-proletarian" peasant poor for which Lenin had been calling began to take shape. The counterrevolution was developing at the same time and at the same pace as the revolution, however, and the resulting crisis was making it clear that "the crux of the matter" for every question of democracy "lies in political power passing into the hands of the proletariat."[50]

Democracy and Insurrection

Throughout the spring the Provisional Government's liberals and the Soviet's democrats were trying hard to cooperate but they were gradually being overwhelmed by popular demands for "peace, land and bread" which they could not satisfy. By the end of April both institutions had sunk into a loud and verbose paralysis. For Lenin the revolution's alternatives had boiled down to the dictatorship of the bourgeoisie and the triumph of "Prussia" or the dictatorship of the proletariat and the transition to communism; there was no middle way, and the twisting and turnings of a petty-bourgeois democracy which was as frightened of the power of the classes which surrounded it as it was reluctant to take power by itself could not resolve the intensifying political crisis.

This deadlock could not last much longer, and it finally exploded at the end of June. Under Lenin's ceaseless prodding the Bolsheviks had been advocating a "democratic peace," the nationalization of the land, worker control of industry, better living conditions, an eight-hour day, higher wages, and—above all—the transfer of power to the Soviets. Their success was reflected in the increase in their strength: the party numbered about two thousand when the February Revolution broke out, was sixteen thousand strong in April and had thirty-two thousand active members by June.[51] It would soon be tested, for the Provisional Government's silence in matters of interest to the workers and peasants was outdone by the energy with which it announced yet another offensive against the Germans in Galicia on June 18. Brutal suppression of opposition in the army and the intensifying social crisis in the cities precipitated a series of massive demonstrations. As in April, large numbers of workers and soldiers were ready to overthrow the government and had considerable Bolshevik support.

Backed by the Soviet's Menshevik and SR leadership, the Provisional Government went on the offensive against the Bolsheviks, whom it now took the occasion to blame for the presence of half a million workers in the streets of the capital and whose leadership it openly accused of being German agents. *Pravda*'s printshop was destroyed, orders were issued for the arrest of Lenin and other party leaders, and attempts were made to forcibly disarm

Bolshevik army units. The bourgeoisie's effort to end the revolution soon broadened as the government announced its intention to rid Petrograd of "armed mobs," attacked the labor press, arrested hundreds of activists, and disbanded land committees in the provinces. It staged old-fashioned Great-Russian *pogroms* against the restive Finns and Ukrainians, encouraged factory managers to lock out workers and suppress the factory committees, and sanctioned General Kornilov's effort to restore "order" and the death penalty in the army.

The June Offensive and the July Days which followed marked a decisive parting of the ways. Faced with a spreading social crisis, an insurrectionary working class, and a rapidly developing reaction, the right wing of petty-bourgeois democracy turned to the bourgeoisie and closed ranks behind an openly counterrevolutionary regime as Alexander Kerensky became Prime Minister in a coalition government of moderate "socialists" and liberals. Convinced that the moment to strike had arrived, the newly emboldened Cadets demanded an end to social reforms, adherence to the war effort, and dispersal of the soviets, trade unions, land and factory committees, and other organs of popular power. Nineteenth-century liberals had often called on the democrats for assistance when they had been unable to suppress the popular movement by themselves. In return for a few insignificant concessions which in no way satisfied popular grievances or compromised the essentials of bourgeois rule, a unified bloc of propertyowners had been able to consolidate power, head off the threat of social revolution, and make the necessary accommodations with the established order. Far from serving as an alternative to counter-revolution, the democrats had often prepared the ground for it. For Lenin 1917 offered the same lesson as 1848 had for Marx and Engels:

> Here we had, in the purest form, the self-deception of the petty-bourgeois masses and the deception of them by the bourgeoisie with the aid of the Socialist-Revolutionaries and Mensheviks. These parties both claim to be "revolutionary democrats." But in fact it was they who placed the people's fate in the hands of the counter-revolutionary bourgeoisie, the Cadets; it was they who deserted the revolution to continue the imperialist war, who deserted democracy to make "concessions" to the Cadets on the issue of power (take, for instance, the "confirmation" from above of the election of authorities by the local population), on the land issue (the Mensheviks' and Social-Revolutionaries' renunciation of *their own* programme, namely, to support the revolutionary actions of the peasantry, *including confiscation* of the landed estates), and on the national question (defense of the undemocratic attitude of the Cadets towards the Ukraine and Finland).
>
> The petty-bourgeois masses cannot help vacillating between the bourgeoisie and the proletariat. This has been the case in all countries, especially between

1789 and 1871. And it is also the case in Russia. The Mensheviks and Socialist-Revolutionaries have *induced the masses* to submit to the policy of the counter-revolutionary bourgeoisie.[52]

"All power to the soviets" had been Lenin's slogan throughout the period of dual power, but a July alliance of all bourgeois Russia had temporarily halted the revolution's progress and rendered the slogan obsolete. The revolution's future was now in the hands of the proletariat and the "semi-proletarian" poor peasantry.[53] The soviets' failure in July notwithstanding, they were bound to be central to any future movement. The political crisis was a crisis of the Petrograd Soviet's petty-bourgeois leadership rather than of the institution as such:

> Soviets may appear in this new revolution, and indeed are bound to, but *not* the present Soviets, not organs collaborating with the bourgeoisie, but organs of revolutionary struggle against the bourgeoisie. It is true that even then we shall be in favor of building the whole state on the model of the Soviets. It is not a question of Soviets in general, but of combatting the *present* counter-revolution and the treachery of the *present* Soviets [54]

The crisis intensified dramatically in the beginning of August with a flood of land seizures in the countryside, increasingly militant strikes and demonstrations from factory workers, accelerating disintegration of the army, insistent demands for autonomy from the Finns and Ukrainians, and a series of military defeats which culminated in the German capture of Riga on August 21. Trapped between the risks of stimulating the masses through naked repression and his inability to sustain a reform program of any kind, Kerensky tried to save the situation by forging an openly counterrevolutionary alliance between the liberals and the Right and establishing a "strong" government which would eliminate the Soviets, bring the revolution to a halt, and drive the population to a defense of the motherland. By the middle of August active planning for a Bonapartist military solution had begun.[55]

The soviets had blocked the revolution's development as their petty-bourgeois leaders had drifted rightward in July, but they were central to the workers' defeat of Kornilov's attempted *coup* in August. Lenin now proposed a series of steps which could avert the "impending catastrophe." Nationalizing the banks, organizing the population into consumers' syndicates, and abolishing commercial secrecy could be carried out by the soviets from below, establish public control over production, and strengthen the workers. Given Russia's transition to "state monopoly capitalism" in conditions of imperialism and war, he was confident that these "American" measures would begin the transition to socialism which had been delayed by the petty bourgeoisie's confusion. The task was still "to *substitute* for the

Junker-capitalist state, for the landowner-capitalist state, a *revolutionary-democratic* state, i.e., a state which in a revolutionary way abolishes *all* privileges and does not fear to introduce the fullest democracy in a revolutionary way." But such a state would go beyond February because Lenin now interpreted the Paris Commune to mean that the "purely repressive" apparatus of minority domination could be broken only as the soviet effort to develop an indispensable administrative apparatus brought them to the outer limits of bourgeois politics. "You will find", he observed, "that, given a really revolutionary-democratic state, state-monopoly capitalism inevitably and unavoidably implies a step, and more than one step, towards socialism!"[56] Imperialism had put the transition to communism on the order of the day:

> Imperialist war is the eve of socialist revolution. And this not only because the horrors of war give rise to proletarian revolt—no revolt can bring about socialism unless the economic conditions for socialism are ripe—but because state-monopoly capitalism is a complete *material* preparation for socialism, the *threshold* of socialism, a rung on the ladder of history between which and the rung called socialism *there are no intermediate rungs.*[56]

This suggestion that monopoly in economics and state supervision in wartime made democratic control a precursor and a condition of socialism reserved an important role for the newly invigorated soviets.[58] In April Lenin had called them the revolutionary-democratic dictatorship of the workers and peasants and wanted them to assume power so as to begin the transition to socialism. In July he had dismissed them when their leadership fled into the arms of the counterrevolution. Now in September, after the defeat of Kornilov and on the eve of the seizure of power, he pointed to the split in the ranks of the peasant democrats which could transform the soviets into the foundation of a more developed transitional state than had been possible in April. The task was "smashing the resistance of the capitalists, of displaying truly supreme courage and determination in the exercise of power, and of securing the enthusiastic, selfless and truly heroic support of the masses both in the army and among the peasants."[59] The very existence of the soviets had proven incompatible with any form of bourgeois democracy. An accelerating revolutionary crisis was about to confirm that the lessons of the Paris Commune required a soviet republic in Russia:

> "Power to the Soviets" means radically reshaping the entire old state apparatus, that bureaucratic apparatus which hampers everything democratic. It means removing this apparatus and substituting for it a new, popular one, i.e., a truly democratic apparatus of Soviets, i.e., the organized and armed majority of the people—the workers, soldiers and peasants. It means allowing the majority of the people initiative and independence not only in the election

of deputies, but also in state administration, in effecting reforms and various other changes.[60]

By now Lenin regarded the soviets as far more than democratic insurrectionary bodies. His view that they were the embryos of proletarian state power distinguished him from most of the Left, for such a view implied that they were more than an institution through which the people could defend themselves in and against a bourgeois state. Lenin's soviets fused democracy and dictatorship because they expressed his interdependent rejection of existing institutions and his orientation toward the seizure of state power and the initiation of social revolution. His attitude toward them concentrated his understanding of the dictatorship of the proletariat as it directly brought Marx and Engels's analysis of the Paris Commune to bear on the progress of the Russian Revolution.

State and Revolution

Since his April return Lenin had been compelled to endlessly restate what he understood to be the central lessons of the Marxist theory of the state. The insistence with which he repeated the necessity to smash the existing political structure and build a new one modeled on the Commune reflected his concern that theoretical confusion in the party about this most basic of questions would block any further development of the revolutionary process. So convinced was he of the importance of clarity that now, at a crucial turning point in the revolution and from his hiding place in Finland, he sought to clarify his position by presenting what Marx and Engels had said on the subject. He had been collecting material for a discussion of "the Marxist theory of the state and the tasks of the proletariat in the revolution" for some time, and *The State and Revolution* was his reassertion of theoretical orthodoxy in a struggle which threatened to further divide the Bolsheviks at a crucial juncture.

Often misinterpreted as either an uncharacteristic semianarchistic utopianism or as a self-serving attempt to establish his claim to theoretical orthodoxy in support of a relentless personal drive for power, *The State and Revolution* was written to prepare the working class and the Bolsheviks for the insurrection that the resolution of the Kornilov affair had clearly made inevitable.[61] Its central theme was a familiar one: the proletarian dictatorship could not emerge in the course of a gradual "withering away" of the bourgeois state but only as it was "smashed." This, "the chief and fundamental point in the Marxist theory of the state," separates revolutionary Marxism from all varieties of petty-bourgeois democracy and situates the theory of the proletarian dictatorship at the heart of the socialist project. Lenin expected the dictatorship of the proletariat to take a variety of forms depending on specific circumstances, but the Commune model was the most vivid example of proletarian power to date and should be studied for that reason. Its lessons could not be implemented all at once and he was careful to warn of the dangers of expecting too much too soon. All talk of abolishing the bureaucracy immediately was "utopian nonsense," but the Commune had been a state whose disappearance had begun *as soon as* it began to replace the structures of the bourgeois state with the self-acting people of Paris. Its ultimate meaning may have rested in its preparation for the abolition of classes and its own disappearance, but it was also true that

> [t]o prevent the true meaning of his struggle against anarchism from being distorted, Marx expressly emphasized the "revolutionary and *transient* form" of the state which the proletariat needs. The proletariat needs the state only temporarily. We do not at all differ with the anarchists on the question of the abolition of the state as the *aim*. We maintain that, to achieve this aim, we must temporarily make use of the instruments, resources and methods of state power *against* the exploiters, just as the temporary dictatorship of the oppressed class is necessary for the abolition of classes.[62]

Lenin's purpose was to demonstrate that the transfer of power to the workers would do considerably more than replace Kerensky's ministers and bureaucrats with socialist ones. By reasserting the necessity to "break" the old state and erect a new one, and by connecting this claim to Marx and Engels's work and to the history of the Paris Commune, he reminded his readers on the eve of an insurrection that almost everyone knew to be coming that a soviet republic would be the specific form of the proletarian dictatorship in Russia. The future of the Constituent Assembly illustrated how his thinking had developed.

The Bolsheviks had been calling for a Constituent Assembly since 1905; indeed, it was one of the "three pillars" of party propaganda. Between April and October Lenin promised repeatedly that the Bolsheviks would convene it to ensure as rapid a transition to a democratic republic as possible, and he often chided the Provisional Government for its failure to organize elections. But he was no less insistent in his calls for the soviets to seize power "from below" throughout this period and claimed that their legitimacy was rooted in their nonparliamentary character. He addressed the apparent contradiction between these two positions by denying that there was one. Only if the soviets seized power could the Constituent Assembly have any political standing. The question was not whether the soviets *or* a Constituent Assembly would organize and use state power. The question was how the soviets *and* an Assembly could rule together, and Lenin's support for elections did not conflict with his post-April position that the soviets would be the backbone of any new state. Even if it was a bourgeois institution suited only to bourgeois republics, a Constituent Assembly could play an important role in uprooting the vestiges of feudalism—but only *as part of the transition to a soviet republic*, only if it was backed up by the soviet seizure of power which would ultimately supplant it.

The population's massive reaction to the events of late August convinced Lenin that the poor peasants and revolutionary democrats were finally prepared to follow the proletariat's leadership against the conferences, preparliaments, studies, commissions, and promises of the Provisional Government—just as he had been convinced in July that they were not. This evolution was revealed in the soviets, where the Left SRs and Menshevik Internationalists broke with a leadership which even now was trying to work out an agreement with the Provisional Government. The long struggle for control of the Petrograd and Moscow Soviets was finally resolved when a Bolshevik motion was carried on September 1 in the capital and on September 5 in Moscow, after which the discredited Menshevik-SR Presidium of the Petrograd Soviet was replaced by one which had a majority of Bolsheviks. Lenin now intensified his call for an uprising as the revolution neared its *dénouement* and repeated his earlier contention that in certain kinds of environments an insurrection could do what no other form of democratic political activity could accomplish:

> To be successful, insurrection must rely not upon conspiracy and not upon a party, but upon the advanced class. That is the first point. Insurrection must rely upon a *revolutionary upsurge of the people*. That is the second point. Insurrection must rely upon that *turning-point* in the history of the growing revolution when the activity of the advanced ranks of the people is at its height, and when the *vacillations* in the ranks of the enemy and *in the ranks of the weak, half-hearted and irresolute friends of the revolution* are strongest. That is the third point. And these three conditions for raising the question of insurrection *distinguish Marxism from Blanquism*.[63]

All of these conditions were now in place, Lenin argued, and he repeated his claim that the final victory of democracy had come down to the overthrow of the Provisional Government. Winning what Marx and Engels had called "the battle for democracy" required a clean break with the existing political structure and "the immediate transfer of all power to *revolutionary democrats, headed by the revolutionary proletariat*."[64] This slogan was not new of course, but things had changed dramatically since the spring:

> Apparently, many leaders of our Party have failed to note the *specific* meaning of the slogan which we all adopted and which we have repeated endlessly. The slogan is "All Power to the Soviets." There were periods, there were moments during the six months of the revolution, when this slogan did

not mean insurrection. Perhaps those periods and those moments blinded some of our comrades and led them to forget that now, at least since the middle of September, this slogan for us has become *equivalent to a call for insurrection.*[65]

The real home of democracy was in factories and the barracks, Lenin pointed out; the workers were far stronger outside the soviets than they were inside them, and the Bolsheviks' relatively late victory in the elections registered the proletariat's increased extraparliamentary ability to influence the masses of the population. This made it particularly important to avoid the temptation to retreat to parliamentary politics and accept the bourgeois contention that "the people" can make their wishes known only through elections. The Bolsheviks' place was at the thousands of meetings, strikes, and demonstrations that were taking place all over the country, and Lenin insisted that the Party learn from the Communards' mistakes and boycott the desperate Provisional Government's hastily called Democratic Conference. "Parliamentarism should be used, especially in revolutionary times, not to waste valuable time over representatives of what is rotten, but *to use the example of what is rotten to teach the masses.*"[66] More than ever, democracy was to be found outside parliament—in the factories and in the streets. It remained essential to break the existing state. What had changed was the orientation of the democrats. Clarity was essential:

> The state, dear people, is a class concept. The state is an organ or instrument of violence exercised by one class against another. So long as it is an instrument of violence exercised by the bourgeoisie against the proletariat, the proletariat can have only one slogan: *destruction* of this state. But when the state will be a proletarian state, when it will be an instrument of violence exercised by the proletariat against the bourgeoisie, we shall be fully and unreservedly in favor of a strong state and of centralism.[67]

The anticapitalist but not-yet-socialist measures Lenin had been advocating for months would be implemented by the workers themselves through their soviets. "This new kind of state machinery was created by the Paris Commune, and the Russian Soviets of Workers', Soldiers' and Peasants' Deputies are a 'state apparatus' of the *same* type" because they personify the lesson of the Commune:

> The proletariat *cannot* "lay hold of" the "state apparatus" and "set it in motion." But it can *smash* everything that is oppressive, routine, incorrigibly bourgeois in the old state apparatus and substitute its *own*, new apparatus. The Soviets of Workers', Soldiers' and Peasants' Deputies are exactly this apparatus.[68]

Because they were the direct creation of the population, the soviets could provide a vitality which "cannot be replaced by anything else." Their accountability through the elective principle and the immediate recall of their leadership "without any bureaucratic formalities" would enable the most energetic elements of the population to draw other classes into political activity on the basis of as advanced a democratic program as the circumstances would allow. This would make it possible "to combine the advantages of the parliamentary system with those of immediate and direct democracy, i.e., to vest in the people's elected representatives both legislative *and* *executive* functions. Compared with the bourgeois parliamentary system, this is an advance in democracy's development which is of world-wide, historic significance."[69] The revolution's past and future was that of the soviets. "If the creative enthusiasm of the revolutionary classes had not given rise to the Soviets, the proletarian revolution in Russia would have been a hopeless cause, for the proletariat could certainly not retain power with the old state apparatus, and it is impossible to create a new apparatus immediately."[70]

It was also impossible to introduce socialism immediately, Lenin argued on the eve of October. The party's minimum program remained in place and it was clear that Russian society would be capitalist in nature for some time after the workers' seizure of political power. No one could tell in advance precisely when bourgeois social relations could be uprooted and the initial transitional steps would yield to more advanced measures. After all, the Russian Revolution stood on the edge of something entirely new. What was abundantly clear, however, was that the passage of state power into the hands of the workers was essential. First let us nationalize the land, banks, and syndicates, organize workers' control of production, and implement the rest of the transitional measures, Lenin said, then we shall see. The lessons of the Paris Commune and Marxist theory notwithstanding, Russia was on the eve of an event whose future could not be fully known. "To go further, to venture into a discussion of separate and concrete measures, seems to me inexpedient. Many things will become clearer *after* the basic measures of the new type have been carried out, *after* the nationalization of banks, *after* the introduction of workers' control; experience will tell us *a lot more*, for it will be the experience of millions, the experience of building a new system of economy with the conscious participation of millions."[71] Until then it was important to avoid unnecessarily precise commitments and keep one's powder dry. The proclamation "to the citizens of Russia" which announced the overthrow of the Provisional Government and the passage of power into the hands of the Petrograd Soviet could go no further than to commit the new government to "the immediate offer of a democratic peace, the abolition of landed proprietorship, workers' control over production, and the establishment of Soviet power."[72]

"We must now set about building a proletarian socialist state in Russia," Lenin soberly told the delirious members of the Petrograd Soviet after the insurrection of October 25.[73] The workers and poor peasants had won "the battle of democracy" for the moment, but a proletarian state was not yet in place and the social revolution had not yet begun. The benefit of hindsight would allow him to say later that the overthrow of the Provisional Government had been the easy part of the revolution. The hard part lay ahead, and it would prove far more difficult than he, Marx, or Engels had ever imagined.

NOTES

1. Karl Marx, "The Civil War in France," Karl Marx and Frederick Engels, *Collected Works* (New York: Progress Publishers, 1975–), 22:328. Unless otherwise noted, all references to Marx and Engels will be to the *Collected Works*.

2. *Ibid.*, 333. For a contrary view see, *inter alia*, Frederic L. Bender, "The Ambiguities of Marx's Concepts of 'Proletarian Dictatorship' and 'Transition to Communism,' " *History of Political Thought*, 11:3 (November 1981): 525–55, and George Lichtheim, *The Origins of Socialism* (New York: Praeger, 1969).

3. "The Civil War in France," 22:330–31.

4. *Ibid.*, 322–23.

5. *Ibid.*, 331.

6. *Ibid.*, 334.

7. Letter to Dr. Kuglemann of 13 December 1870 in Hal Draper, ed., *Karl Marx and Friedrich Engels: Writings on the Paris Commune* (New York: Monthly Review Press, 1971), 220.

8. "The Civil War in France," 22:331.

9. *Ibid.*, 331.

10. *Ibid.*

11. *Ibid.*

12. *Ibid.*

13. *Ibid.*

14. *Ibid.*, 332.

15. *Ibid.*, 337.

16. *Ibid.*, 337–38.

17. *Ibid.*, 332.

18. *Ibid.*

19. *Ibid.*, 333.

20. *Ibid.*, 334.

21. Letter from Marx to Kuglemann of 6 April 1871, Hal Draper, ed., 221.

22. "The Civil War in France," 22:323–28.

23. Letter to Liebknecht of 6 April 1871, in Hal Draper, ed., 220.

24. *Ibid.*, 221.

25. "The Civil War in France," 22:336.

26. *Ibid.*, 334–35.

27. *Ibid.*, 335.

28. "Letters From Afar," *Collected Works* (Moscow: Progress Publishers, 1960–72), 23:305. Unless otherwise noted, all subsequent references will be to this edition.

29. *Ibid.*, 324.

30. *Ibid.*, 306.

31. Almost all histories of the Russian Revolution contain a great deal of material about the Bolsheviks' initial assessment of the February Revolution. See, for example, Edward Hallett Carr, *The Bolshevik Revolution* (New York: Macmillan, 1950), 1:70–77, and William Henry Chamberlin, *The Russian Revolution 1917–1921* (New York: Macmillan, 1935), 1:chap. 5.

32. "The Tasks of the Proletariat in the Present Revolution," 24:22.

33. *Ibid.*, 23.

34. *Ibid.*

35. "The Tasks of the Proletariat in Our Revolution," 22:60–61.

36. *Ibid.*, 62.

37. "The Dual Power," 24:39.

38. "Has Dual Power Disappeared?" 24:447–48.

39. "Resolution of the Central Committee of the RSDLP (Bolsheviks) Adopted in the Morning of April 22 (May 5), 1917," 24:210–11.

40. "Letters From Afar," 23:325.

41. "Congress of Peasant Deputies," 24:170.

42. "Political Parties in Russia and the Tasks of the Proletariat," 24:96–100.

43. "The Tasks of the Proletariat in Our Revolution," 22:69.

44. " 'Report on the Current Situation' delivered to the April All-Russia Conference of the Bolshevik Party," 25:241.

45. See Franco Venturi, *Roots of Revolution: A History of the Populist and Socialist Movements in Nineteenth-Century Russia* (Chicago: University of Chicago Press, 1983).

46. "A 'Voluntary Agreement' Between Landowners and Peasants?" 24:134.

47. "Speech on the Agrarian Question," 24:498.

48. *Ibid.*, 497.

49. "A Basic Question," 24:194.

50. "From a Publicist's Diary," 25:278–86.

51. Alexander Rabinowitch, *The Bolsheviks Come to Power: The Revolution of 1917 in Petrograd* (New York: Norton, 1978), xxvi–ix.

52. "To What State Have the Socialist-Revolutionaries and the Menshiviks Brought the Revolution?" 25:119–20.

53. "The Political Situation: Four Theses," 25:178–80.

54. "On Slogans," 25:191.

55. Alexander Rabinowitch, chaps. 6, 7.

56. "The Impending Catastrophe and How to Combat It," 25: 361–62.

57. *Ibid.*, 363.

58. See Neil Harding, *Lenin's Political Thought, Theory and Practice in the Socialist Revolution* (New York: St. Martin's Press, 1981), 2:chaps. 1–6.

59. "One of the Fundamental Questions of the Revolution," 25: 377.

60. *Ibid.*, 372.

61. There are nearly as many different interpretations of Lenin's motives as there are interpreters. See, for example, Richard Adamiak, "The 'Withering Away' of the State: A Reconsideration," *Journal of Politics*, 32:1 (1970): 3–18; Rodney Barfield, "Lenin's Utopianism: State and Revolution," *Slavic Review*, 30:1(1971): 45–56; Solomon Bloom, "The Withering Away of the State," *Journal of the History of Ideas*, 8:1: 113–21; Robert Daniels, "The State and Revolution: A Case Study in the Genesis and Transformation of Communist Ideology," *American Slavic and East European Review*, 12:1(1953): 22–45; Louis Fischer, *The Life of Lenin* (New York: Harper, 1964), chap. 6; A.J. Polan, *Lenin and the End of Politics* (Berkeley: University of California Press, 1984); Adam Ulam, *The Bolsheviks* (New York: Macmillan, 1965), chaps. 6,7; Sheldon Wolin, *Politics and Vision* (Boston: Little, Brown, 1960), chap. 10.

62. "The State and Revolution," 25:441.

63. "Marxism and Insurrection," 26:22–23.

64. *Ibid.*, 26.

65. "Letter to Bolshevik Comrades Attending the Congress of Soviets of the Northern Region," 26:184–85.

66. "Heroes of Fraud and the Mistakes of the Bolsheviks," 26:50.

67. "Can the Bolsheviks Retain State Power?" 26:116.

68. *Ibid.*, 102.

69. *Ibid.*, 103–4.

70. *Ibid.*, 104.

71. "Revision of the Party Platform," 26:173.

72. "To the Citizens of Russia!" 26:236 .

73. Newspaper Report of a "Report on the Tasks of the Soviet Power," delivered at the meeting of the Petrograd Soviet of Workers' and Soldiers' Deputies 25 October (7 November), 1917, 26:240.

Part III

Problems of Communism

Chapter 6

Democracy, Dictatorship and War

Most communists were totally unprepared for the October Revolution and it was not immediately clear how much theoretical guidance Marx or Engels could provide. After all, they had spent the great majority of their time analyzing capitalism and had offered relatively few direct comments about the nature of communist society. But it is easy to read more into this than is appropriate. Their materialist outlook and distaste for *émigré* intellectualism did discourage any temptation they may have felt to engage in idle speculation, but they had more to say about the economics and politics of the future than is often recognized. The Marxism which Lenin inherited was considerably more than a critique of capitalism; it contained the germs of a full-fledged theory of communism as well. Lenin's substantial development of these germs came from his ability to extract the theory's revolutionary core and apply it to the sort of situation of which Marx and Engels had been largely unaware.

The central projection that the workers' political victory would precede and make possible the social revolution implied that the basic structures of capitalist society would continue to exist even after the "overthrow" of the bourgeoisie. An unavoidable if temporary coexistence between a proletarian state and a bourgeois society on the one hand and between emerging elements of communism and surviving remnants of capitalism on the other would complicate an already difficult transitional environment opened up by the seizure of power. The relationship between these contradictory and mutually exclusive opposites imparted to the theory of the dictatorship of the proletariat the undertone of permanent emergency which had reflected the short history of the Paris Commune and which would do the same in Soviet Russia. Born out of the insoluble crisis of the old, communism itself would be marked by a tension between past and future which pushed it forward and simultaneously held it back. Its theory of the dictatorship of the proletariat could not fail to be affected by complexities at which Marx and Engels had hinted but with which only Lenin had to deal.

The Dialectics of Transition

Having finally won "the battle of democracy" in October, the Russian workers had conquered political power—but even this victory did not and could not guarantee that they would be able to begin transforming society. Marx and Engels had anticipated that an uninterrupted social revolution would establish and develop the foundations of a classless society. Even after the Paris Commune it was not entirely clear what these structures would look like, but one distinctive communist claim continued to stand out against the anarchists' desire to abolish the state immediately upon its seizure:

> In its struggle against the collective power of the possessing classes the proletariat can act as a class only by constituting itself a distinct political party, opposed to all the old parties formed by the possessing classes.
>
> This constitution of the proletariat into a political party is indispensable to ensure the triumph of the social revolution and of its ultimate goal: the abolition of classes.
>
> The coalition of the forces of the working class, already achieved by the economic struggle, must also serve, in the hands of this class, as a lever in its struggle against the political power of its exploiters.
>
> As the lords of the land and of capital always make use of their political privileges to defend and perpetuate their economic monopolies and to enslave labor, the conquest of political power becomes the great duty of the proletariat.[1]

If the proletarian revolution would begin with the seizure of political power and would develop on the basis of its continuous use, this "conquest" would necessarily be premature and ahead of its time. The Marxist account of the transition from capitalism to communism began with the expectation that the social foundations of a classless society are not and cannot be prepared in capitalism. Communism would have to be built *de novo*, its foundations laid down in a social environment which would never be ready for them if taken by itself. A workers' state would have to initiate the assault on property, but communism would necessitate considerably more than proletarian political power and social ownership of the means of production—whatever that meant. Marx and Engels expected that this process would be complex and difficult and this is why they conceived of the dictatorship of the proletariat as the political expression of *the entire transition to communism* rather than as one of several strategies for guiding that transition. It had been clear from the beginning that proletarian state power would be required if an undeveloped communism whose foundations were not in place was to confront an established capitalism whose roots remained intact even after the bourgeoisie had been driven from political power. A powerful workers' state would be needed even as communism took shape. Neither man could foresee all the complications in such a situation, but their understanding that it would be difficult lay behind Marx's famous observation that "between capitalist and communist society lies the period of the revolutionary transformation of the one into the other. Corresponding to this is also a political transition period in which the state can be nothing but *the revolutionary dictatorship of the proletariat.*"[2] He had thought that the Paris Commune represented "the political form at last discovered" under which the workers could work out their economic emancipation; this later formulation specifically identified the dictatorship of the proletariat as the politics of the entire transition from capitalism to communism. Emerging "after prolonged birth pangs from capitalist society," its first stage—which Lenin would call "socialism"—would develop on a foundation of private property which was fundamentally and profoundly hostile to it. This deep conflict with its setting would shape both its structure and its content.[3]

"What we have to deal with here," Marx went on, "is a communist society, not as it has *developed* on its own foundations, but, on the contrary, just as it *emerges* from capitalist society; which is thus in every respect, economically, morally and intellectually, still stamped with the birth marks of the old society from whose womb it emerges."[4] The full contradictoriness of communism's "first stage" is revealed in this formulation. Socialism will be a phase of *communism* even as it would be marked by the capitalism from which it arose. As incomplete and contradictory as it is, it can be fully understood only in terms of its progress toward the classless society which its initial social structure seems to make impossible. The abolition of classes may require "the political domination of the proletariat" as a first step, but Marx and Engels had always been describing a revolution with a social and economic content.[5] Political power might permit the workers to impose their will on society, but it remained true that "the *class rule* of the workers over the resisting strata of the old world can only continue until the economic basis that makes the existence of classes possible has been destroyed."[6] The proletarian state's *raison d'être* was to enable the workers to begin the task of social transformation, and the form and content of communist politics would have to be evaluated in light of the revolution's "ultimate general result." Just as crisis and revolution fused the political and social revolutions, so would the contradictions inherent in the circumstances of its birth make proletarian democracy and proletarian dictatorship mutually interdependent aspects of socialism.

"In politics there are only two decisive powers: organized state power, the army, and the unorganized, elementary power of the popular masses," observed Engels.[7] The Paris Commune had begun to break the first so as to unleash the second, since the transition to communism would depend as much on the popular character of the workers' state as on its coerciveness. Democracy and dictatorship would be required, for Marx and Engels expected the class struggle to continue in new and often more intensified circumstances after the seizure of power than before it, the building of communism to be a fierce struggle even if it would benefit the vast majority, and the propertied minority to remain powerful far beyond its numbers even after its political defeat. The democrats continued to argue from a nonclass standpoint about "pure" democracy, but Engels defined it in terms of social revolution even on the eve of his death. "Where it is a question of a complete transformation of the social organization, the masses themselves must also be in it, must themselves already have grasped what is at stake, what they are going in for, body and soul. The history of the last fifty years has taught us that. But in order that the masses may understand what is to be done, long, patient work is required."[8] A proletarian state was indispensable if the workers are to organize the "masses" for a social revolution which begins with their capture of political power but must gather momentum as it moves to its more difficult project of social transformation.

The Commune had only begun to fuse proletarian democracy with proletarian repression. Its history had demonstrated that the class struggle would not end with the workers' seizure of power but would merely assume a new form. A powerful workers' state will be indispensable throughout the entire transitional period between class society and fully developed communism precisely because of the mismatch between the proletariat's historically unprecedented ends and its more limited and historically conditioned means:

> . . . as long as other classes, and the capitalist class in particular, still exist, and as long as the proletariat fights against them (for its enemies and the old organization of society do not vanish as a result of its coming to power) it must employ *coercive* measures, that is, government measures; so long as it is still a class itself, and the economic conditions which give rise to the class struggle and the existence of classes have not yet disappeared, and must be forcibly

removed or transformed, and the process of their transformation accelerated by the use of force.[9]

If the bourgeois state had been a weapon in the hands of a relatively small propertied minority, the democratic character of the proletarian state will change only the direction of its coercive activity. No matter how popular it is, it can never be the full embodiment of freedom; created by class society, it "is only a transitional institution which is used in the struggle, in the revolution, to hold down one's adversaries by force, [and] it is pure nonsense to talk of a free people's state: so long as the proletariat still *uses* the state, it does not use it in the interests of freedom but in order to hold down its adversaries, and as soon as it becomes possible to speak of freedom the state as such ceases to exist."[10] The difficult circumstances of its birth placed the workers in the contradictory position of strengthening their state in the short run so as to accelerate its disappearance in the long, for the economic foundations which would guarantee its survival could be established and defended only by political power. Engels knew that the circumstances by which the workers would come to power would guarantee the primacy of politics throughout the entire transition, since

> after the victory of the Proletariat the only organization the victorious working class finds ready-made for use is that of the State. It may require adaptation to the new function. But to destroy that at such a moment, would be to destroy the only organism by means of which the victorious working class can exert its newly conquered power, keep down its capitalist enemies and carry out that economic revolution of society without which the whole victory must end in a defeat and in a massacre of the working class like that after the Paris Commune.[11]

Marx and Engels never described the complexities of the transition from capitalism to communism in detail because they were not given to idle speculation and because the actual course of events never forced them to do so. But it was clear that it would be characterized by an intense class struggle which would be more likely to intensify than diminish as it progressed. Its "socialist" first stage cannot describe a society from which every form of exploitation has disappeared; at best it can describe a general historical tendency toward freedom. Petty commodity production, bourgeois property, wage labor, and the separation of the producers from the means of production will characterize "socialism" for some time. The seizure of power will not guarantee the final victory of the majority, changes in property relations will not follow automatically upon political transformations, and the workers' defeat is always possible even after their political "victory." Defeating the counterrevolution was as important a task of the workers' state as was constructing the foundations of a new society. Repression of the bourgeoisie and democracy for the workers would be as interdependent and as necessary as destruction of the old and construction of the new would be. This is why Engels insisted that communists must be as clear as their bourgeois predecessors had been about the likelihood of force. He drew the line between communism and the "anti-authoritarianism" of the anarchists in his classic distinction between the workers' short-term and long-term goals:

> All Socialists are agreed that the political state, and with it political authority, will disappear as a result of the coming social revolution, that is, that public functions will lose their political character and be transformed into the simple administrative functions of watching over the true interests of society. But the anti-authoritarians demand that the authoritarian political state be abolished at one stroke, even before the social conditions that gave birth to it have been destroyed. They demand that the first act of the social revolution shall be the abolition of authority. Have these gentlemen ever seen a revolution? A revolution is certainly the most authoritarian thing there is; it is the act whereby one part of the population imposes its will upon the other part by means of rifles, bayonets and cannon—authoritarian means, if such there be at all; and if the victorious party does not want to have fought in vain, it must maintain this rule by means of the terror which its arms inspire in the reactionaries. Would the Paris Commune have lasted a single day if it had not made use of this authority of the armed people against the bourgeois? Should we not, on the contrary, reproach it for not having used it freely enough?[12]

Even in an advanced country like France, the proletariat's ability to transform society would be limited by the weight of the past and the contradictions of the present. This made the question of the state more important than it had been in any earlier revolution. The bourgeoisie may have its roots in market processes and the operations of the existing social order, but this was not and could not be true of the workers. The Paris Commune had only hinted at what might be possible if state power were enlisted on the side of social revolution. "Why do we fight for the dictatorship of the proletariat if political power is economically impotent?" Engels asked rhetorically toward the end of his life. He provided the answer. "Force (that is, state power) is also an economic power!"[13] It remained for Lenin to extract what lessons he could from the Commune's history as he tried to understand what political power could accomplish if organized in a soviet republic and brought to bear on social transformation. The deeply contradictory motion of the October Revolution would soon substantiate his view that communism's revolutionary quality would necessitate a sharp break with the past from which it had emerged but to which it remained connected.

October and the Soviet Republic

"We need revolutionary *government*, we need (for a certain transitional period) a *state*," Lenin declared as soon as he heard of the February Revolution "from afar." What makes communists different from anarchists, he continued as he developed the implications of Engels's earlier words, "is that we are *for*, and the anarchists *against*, utilizing revolutionary forms of the state in a revolutionary way for the struggle for socialism," a struggle which began in October and whose outcome remained in doubt for some time.[14]

The enormous difficulties Lenin now faced resulted from the fusion of counterrevolution, foreign intervention, and the very backwardness which had precipitated the revolution in the first place. The workers may have "seized" political power in October, but it was clear that both the economy and the state would remain substantially unchanged for some time and that it would be far more difficult to even begin the attack on bourgeois relations of production than he had anticipated. The increasingly violent contradictions between the first elements of communism, confined to the political arena for the moment, and the powerful legacy of the past would dominate the entire period. In these conditions Lenin regarded political power as the most important weapon the workers had even as he remained committed to *The State and Revolution*'s view that the commune state would begin to "wither away" immediately upon its consolidation.

Overthrowing the Provisional Government had been comparatively easy but the absence of detailed theoretical and practical experience made it difficult to guide the transition from a capitalism which was familiar to a socialism whose economic foundations would not be in place for years. The situation became more dangerous as time went on, for the new government began the advance to a socialist society as it was compelled to fight for its survival in an increasingly difficult environment. Lenin's conviction that the dictatorship of the proletariat would take the form of a soviet republic guided his early thinking about the connection between proletarian dictatorship and proletarian democracy and was expressed with particular clarity in his crucial decision to disperse a Constituent Assembly which was unable to register the rapid changes in the population's political attitudes and had thus become an obstacle to the same democracy to which it had been indispensable only a few months earlier.

The October Revolution had changed everything because it had placed socialism on the agenda. All the old terms of political discourse had been turned on the heads. The workers' seizure of power had rendered bourgeois democracy unequivocally counterrevolutionary and antidemocratic because of its connection to a capitalist society whose uprooting was now the revolution's pressing and immediate project. As unstable as it was, the workers' victory had transformed all the democratic institutions associated with the bourgeoisie. "Every direct or indirect attempt to consider the question of the Constituent Assembly from a formal, legal point of view, within the framework of ordinary bourgeois democracy and disregarding the class struggle and civil war, would be a betrayal of the proletariat's cause, and the adoption of the bourgeois standpoint."[15] The problems of Russian society could not be solved in the "old," bourgeois, fashion; only the complete victory of the workers and peasants over the bourgeoisie and landowners could guarantee the democratic content and socialist potential of February and October. This is why Lenin insisted that the broader interests of the revolution and democracy must now take precedence over the narrowly defined formal rights of the Constituent Assembly. Only a new Assembly *elected on the basis of the October Revolution* could serve democracy—and it could do so only by accepting soviet power and agreeing to implement Lenin's Decrees on Land and Peace and the Declaration of the Rights of the Working and Exploited People, the soviet republic's first political program and the legal foundation of its legitimacy.

Issued only two days after the October Revolution, the Decree on Peace announced the new government's intention to immediately conclude a "democratic" peace without annexations or indemnities, denounced the secret treaties and the negotiations which had produced them, and promised to publish all agreements into which the Provisional Government had entered. The Decree on Land adopted the agrarian program of the peasant democrats as a transitional measure, proclaimed the immediate and uncompensated abolition of the landed estates, and transferred control of them to local revolutionary land committees and peasant soviets pending the convocation of a Constituent Assembly which would decide how to organize land reform.[16] The Declaration of the Rights of the Working and Exploited People proposed that this Constituent Assembly declare itself in solidarity with the October Revolution and summarized the contradiction between bourgeois and proletarian democracy with exceptional clarity. It vested all political power in the soviets and proclaimed Russia a "Republic of Soviets of Workers', Soldiers' and Peasants' Deputies." Further provisions established the new state as a voluntary federation of Soviet republics, implemented the Decrees on Land and Peace, proclaimed workers' control as the first step toward state ownership of the means of production and the banks, disarmed the propertied classes and organized a Red Army, granted independence to Finland and self-government to Armenia, and denounced the loans to Western banks entered into by previous governments. It noted that the Constituent Assembly had been elected before "the people" had overthrown the Provisional Government and invited it to declare that "its own task is confined to establishing the fundamental principles of the socialist reconstruction of society."[17] The Assembly surprised no one when it declined to do so and was promptly dispersed by the Bolshevik and Left-SR leadership of the Third All-Russian Congress of Workers' and Soldiers' Soviets on January 6, 1918. With its dismissal the bourgeoisie was finally driven from national political life and "dual power" brought to an end.

The Constituent Assembly could have served democracy, said Lenin, but *only* as part of the transition to a Soviet Republic. Its dissolution signified the revolution's final break with bourgeois democracy and removed the last obstacle to the creation of a modern commune state based on soviets of workers and peasants. Now a revolutionary soviet political structure confronted a ruined society which remained untouched by the political events in Petrograd and Moscow. "We have always known, said and emphasized," Lenin declared, "that socialism cannot be 'introduced', that it takes shape in the course of the most intense, the most acute class struggle—which reaches heights of frenzy and desperation—and civil war; we have always said that a long period of 'birth-pangs' lies between capitalism and socialism; that a special state (that is, a special system of organized coercion of a definite class) corresponds to the transitional period between the bourgeois and the socialist society, namely, the dictatorship of the proletariat. What dictatorship implies and means is a state of simmering war, a state of military measures of struggle against the enemies of the proletarian power. The Commune was a dictatorship of the proletariat, and Marx and Engels reproached it for what they considered to be one of the causes of its downfall, namely, that the Commune had not used its armed force with *sufficient* vigor to suppress the resistance of the oppressors."[18] The proletarian dictatorship now described an entire complicated transitional period during which the old and the new coexisted in a permanently unstable unity. The workers' possession of political power could be decisive in such an environment. Its dictatorial quality was a function of the unprecedented difficulties which prompted Lenin's momentary emphasis on its "negative" tasks of suppression:

... during every transition from capitalism to socialism, dictatorship is necessary for two main reasons, or along two main channels. Firstly, capitalism cannot be defeated and eradicated without the ruthless suppression of the resistance of the exploiters, who cannot at once be deprived of their wealth, of their advantages of organization and knowledge, and consequently for a fairly long period will inevitably try to overthrow the hated rule of the poor; secondly, every great revolution, and a socialist revolution in particular, even if there is no external war, is inconceivable without internal war, i.e., civil war, which is even more devastating than external war, and involves thousands and millions of cases of wavering and desertion from one side to another, implies a state of extreme indefiniteness, lack of equilibrium and chaos. And of course, all the elements of disintegration of the old society, which are inevitably very numerous and connected mainly with the petty bourgeoisie (because it is the petty bourgeoisie that every war and every crisis ruins and destroys first), are bound to "reveal themselves" during such a profound revolution. And these elements of disintegration *cannot* "reveal themselves" otherwise than in an increase of crime, hooliganism, corruption, profiteering and outrages of every kind. To put these down requires time and *requires an iron hand.*[19]

Lenin's criticisms of bourgeois democracy had always been clear enough, but his recent emphasis on the corrosive effects of Russia's enormous petty bourgeoisie led him to a renewed emphasis on the strength that only the proletariat could bring to the new situation. "The question of the dictatorship of the proletariat is a question of the relation of the proletarian state to the bourgeois state, of proletarian democracy to bourgeois democracy," he continued as he rejected Kautsky's contention that the "democratic" and "dictatorial" ways of building socialism were mutually exclusive.[20] If one reasons like an "ordinary bourgeois," he claimed, then one thinks of democracy as a pure, non-class political formation which reflects the numerical relation between majority and minority. But a Marxist must define democracy in terms of the relations between exploiter and exploited. The fundamental question was still *"For what class?"* and the democrats' error lay in their acceptance of the bourgeois claim that classes settle things with each other and with the rest of society on the basis of majority rule rather than on the basis of economic power. Kautsky had asked why the Bolsheviks had not waited until they had a numerical majority in the Constituent Assembly before they dismissed it. Lenin's answer was characteristic of his approach to the entire question: *because we will never become the majority until we seize power and begin to expropriate the bourgeoisie.* In the absence of social revolution, numbers alone cannot express democracy; "the proletariat must first overthrow the bourgeoisie and win *for itself* state power, and then use that state power, that is, the dictatorship of the proletariat, as an instrument of its class for the purpose of winning the sympathy of the majority of the working people."[21] In the current environment, "proletarian dictatorship is the sole means of defending the working people against the oppression of capital, the violence of bourgeois military dictatorship, and imperialist war. Proletarian dictatorship is the sole step to equality and democracy in practice, not on paper, but in life, not in political phrase-mongering, but in economic reality."[22] But even political victory is not enough. Even if the "people" do monopolize political power, the future will be in doubt until they have begun to attack the real sources of their exploitation:

> In these circumstances, to assume that in a revolution which is at all profound and serious the issue is decided simply by the relations between the majority and the minority is the acme of stupidity, the silliest prejudices of a common liberal, an attempt to *deceive the people* by concealing from them a

well-established historical truth. This historical truth is that in every profound revolution, the *prolonged, stubborn and desperate* resistance of the exploiters, who for a number of years retain important practical advantages over the exploited, is the *rule*. Never—except in the sentimental fantasies of the sentimental fool Kautsky—will the exploiters submit to the decisions of the exploited majority without trying to make use of their advantages in a last desperate battle, or series of battles.[23]

These formulations lay behind Lenin's famous and familiar definition of the dictatorship of the proletariat. "The revolutionary dictatorship of the proletariat is rule won and maintained by the use of violence by the proletariat against the bourgeoisie, rule that is unrestricted by any laws."[24] The soviet republic's legitimacy rested exclusively on the October insurrection and could be deepened only in its assault on a capitalism which remained in place. This would necessitate the sort of "despotic" and "terroristic" coercive methods at which Marx and Engels had hinted, measures which could save communism only if democratically organized and implemented. This implied that the dictatorship of the proletariat would be an alliance between the workers and the peasants, and it remained to organize the relationship between the proletarian state and these "nonproletarian masses" whose support Lenin had always regarded as indispensable to the success of the socialist project.

"War Communism"

Lenin had defined the "revolutionary-democratic dictatorship of the workers and peasants" as a political formation which would eliminate the remnants of medievalism from a society whose bourgeoisie was spent as a democratic force but whose proletariat was not yet ready to wield state power by itself. His 1905 version of Marx and Engels's 1848 call for a "people's" revolution, it had looked past the traditional bourgeois republic to complete the democratic revolution in agriculture. By April 1917 he was saying that the revolution's bourgeois shell had been decisively ruptured and that agrarian democracy could not be won unless organized by a soviet republic. But the peasantry continued to support the rural democrats' plans for land reform even after October, and this persuaded him to base the Bolshevik agrarian program on that of the SRs. His Decree on Land thus represented the most comprehensive and revolutionary statement of peasant democracy taken as a whole.

Lenin had long fought against the notion that equalization of landholdings was socialism but this did not prevent him from defending the Decree as the kind of transitional measure which, *since it was promulgated by a workers' government*, could assist the transition to socialism. It organized a measure of public control over agriculture even if it did not and could not establish socialism in the countryside. In effect, the "proletarian dictatorship" had become a "workers' and peasants' state," a formulation which expressed the workers' need for rural support and now seemed to define their role as one of leadership. "For the proletariat to *impose* such transitional measures would be absurd," Lenin warned some of the "leftists" in the party; "it is obliged, in the interests of the victory of socialism, to *yield* to the small working and exploited peasants in the choice of these transitional measures, for they could do *no harm* to the cause of socialism."[25] Similar measures promulgated by a bourgeois government would strengthen capitalist social relations, but a proletarian state could use them in the transition to socialism; "equal land tenure and like measures *cannot* prejudice socialism if the power is in the hands of a workers' and peasants' government, if workers' control has been introduced, the banks nationalized, a workers' and peasants' supreme economic body set up to direct (regulate) the *entire* economic life of the country, and so forth."[26] The Decree on Land could go no further than "state capitalism," but, *when organized by a soviet republic,* state capitalism can serve socialism.[27] Everything depended on political power. A proletarian state could initiate such a radical political transformation that what used to serve capitalism and the bourgeoisie could now be made to serve communism and the proletariat.

By the spring of 1918 civil war and economic crisis had raised the struggle in the countryside to a new level. Only six percent of the grain allocated to Moscow and Petrograd was being delivered as prosperous peasants held their crops back from the market. This sort of resistance had doomed every nineteenth-century European working-class revolution, and Lenin knew that the time had come to break the peasantry's political unity and begin to forge an explicitly socialist alliance between the urban workers and the rural "semi-proletariat." Radical measures were necessary if the workers were to avoid starvation at the moment of victory. The "worker-peasant alliance" was coming under severe strain and the backing of the rural poor had become necessary for the consolidation of the "dictatorship of the proletariat." Now it was time to organize this support and take the severe measures against the rural bourgeoisie which the developing crisis had made necessary. The workers would have to rally the majority of the laboring population behind its program for social revolution, but they would be able to do so only *after* the seizure of power. "Only the proletariat could rout the bourgeoisie," Lenin observed later, "and only after routing the bourgeoisie could the proletariat definitely win the sympathy and support of the petty-bourgeois strata of the population by using an instrument like state power."[28]

For Lenin the committees of urban workers and poor peasants which spontaneously began to requisition and distribute the prosperous peasants' surplus signaled the end of the bourgeois revolution in agriculture. Directed against speculation and hoarding, they initiated "War Communism," accelerated the division of the peasantry into its bourgeois and proletarian wings, and began the transition to socialism in the countryside. As Marx had anticipated, the threat of famine had forced the revolution to become more radical. Shaped by the dialectics of proletarian revolution in a backward countryside, War Communism marked the threshold of the direct struggle for a classless society:

> In a country where the proletariat could only assume power with the aid of the peasantry, where the proletariat had to serve as the agent of a petty-bourgeois revolution, our revolution was largely a *bourgeois* revolution until the Poor Peasants' Committees were set up, i.e., until the summer and even the autumn of 1918. . . . [O]nly when the October Revolution began to spread to the rural districts and was consummated, in the summer of 1918, did we acquire a real proletarian base, only then did our revolution become a *proletarian revolution in fact*, and not merely in our proclamations, promises and declarations.[29]

War Communism also precipitated the final break with the Left SRs, who had remained in both the government and the soviets until the summer of 1918. The peasant democrats opposed the Bolsheviks' attempts to organize the rural population along class lines, violently objected to any state encouragement of large-scale farms formed from confiscated estates, and generally regarded the forced requisitions as a war waged by the proletariat against the entire peasantry. They were outlawed after they assassinated the German ambassador Mirbach and their disappearance removed the last obstacle to the development of a purely Bolshevik agrarian policy.

Lenin's approach to the proletarian dictatorship now led him to concentrate on developing the alliance between the urban and rural workers, but he still had to keep the important "middle peasantry" in mind. A large stratum standing between the forty percent of the rural population who owned so little land that they were unable to support their families unless they hired themselves out for a wage and the ten percent who owned enough so they could produce for the market and hire laborers to work for them, the middle peasantry had become indispensable to the survival of a revolution and the success of a communism which seemed to work against its long-term interests. It remained at the center of Lenin's thinking long after the counterrevolution had been defeated; indeed, the "new economic policy" he recommended to the Party's Tenth Congress was designed to undo some of the damage War Communism had inflicted on this huge stratum of small proprietors. Despite the workers' dependence on the peasants, he was confident that the state's proletarian character had opened the way to a "socialist" solution to the food crisis—the compulsory delivery of grain at fixed prices. Given the emergency conditions of the period, he was convinced that a "capitalist" solution—the sale of grain on the open market—would have jeopardized the revolution's future. Organized public control of the market's disruptive anarchy remained as central to his thinking as it had been to that of Marx and Engels and expressed a good deal of the content of the transition to socialism.

Lenin's 1918 claim that War Communism had begun the socialist transformation of the countryside turned out to be premature. Even with its forced requisitions, the division and redistribution of the landed estates dominated rural life for some time and was instrumental in solidifying support for the Bolsheviks among the peasantry as a whole. There was nothing "socialist" in land reform; taken by itself, the destruction of the landed estates did no more than consolidate the "bourgeois" revolution in agriculture. Even if it was organized by a workers' state and made possible the approach to rural socialism, the civil war permitted little else for the moment. Paradoxically, the most important short-term result of the proletarian state's agrarian policy was a tremendous expansion of the middle peasantry. In the countryside, as everywhere else in a ruined society, the "construction of socialism" proceeded more slowly than Lenin had ever expected. The civil war forced him to look for allies everywhere, and the same sort of measures which had characterized his policy toward the peasantry marked his attitude toward bureaucrats, "experts," and the intelligentsia as well.

Efficiency and Expertise

Their emphasis on politics notwithstanding, Marx and Engels knew that liberating the productive powers "fettered" by private property would require much more than organizing a workers' state and converting the means of production to public property. They tended to assume that democratic proletarian revolutions in advanced societies would make it relatively simple to repress the bourgeoisie and construct communist social relations. Lenin's analysis of imperialism had modified this optimism to some extent, but he expected that even if socialism could now be built in backward countries the final victory of the Russian workers would depend on support from insurrections in Western Europe. It soon became clear that the encircled Russians stood alone, and the enormous problems encountered in tapping and organizing the energy of an exhausted and mutilated society became the chief dilemma of the proletarian dictatorship. Lenin knew that this could not be done on orders from above, that bureaucratic methods would surely fail, and that everything would depend on the energy, initiative, and creativity of the entire laboring population. Smashing the bourgeois state, even socializing the ownership of the means of production, would not suffice; "we must understand that only now that we have removed the external obstacles and broken down the old institutions have we come face to face with the primary task of a genuine proletarian revolution in all its magnitude, namely, that of organizing tens and hundreds of millions of people."[30]

Soon after October Lenin began to consider how competition, reviled by many of his colleagues as a divisive and obsolete feature of capitalist society, might be transformed into an instrument for building socialism. In and of itself, he said, competition is no more inherently bourgeois than land reform; the proletarian character of the state can change the political environment so decisively that it can be transformed into its opposite. "Far from extinguishing competition, socialism, on the contrary, for the first time creates the opportunity for employing it on a really *wide* and on a really *mass* scale, for actually drawing the majority of working people into a field of labor in which they can display their abilities, develop their capacities, and reveal those talents, so abundant among the people whom capitalism has crushed, suppressed and strangled in thousands and millions."[31] Everything would depend on severing competition's connection to private profit and individual advantage, and this could only be done if the bourgeoisie was expropriated and consistent proletarian supervision of economic life was organized through the activity of the workers' state. "There are a great many talented organizers among the peasants and the working class," Lenin wrote, "and they are only just beginning to become aware of themselves, to awaken, to stretch out towards great, vital, creative work, to tackle with their own forces the task of building socialist society. One of the most important tasks today, if not the most important, is to develop this independent initiative of the workers, and of all the working and exploited people generally, develop it as widely as possible in creative *organizational* work. At all costs we must break the old, *absurd*, savage, despicable and disgusting prejudice that only the so-called 'upper classes', only the rich, and those who have gone through the school of the rich, are capable of administering the state and directing the organizational development of modern society."[32] What Lenin would come to call "accounting and control" had become the chief economic tasks of every soviet and could serve socialism only because the political environment had changed:

> Accounting and control, if carried on by the Soviets of Workers', Soldiers' and Peasants' Deputies as the supreme state power, or on the instructions, on the authority, of this power—widespread, general, universal accounting and control, the accounting and control of the amount of labor performed and of the distribution of products—is the *essence* of socialist transformation, once the political rule of the proletariat has been established and secured.
>
> The accounting and control essential for the transition to socialism can be

exercised only by the people. Only the voluntary and conscientious co-operation of the *mass* of the workers and peasants in accounting and controlling *the rich, the rogues, the idlers and the rowdies*, a co-operation marked by revolutionary enthusiasm, can conquer these survivals of accursed capitalist society, these dregs of humanity, these haplessly decayed and atrophied limbs, this contagion, this plague, this ulcer that socialism has inherited from capitalism.[33]

Only soviets could make the modern technical skills available to every worker and peasant which could enable them to exercise the all-round control of the economy for which Lenin was calling. The complicated dynamics of the Marxist theory of the state now began to play themselves out in Lenin's suggestion that, as parasitical and antidemocratic as the bourgeois state had been, a soviet republic could stimulate and organize the all-round democratic supervision of the entire society. This would require an assault on everything associated with the bureaucratic state because only the broadest popular participation from below could overcome the weight of the past. It was natural that Lenin should draw theoretical support from the Paris Commune, the workers' first attempt to fuse technical expertise with popular activity. The Russian Revolution had reached the point at which the peaceful organization of nationwide accounting and control had become as important a means to curb the bourgeoisie and "smash" its state as had been War Communism's coercive methods of direct expropriation and political repression:

The programme of this accounting and control is simple, clear and intelligible to all—everyone to have bread; everyone to have sound footwear and good clothing; everyone to have warm dwellings; everyone to work conscientiously; not a single rogue (including those who shirk their work) to be allowed at liberty, but kept in prison, or serve his sentence of compulsory labor of the hardest kind; not a single rich man who violates the laws and regulations of socialism to be allowed to escape from the fate of the rogue, which should, in justice, be the fate of the rich man. "He who does not work, neither shall he eat"—this is the *practical* commandment of socialism.[34]

The same contradictions appeared in other areas. The workers' revolution now required the discipline and mobilization of labor, a longer working day, the application of "Taylorism," material incentives like piecework, and other measures which Lenin had denounced before October but which he now defended. Raising the productivity of labor had become a matter of survival. Once again Lenin fell back on the claim that the October Revolution had so altered the political environment that what had been instruments of oppression and exploitation were now tools of liberation. The coexistence of some elements of communism and the remnants of capitalism complicated an already-difficult situation as it raised the possibility of using the latter to strengthen the former. The soviet state was all the workers had, and the added burden of a backward social order illustrated how much more complex real life was than the most sophisticated of political slogans. There was so little room in which to maneuver that only a proletarian dictatorship could make the past serve the future. Things would have been difficult enough in a developed social order, but the pervasive backwardness in which the soviet republic had to be built only made things that much worse:

> The Russian is a bad worker compared with people in advanced countries. It could not be otherwise under the tsarist regime and in view of the persistence of the hangover from serfdom. The task that the Soviet government must set before the people in all its scope is—learn to work. The Taylor system, the last word of capitalism in this respect, like all capitalist progress, is a combination of the refined brutality of bourgeois exploitation and a number of the greatest scientific achievements in the field of analyzing mechanical motions during work, the elimination of superfluous and awkward motions, the elaboration of correct methods of work, the introduction of the best system of accounting and control, etc. The Soviet Republic must at all costs adopt all that is valuable in the achievement of science and technology in this field. The possibility of building socialism depends exactly on our success in combining the Soviet power and the Soviet organization of administration with the up-to-date achievements of capitalism. We must organize in Russia the study and teaching of the Taylor system and systematically try it out and adapt it to our own ends. At the same time, in working to raise the productivity of labor, we must take into account the specific features of the transition period from capitalism to socialism, which, on the one hand, require that the foundations be laid of the socialist organization of competition, and, on the other hand, require the use of compulsion, so that the slogan of the dictatorship of the proletariat shall not be desecrated by the practice of a lily-livered proletarian government.[35]

The past constantly extracted its dues from the present as the course of the Russian Revolution bore out Marx and Engels's observation that the foundations of communism could be built only if a workers' state organized the use of capitalism's methods in the struggle against class society. Nowhere was this more clear than in the debate over industrial management. A significant stream of Bolshevik thought assumed that all industrial decisions would be made by the workers collectively, and Lenin's call for "one-man management" now struck many party veterans as a serious violation of socialist theory and democratic practice. He answered, quoting Engels, that all modern industrial enterprises demand unity and discipline. Socialism is inconceivable without large-scale industry, and industry cannot be organized democratically. But this does not mean that industrial democracy is impossible, he said. The Paris Commune had begun to demonstrate that wide participation by citizens in public affairs is compatible with absolute clarity about who is responsible for implementing decisions democratically arrived at. If managers are controlled by and accountable to the workers, their undivided authority in the factory need not conflict with democracy. "The masses must have the right to choose responsible leaders for themselves. They must have the right to replace them, the right to know and check each smallest step of their activity. They must have the right to put forward any worker without exception for administrative functions. But this does not mean that the process of collective labor can remain without definite leadership, without precisely establishing the responsibility of the person in charge, without the strictest order created by the single will of that person."[36] Making decisions and implementing them are two different things. Only proletarian political power can ensure that democracy will be well served by the efficient execution of democratic decisions:

> We must consolidate what we ourselves have won, what we ourselves have decreed, made law, discussed, planned—consolidate all this in stable forms of *everyday labor discipline*. This is the most difficult, but the most gratifying task, because only its fulfillment will give us a socialist system. We must learn to combine the "public meeting" democracy of the working people—turbulent, surging, overflowing its banks like a spring flood—with *iron* discipline while at work, with *unquestioning obedience* to the will of a single person, the Soviet leader, while at work.[37]

The problem of the "bourgeois experts" provided another example of how complex the transition to socialism was turning out to be. Simply recovering from the consequences of international and civil war required a level of technical and administrative expertise which the proletariat did not possess. In the medium and long run it was essential to form an army, raise the productivity of labor, organize control and accounting, and set in place the foundations of a modern economy. The administrative and technical simplification of a modern economy might, *when organized by soviet power*, bring these skills within the reach of every citizen. In the meantime there was a revolution to defend and a new society to build—and the only source of indispensable technical, scientific, and administrative expertise was the very bourgeoisie against which it was to be directed. Socialists used to think that the new society could be built only by first creating completely new, "socialist," people. But this approach, said Lenin, is for "young ladies." It may be true that communism can be built only with soviet methods, but its raw materials can come from nowhere else than bourgeois society.

Once again proletarian democracy was critical. The "old," bourgeois, way of appealing to experts is to pay them high salaries, and Lenin contrasted it to the "new," proletarian, method of "creating the conditions of national accounting and control from below, which would inevitably and of itself subordinate the experts and enlist them for our work."[38] But it was not yet possible to organize things in this "new" way, and the experts were needed now. "We cannot wait twenty years until we have trained pure, communist experts, until we have trained the first generation of Communists without blemish or reproach. No, excuse me, but we must build now, in two months and not in twenty years' time, so as to be able to fight the bourgeoisie."[39] Fully imbued with the expectations they inherited from the old society, the experts would have to be paid. Once again it was obvious that "this measure is a compromise, a departure from the principles of the Paris Commune, and of every proletarian power, which calls for the reduction of all salaries to the level of the wages of the average workers, which urge that careerism be fought not merely in words, but in deeds."[40] The complicated exigencies of the period implied that it might be necessary to move away from the Commune state in order to save the soviet republic.

There was no doubt that what Lenin called a compromise was really a step backward and that it stood in direct contradiction to everything Marx and Engels had written about the Commune's historical tendencies. But there was no choice in the matter and he was confident that inequality, bureaucracy, and corruption could be controlled by the political dominance of the proletariat. It might be necessary to pay "tribute" to the bourgeoisie for the moment, but even here soviet power might help construct socialist relations of production. "It is not enough to suppress the exploiters," Lenin observed. "One must also learn from them."[41] Given working-class political power and Russia's dreadful backwardness, concessions to the bourgeoisie could be used against the bourgeoisie. It is true that "a capitalist who retains private property and exploitative relations cannot be anything but a foreign body in a socialist republic,"[42] but "we have no right to neglect anything that may, in however small a measure, help us to improve the condition of the workers and peasants."[43] Given a soviet state, paying the experts might strengthen the bourgeoisie in the short run but could fortify the proletariat in the long.

Three years of emergency had converted the revolution into a desperate struggle for efficiency and expertise. Russia's backwardness had forced the soviet government to make entirely unexpected concessions to the capitalist past. The country would have to cease being backward before she could become communist, for the contradictory logic of imperialism had fixed the world's first socialist revolution in a society which was now forced to produce its most basic means of production while simultaneously beginning the advance to communism. With the end of the civil war in 1920 the economic task of the proletarian dictatorship "consists in laying the foundations of socialism in large-scale industry, in reorganizing the old capitalist economy with the capitalists putting up a stubborn resistance in millions and millions of different ways. There is, however, not yet anything communist in our economic system."[44] Solutions to the revolution's daunting economic problems could serve socialism only if organized by a political structure which fused revolutionary democracy with revolutionary dictatorship. If he knew anything at all, Lenin knew that this structure could only be Marx's revolutionary dictatorship of the proletariat.

The Price of Backwardness

Even if it had occurred in an advanced society, the socialist revolution's immediate prospects would have been more difficult than those of its bourgeois predecessors. In Russia it had occurred before the foundations of socialism had even been created, and this meant that the same conditions which had precipitated the October Revolution would simultaneously make it difficult to consummate. "The more backward the country which, owing to the zigzags of history, has proven to be the one to start the socialist revolution, the more difficult it is for that country to pass from the old capitalist relations to socialist relations," Lenin observed.[45] Political victory was only the first step. A soviet republic neither required nor guaranteed a socialist society in the short run, and much more effort would be needed to transform a bourgeois social order which remained very strong even if it was supposed to be historically obsolete.

Russia's backwardness had tended to merge many democratic currents together, and Lenin's understanding of the dictatorship of the proletariat as a network of alliances stood behind his observation that "the essence of proletarian dictatorship is not in force alone, or even mainly in force."[46] Its ultimate purpose is the abolition of private property and class society, but the workers cannot accomplish this by themselves. Even beginning the advance to a classless society required "a long, difficult and stubborn *class struggle*, which, *after* the overthrow of capitalist rule, *after* the destruction of the bourgeois state, *after* the establishment of the dictatorship of the proletariat, *does not disappear* (as the vulgar representatives of the old socialism and the old Social-Democracy imagine), but merely changes its form and in many respects becomes fiercer."[47] The bourgeoisie might be relatively small but it remains powerful far beyond its numbers. If the proletarian dictatorship describes the workers' leadership of the vast majority, even its democratic character does not guarantee that it will be able to accomplish its task easily:

> The dictatorship of the proletariat is not the end of class struggle but its continuation in new forms. The dictatorship of the proletariat is class struggle

waged by a proletariat that is victorious and has taken power into its hands against a bourgeoisie that has been defeated but not destroyed, a bourgeoisie that has not vanished, not ceased to offer resistance, but that has intensified its resistance. The dictatorship of the proletariat is a specific form of class alliance between the proletariat, the vanguard of the working people, and the numerous non-proletarian strata of the working people (petty bourgeoisie, small proprietors, the peasantry, the intelligentsia, etc.), or the majority of these strata, an alliance against capital, an alliance whose aim is the complete overthrow of capital, complete suppression of the resistance offered by the bourgeoisie as well as of attempts at restoration on its part, an alliance for the final establishment and consolidation of socialism. It is a specific kind of alliance which takes shape in a specific situation, namely, amidst fierce civil war; it is an alliance between firm supporters of socialism and its vacillating allies, sometimes "neutrals" (in which case instead of an agreement on struggle the alliance becomes an agreement on neutrality); an alliance between economically, politically, socially, and spiritually different classes.[48]

When all was said and done, victory in the civil war had accomplished little more than to redefine the parameters of a crisis which was rapidly becoming permanent. Effective economic planning had been impossible for three years, industrial and agricultural production had almost disintegrated, the proletariat which supposedly wielded state power was melting away, trade relations between town and country were almost nonexistent, compulsion in grain acquisition and labor allocation had strained the alliance with the peasantry to the breaking point, and wages were increasingly being paid in kind as money disappeared. The transition to socialism, which had begun in October 1917 and was supposed to lead to the conscious satisfaction of all human needs, appeared instead to have precipitated a backward turn toward a natural economy. It was all well and good to talk of the complexities of the situation, declaim about Russia's backwardness and point to the destructiveness of years of war, but with the military phase of the revolution coming to an end economic construction would clearly be the next battlefield.

Lenin had taken a step toward the middle peasants because, War Communism notwithstanding, it had not been possible to begin the direct struggle for rural socialism in 1918. He had underestimated how many middle peasants there would be after the landlords had been expropriated. Marxist theory had always maintained that land reform would strengthen the rural petty bourgeoisie in the short run and Russia's experience had confirmed this projection. The civil war had forced the peasants to defer their dreams of independence, and now Lenin had no choice but to take account of them.

The alliance with the middle peasantry would continue precisely because the drive against the landlords had been so successful. Small proprietorship dominated the countryside now and would continue to do so for some time.

The revolution's immediate task was to raise the productivity of this middle peasant economy, and this came to define Lenin's "New Economic Policy." The risks of further postponing the struggle for socialism in agriculture were as clear as they were necessary, and once again he fell back on the discipline of the proletariat, the organization of its party, and the character of its state to steer the revolution through a stage which was as difficult and dangerous as its predecessors because the obstacles to its completion were so deeply rooted. The economy's lag behind the political order guaranteed that capitalism would spontaneously regenerate itself even under the "dictatorship of the proletariat." The revolution's difficulties intensified as its stakes rose and its progress accelerated. The bourgeoisie itself had been defeated but the threat it posed lived on in the ocean of small property which surrounded the exhausted workers. The struggle to transform the petty bourgeoisie would be far more difficult and protracted than the direct struggle to expropriate the bourgeoisie proper. If anything, the workers would have to be more organized and more dictatorial with their former allies than they had been against their obvious enemies:

> We in Russia (in the third year since the overthrow of the bourgeoisie) are making the first steps in the transition from capitalism to socialism or the lower stage of communism. Classes still remain, and will remain everywhere *for years after* the proletariat's conquest of power. Perhaps in Britain, where there is no peasantry (but where petty proprietors exist), this period may be shorter. The abolition of classes means, not merely ousting the landlords and the capitalists— that is something we accomplished with relative ease; it also means *abolishing the small commodity producers*, and they cannot be *ousted*, or crushed; we *must learn to live* with them. They can (and must) be transformed and re-educated only by means of very prolonged, slow, and cautious organizational work. They surround the proletariat on every side with a petty-bourgeois atmosphere, which permeates and corrupts the proletariat, and constantly causes among the proletariat relapses into petty-bourgeois spinelessness, disunity, individualism, and alternating moods of exultation and dejection. The strictest centralization and discipline are required within the political party of the proletariat in order to counteract this, in order that the *organizational* role of the proletariat (and that is its *principal* role) may be exercised correctly, successfully and victoriously. The dictatorship of the proletariat means a persistent struggle—bloody and bloodless, violent and peaceful, military, economic, educational and administrative—against the forces and traditions of the old society. The force of habit in millions and tens of millions is a most formidable force. Without a party of iron that has been tempered in the struggle, a party enjoying the confidence of all honest people in the class in question, a party capable of watching and influencing the mood of the masses, such a struggle cannot be waged successfully. It is a thousand times easier to vanquish the

centralized big bourgeoisie than to "vanquish" the millions upon millions of petty proprietors; however, through their ordinary, everyday, imperceptible, elusive and demoralizing activities, they produce the *very* results which the bourgeoisie needs and which tend to *restore* the bourgeoisie. Whatever brings about even the slightest weakening of the iron discipline of the party of the proletariat (especially during its dictatorship), is actually aiding the bourgeoisie against the proletariat.[49]

Marxist theory may have identified the workers as Russia's most "advanced" class, but its state was still faced by a nearly ruined society three years after October. Transforming this society would be made more difficult by a "defeated" bourgeoisie which, fortified by the persistence of small property, remained stronger in many ways than the supposedly victorious proletariat. The revolution was approaching yet another dangerous turning point as it neared victory in the civil war. Many mistakes had been made and in some ways society had moved backward during the difficult years of "war communism," but some important accomplishments were in place. The attack on bourgeois social relations could now develop in earnest, but this would require a serious analysis of a deeply contradictory situation and a willingness to make important compromises in theory and practice. Like Marx and Engels, Lenin had always known that a proletarian state might protect the revolution in the short run but that only a developed socialist economy could make communism possible in the long. The construction of such a society now required a systematic campaign whose immediate aim would be a massive improvement in the very small-scale peasant farming which was socialism's most dangerous enemy. The difficulties of relying upon "old," "bourgeois," methods to build the future would continue to haunt Lenin even if he retained his confidence that the workers' monopoly of state power would enable them to accomplish the task.

NOTES

1. Karl Marx and Frederick Engels, "Resolution on the Rules," *Selected Works in Three Volumes* (Moscow: Progress Publishers, 1969), 2:291.

2. "Critique of the Gotha Programme," *ibid.*, 3:26.

3. *Ibid.*, 19.

4. *Ibid.*, 17.

5. "On the Political Action of the Working Class," Karl Marx and Frederick Engels, *Collected Works* (New York: Progress Publishers, 1975–), 22:417.

6. Karl Marx, "Conspectus of Bakunin's Book *State and Anarchy*," *Anarchism and Anarcho-Syndicalism: Selected Writings by Marx, Engels, Lenin* (New

York: International Publishers, 1972), 152. See also Marx, Letter to Bolte, 23 November 1871, *Selected Works in Three Volumes*, 2:423–24.

7. "The Role of Force in History," *Selected Works in Three Volumes*, 3:398.

8. "Introduction to Karl Marx's Work *The Class Struggles in France, 1848–1850*," Karl Marx and Frederick Engels, *Selected Works in One Volume* (New York: International Publishers, 1968), 664.

9. Marx, "Conspectus of Bakunin's Book *State and Anarchy*," 146.

10. Letter to Bebel of 18–28 March 1875, *Selected Works in Three Volumes*, 3:34–35.

11. Engels, "On the Occasion of Karl Marx's Death," *Anarchism and Anarcho-Syndicalism*, 172.

12. "On Authority," *Anarchism and Anarcho-Syndicalism*, 378–79. See also Engels's letter to Paul Lafargue, 30 December 1871, *ibid.*, 58–59.

13. Letter to Schmidt, 27 October 1890, *Selected Works in Three Volumes*, 3:494.

14. "Letters From Afar," *Collected Works* (Moscow: Progress Publishers, 1960–72), 23:325. Unless otherwise noted, all subsequent references will be to this edition.

15. "Theses on the Constituent Assembly," 26:382.

16. "Decree on Peace," 26:249–53 and "Decree on Land," 26:258–61.

17. "Declaration of Rights of the Working and Exploited People," 26:423–25.

18. "Fear of the Collapse of the Old and the Fight for the New," 26:401.

19. "The Immediate Tasks of the Soviet Government," 27:264.

20. "The Proletarian Revolution and the Renegade Kautsky," 28:232.

21. "Elections and the Dictatorship of the Proletariat," 30:263.

22. "Greetings to Italian, French and German Communists," 30:57.

23. "The Proletarian Revolution and the Renegade Kautsky," 253–54.

24. *Ibid.*, 236.

25. "Alliance Between the Workers and the Working and Exploited Peasants," 26:334.

26. *Ibid.*, 335.

27. " 'Left-Wing' Childishness and the Petty-Bourgeois Mentality," 27:336–39.

28. "Elections and the Dictatorship of the Proletariat," 30:270.

29. "Report of the Central Committee to the Eighth Congress of the R.C.P. (B)," 29:157.

30. "Speech of Greeting to the First All-Russia Congress on Adult Education," 29:338.

31. "How to Organize Competition?" 26:404.

32. *Ibid.*, 409.

33. *Ibid.*, 410.

34. *Ibid.*, 414.

35. "The Immediate Tasks of the Soviet Government," 27:259.

36. "Original Version of the Article 'The Immediate Tasks of the Soviet Government,' " 27:212.

37. "The Immediate Tasks of the Soviet Government," 27:271.

38. *Ibid.*, 248.

39. "The Achievements and Difficulties of the Soviet Government," 29:70.

40. "The Immediate Tasks of the Soviet Government," 27:249.

41. "The Achievements and Difficulties of the Soviet Government," 29:72.

42. "Speech at the Eighth All-Russia Congress of Soviets," 31:479.

43. "Report on the Work of the Council of People's Commissars Delivered at the Eighth All-Russia Congress of Soviets," 31:494.

44. "Report on Subbotniks," 30:284, 286.

45. "Political Report of the Central Committee Delivered to the Extraordinary Seventh Congress of the RCP (B)," 27:89.

46. "Greetings to the Hungarian Workers," 29:388.

47. *Ibid.*

48. "Forward to the Published Speech 'Deception of the People with Slogans of Freedom and Equality,'" 29:380–81.

49. "Left-Wing Communism, An Infantile Disorder," 31:43–44.

Chapter 7

Democracy, Dictatorship and Peace

War Communism had saved the revolution but had done little to begin the "transition to socialism." It was clear that Russia's deep social crisis could not be resolved through military means, and a vulnerable proletarian state coexisted uneasily with a ruined society fully two and a half years after the "socialist revolution" was supposed to have begun. The ongoing emergency which had precipitated the revolution had also accelerated and distorted it. In these circumstances, the lack of clear theoretical guidance, of long experience with capitalism, and of support from European revolutions imparted a temporary and artificial quality to the period of which Lenin was constantly aware.

It was clear that War Communism was not socialism; even if organized by a proletarian state, surplus appropriation could do little more than "approach" the transition to socialism. As Lenin began to understand that the entire process would be considerably longer and more difficult than he had anticipated, it became clear that Marx and Engels could provide him with little more than general theoretical orientation. The leaders of an unexpectedly complex revolution were largely on their own, and the result was a more subtle Leninist analysis which defined both the "approach" to the transition and the "transition" itself as definite stages in a single revolutionary process. The theory of the dictatorship of the proletariat grew in sophistication and scope as a complex and protracted revolutionary process forced Lenin to refine it. Tested and enriched by the difficult ambiguities of real life, it developed into the general Marxist summation of the theoretical and practical experiences of the first revolution of its type in history.

Democratic Peasants and Dictatorial Workers

The relationship between Russia's relatively small proletariat and her enormous peasantry had been the revolution's central political problem for many years. It remained so with the end of the civil war, and Lenin continued to place it at the heart of his evolving theory of the revolutionary state. Military victory brought this problematic connection to a head, for a decimated proletariat and an exhausted peasantry needed each other more than ever even as the material basis for their cooperation was rapidly disappearing.

The class basis for War Communism had been the workers' provision of land and protection to the peasants and the latter's supply of food and raw materials for industry under the surplus-appropriation system. But by the end of 1920 the contradictions in this relationship forcibly asserted themselves as the military triumphs which they had made possible stimulated forces which undermined the prospects for rural security and prosperity. Victory brought War Communism into violent collision with the interests of the peasantry as a whole, and it became essential to establish mutually beneficial relations between the dictatorship's core classes. The peasants' deepening resentment and discomfort demanded that a proletarian state protect the small property which Lenin knew would be a tenacious enemy of the socialism he proposed to build with its reluctant help. War Communism had shifted the class struggle in favor of the workers for the moment, but this final period of Lenin's life would be shaped by the continuing struggle between a capitalism which, while wounded, was a long way from being uprooted and a socialism which, while in nominal control of the state, was a long way from consolidation. War Communism had solved nothing in the long run; the end of the civil war notwithstanding, the revolution's most difficult tasks still lay in the future.

The first public suggestion that War Communism be scrapped came in Lenin's 1921 suggestion to the Tenth Party Congress that surplus appropriation be replaced by a "tax in kind" which would encourage the peasants to use most of their surplus for themselves.[1] He intended to ease the burden on agriculture so the enlarged middle peasantry which had been strengthened by the land reform would voluntarily produce more food for the cities and reestablish normal economic connections between industry and agriculture. The suggestion that the state stop requisitioning food and reduce itself to a tax gatherer spoke to the peasants' urgent desire for a measure of economic liberty once the threat of the landlords' return had disappeared. It also reflected the enormous difficulties the revolution was encountering in a society which had virtually ceased to function.

Lenin knew how contradictory and dangerous the New Economic Policy would be, for it would tend to revive and strengthen bourgeois relations of production even if it developed under conditions of proletarian dictatorship. Two antagonistic systems still lived together in the same social formation and if War Communism had benefited the proletariat, the New Economic Policy would now favor the rural small producers. If socialism was to work, then, it would work only in violation of both its own rules and those of its immediate environment. Forced to make concessions to the past in order to serve the future, the workers' state found itself compelled to strengthen bourgeois social relations in order to strike at the market. This made very little sense on the face of it, but Lenin remained confident that the proletarian character of the state would enable the workers to make their unavoidable concessions to the petty bourgeoisie benefit socialism. There was as little choice here as there was in many other areas, for the obvious risk Lenin was running as he moved to protect small property was the price he had to pay if he wanted to revitalize agricultural production.

War Communism had proposed to defeat capitalism by relying on the energy and enthusiasm of the workers and poor peasants, but Lenin's New Economic Policy illustrated his awareness that the struggle would be far more complicated and would take far longer to win than he had initially anticipated. A proletarian "island" exhausted by years of struggle and sacrifice was trying to lead a hostile petty-bourgeois "ocean" toward a socialism it did not yet want. Six years of ruinous war and famine had so weakened the revolution's leading class that its very existence was in doubt. A proletariat which had won "the battle of democracy" and organized the world's first socialist state was on the verge of disappearing. "After an enormous, unparalleled exertion of effort, the working class in a small-peasant, ruined country, the working class which has very largely become declassed, needs an interval of time in which to allow new forces to grow and be brought to the fore, and in which the old and worn-out forces can 'recuperate.' "[2]

But the revolution could not wait. Just when its main forces seemed utterly spent, it had come face to face with its most important and most difficult task. Having defeated the counterrevolution militarily, it had no choice but to begin laying the foundations of a new society. It had gone further than any other revolution in history and yet, even as it was clear that it had to begin the assault on private property, it was just as clear that there was no alternative to a compromise with the peasants. The New Economic Policy was the next stage in the struggle to uproot a capitalism to which it was also necessary to make serious and dangerous concessions. As long as the most basic tasks of industrializing and constructing the means of production would be the revolution's chief economic priority, it would be difficult to avoid Marx and Engels's dilemma that equality could be built only with inequality, that democracy required repression, and that the road to a classless society lay through the class dictatorship of the proletariat.

The workers' October victory had inspired the hope that the direct transition to communist production and distribution was possible. War Communism had encouraged some to think that the foundations of a new society could be built in relatively short order with "shock" methods like surplus appropriation. This was a mistake, Lenin now acknowledged, and it had become clear that the transition from capitalism to communism in a small-peasant country would require a number of intermediate stages. War Communism's surplus appropriation was inhibiting the growth of the rural economy whose survival it had helped make possible. The New Economic Policy was designed to reconstitute a disappearing proletariat which supposedly held political power and encourage the revival of peasant activity which had virtually ground to a halt. The period's unforeseen complications demanded that a victorious proletariat organize a form of state capitalism so as to begin the transition to socialism. Lenin seemed to have no choice but to use the market to defeat the market, and this would make political matters more important than ever.

The difficulty the revolution now faced was related to its very success, for it would have to begin the transformation of society if it was to make any further progress. Marx and Engels had anticipated that the revolutionary process would steadily deepen and become more complicated after the seizure of power. Lenin knew that victory in the civil war had brought the Soviet republic to the precipice before which all earlier revolutions had recoiled or been driven back: eliminating the capitalists and their property. He also knew that its moment of greatest opportunity was also its moment of greatest danger. Despite its accomplishments, the revolution's outcome was in doubt fully four years after its triumphant birth:

> The whole question is who will take the lead. We must face this issue squarely—who will come out on top? Either the capitalists succeed in organizing first—in which case they will drive out the Communists and that will be the end of it. Or the proletarian state power, with the support of the peasantry, will prove capable of keeping a proper rein on these gentlemen, the capitalists, so as to direct capitalism along state channels and to create a capitalism that will be subordinate to the state and serve the state.[3]

This fight to organize state capitalism would be particularly difficult because the old methods of direct assault were no longer appropriate. Military and political victory may have saved the revolution from its open enemies, but the path to communism now lay through stimulating the peasants' personal incentive. It had become essential to lay "an economic foundation for the political gains of the Soviet state," and this meant making it worth the peasants' while to farm land they did not directly own but could freely use.[4] A novel set of difficulties had imposed themselves after the seizure of power, had been deepened by a civil war which had only postponed their solution, and were intensifying as the revolution continued its uneven development.

Toward the end of his life Engels had described relations between workers and peasants in societies where capitalism had produced a politically organized labor movement and simultaneously confronted the rural smallholders with ruin. He knew how easily the bourgeoisie had terrified the peasants by stirring up their insecurity and appealing to their acquisitiveness. Its success in turning them against the "partageux" workers had doomed every significant nineteenth-century proletarian rising. But things had changed considerably, Engels now thought. Capitalism in agriculture was creating the social conditions for an alliance between the peasants and the workers in both France and Germany. As he and Marx had for more than forty years, Engels tried to provide political guidance in a situation where a revolutionary alliance between proletarian communism and petty-bourgeois democracy was as important as it was difficult.

Owning or renting just enough land to sustain his family without hiring wage labor and differing from the proletarian proper in his ownership of tools, the small free peasant, "like every other survival of a past mode of production, is hopelessly doomed. He is a future proletarian" despite his immediate desire to own the land on which he works.[5] In France this "semi-proletariat" had received land and liberty as a result of the bourgeoisie's victory over the feudalists but had suffered greatly from the consequences of that victory.[6] Its extreme poverty and vulnerability made it a potential ally of the proletariat which "functioning as the government must take steps that will directly improve his position and thus win him over to the revolution; these steps moreover further the transition from private to communal ownership of land in such a way, that the peasant comes to it of his own accord on economic grounds. But one must not affront the peasant, for instance by proclaiming the abolition of the right of inheritance or the abolition of his property. . . ."[7] It was essential to proceed with tact and patience, and Engels urged his fellow socialists to think of land reform as a first step toward the communist goal of common possession of the land and of the instruments of agricultural production. The workers' long-term task—and he had no doubt that it would be difficult to accomplish—cannot be "to unite labor with possession" as some defenders of small property desire, but "to transfer the means of production to the producers as their *common possession*. As soon as we lose sight of this the above statement becomes directly misleading in that it implies that it is the mission of socialism to convert the present sham property of the small peasant in his fields into real property, that is to say, to convert the small tenant into an owner and the indebted owner into a debtless owner. Undoubtedly socialism is interested to see that the false semblance of peasant property should disappear, but not in this manner."[8] Socialists must tell the truth and not try to maintain conditions they know to be doomed. This means that

> when we are in possession of state power we shall not even think of forcibly expropriating the small peasants (regardless of whether with or without compensation), as we shall have to do in the case of the big land-owners. Our task relative to the small peasant consists, in the first place, in effecting a transition of his private enterprise and private possession to co-operative ones, not forcibly but by dint of example and the proffer of social assistance for this purpose. And then of course we shall have ample means of showing to the small peasant prospective advantages that must be obvious to him even today.[9]

Engels knew how difficult it would be to convince the peasants that land reform alone would not solve their problems. In theory he expected them to become receptive to cooperation and socialism as capitalism dispossessed and impoverished them, but he also knew that their scattered and precarious conditions of life would render them vulnerable to the bourgeoisie for some time. What can socialists offer them now without lying or being untrue to their socialist aims? he asked rhetorically. "How was the peasant to be helped, not the peasant as a future proletarian but as a present propertied peasant without violating the basic principles of the general socialist programme?"[10]

It would not be sufficient to limit oneself to land reform. Communism's distinctive demand had always been the abolition of individual possession of the means of production, and the peasants must be convinced that only common possession and use can guarantee the independence and security they had always sought. But, mindful of the petty bourgeoisie's historical fear of the workers, the French Social Democrats had tried to present themselves as the most reliable defenders of its immediate economic interests. They were making a serious mistake, Engels warned. "Your attempt to protect the small peasant in his property does not protect his liberty but only the particular form of his servitude; it prolongs a situation in which he can neither live nor die."[11] Communists cannot put themselves in the position of defending conditions which they know are doomed—even if such a policy would appeal to the peasants in the short run. They must say clearly that the course of social development will inevitably ruin the small peasantry, pledge that they will not hasten it by anything they do, and offer the peasants a clear alternative to the pauperization which the bourgeoisie's market offers them.

For Engels cooperation was a transitional step to socialism in agriculture because its immediate advantages could be easily demonstrated. Socialists should "come along and offer the peasants the opportunity of introducing large-scale production themselves, not on account of the capitalists but for their own, common account" because small proprietors could be convinced that "this is in their own interest, that it is the sole means of their salvation."[12] If it could be the transition to large-scale agricultural production, cooperation could help the rural smallholders if and only if unambiguously offered by a working class in possession of political power *as part of the transition to a higher form of agricultural production*. Engels never expected the rural smallholders to become socialists overnight, but he did know how important it was to blunt their resistance to the social changes which the workers would have to initiate.

Although he was responding to a very different situation in 1920, Lenin had Engels's analysis in mind as he confronted the failure of War Communism's siege economy to provide a working relationship with the bulk of the peasantry. Requisitions, state farms, the partial elimination of money, and other measures had helped to save the revolution in the short run but had clearly outlived their usefulness. The history of past revolutions weighed heavily on Lenin as he turned his thoughts to the future. The French Revolution had come to its Thermidor because Robespierre never understood that the Terror had lost its political *raison d'être* after the military victories of 1794. When he refused the prosperous peasants' call for an end to the emergency measures which restricted freedom of trade, they had swept the Jacobins away and halted the revolution's further development.[13] Lenin's decision to retreat was partially motivated by his desire to avoid a confrontation with the same forces which had doomed the Jacobins. A series of ominous peasant disturbances and the more troubling mutiny of the Kronstadt sailors in early March 1921 had highlighted the danger the revolution faced. There was only one way out, he told the Tenth Congress:

> We have to understand that, with the peasant economy in the grip of a crisis, we can survive only by appealing to the peasants to help town and countryside. We must bear in mind that the bourgeoisie is trying to pit the peasants against the workers; that behind the facade of workers' slogans it is trying to incite the petty-bourgeois anarchist elements against the workers. This, if successful, will lead directly to the overthrow of the dictatorship of the proletariat and, consequently, to the restoration of capitalism and of the old landowner and capitalist regime.[14]

It had been theoretically and politically clear for some time that the prospects for communism in agriculture would rise or fall with the workers' ability to gradually lead the small proprietors toward socialized ownership and work. But it was not so simple to organize cooperation in a backward country where the proletariat was a tiny minority—and a badly weakened one at that. The confiscations and reapportionments of 1917–18 had begun to eliminate the landlords and the rural poor and the intervening period had created a large middle peasantry which Russia's economic backwardness would sustain for some time. "When concentrating on economic rehabilitation," Lenin observed in 1921, "we must understand that we have before us a small farmer, a small proprietor and producer who will work for the market until the rehabilitation and triumph of large-scale production. But rehabilitation on the old basis is impossible; it will take years, at least a decade, and possibly longer, in view of the havoc. Until then we shall have to deal, for many long years, with the small producers as such, and the unrestricted trade slogan will be inevitable."[15] In the meantime this unavoidable concession to the "elemental force" of the petty bourgeoisie could be made to serve socialism because the workers held state power and had begun to transform the economy's "commanding heights" of banking, foreign trade, and large-scale heavy industry. The revolution's first transitional stage was lasting much longer than Lenin had expected because a politically advanced proletarian revolution had taken place because of—and despite—an exceedingly backward peasant society:

> There is no doubt that in a country where the overwhelming majority of the population consists of small agricultural producers, a socialist revolution can be carried out only through the implementation of whole series of special transitional measures which would be superfluous in highly developed capitalist countries where wage-workers in industry and agriculture make up the vast majority. Highly developed capitalist countries have a class of agricultural wage-workers that has taken shape over many decades. Only such a class can socially, economically, and politically support a direct transition to socialism. Only in countries where this class is sufficiently developed is it possible to pass directly from capitalism to socialism, without any special country-wide transitional measures.[16]

Given an overwhelmingly peasant society and the failure of socialist revolutions to materialize in the West, this meant that "only agreement with the peasantry can save the socialist revolution in Russia."[17] Such an agreement has to be genuine if it is to work, said Lenin as he echoed Engels' earlier warning that "you can't fool a class." But it would be difficult to conclude because the bulk of the peasants did not want the same thing as the workers. Given the progress of land reform and the general leveling of social conditions in the villages, the middle peasants had been the immediate beneficiaries of the proletarian revolution in the countryside. The proletarian revolution's contradictory course had strengthened small rural property and would continue to do so for some time. This could not fail to complicate and lengthen the approach to the transformation of agriculture:

> it will take generations to remold the small farmer, and recast his mentality and habits. The only way to solve this problem of the small farmer—to improve, so to speak, his mentality—is through the material basis, technical equipment, the extensive use of tractors and other farm machinery and electrification on a mass scale. This would remake the small farmer fundamentally and with tremendous speed. If I say this will take generations, it does not mean centuries. But you know perfectly well that to obtain tractors and other machinery and to electrify this vast country is a matter that may take decades in any case. Such is the objective situation.[18]

Like small proprietors everywhere, Lenin observed, the middle peasants have two simple demands. "The first is a certain freedom of exchange, freedom for the small private proprietor, and the second is the need to obtain commodities and products."[19] Threatened by both the bourgeoisie and the proletariat, they still thought that their small property could be protected if they enjoyed a measure of economic liberty and were sheltered by the state from the ruinous effects of competition and monopoly. Petty-bourgeois democracy had always been based on the vulnerability of small property, and the defensive measures it advocated had always sought to enlist the public power in the defense of the "little man." Their desire to limit what the bourgeoisie could do with its property had made the rural democrats potential allies of the workers, and in the proletarian state they had a real, if temporary, defender.

But the limits of such an alliance were clear. The market's tendency to divide commodity owners into those who own capital and those who own nothing but their labor-power would have a far more dramatic impact on the workers than on the peasants. Its divisive and pauperizing effects would undermine both classes and spontaneously generate capitalism even if it was nominally regulated by a proletarian state. How can a socialist working class—especially one which holds political power—tolerate, let alone encourage, such a state of affairs? "Can freedom of trade, freedom of capitalist enterprise for the small farmer, be restored to a certain extent without undermining the political power of the proletariat?" asked Lenin. His affirmative answer revealed his belief that the workers could satisfy the middle peasants' immediate economic interests without jeopardizing socialism—*provided* they held political power and controlled the most important branches of large-scale industry. Political power became more important to him as the economic contradictions of socialism intensified. He had believed earlier that the revolution could advance more or less in a straight line, but it had become clear that an undetermined number of transitional stages remained and that additional measures would be required.

Not long after October Lenin had developed a preliminary analysis of how "state capitalism" could serve as a transition to socialism if organized by a proletarian state, and he returned to that analysis now. In a deeply petty-bourgeois society from which the bourgeoisie had largely been eliminated, he did not doubt that the anarchic disruptiveness of small commodity production was now socialism's chief enemy. State capitalism and socialism shared a commitment to public control and regulation of the marketplace. This might make it possible to satisfy the peasants in the short run and control their destructiveness in the long.

If state capitalism could make the rural petty bourgeoisie's revival serve communism, it would have to be wielded by a proletarian dictatorship. This led Lenin to define the revolution's present stage as a struggle between private capital and small production in the service of capitalism on one hand against state capitalism and a workers' state in the service of socialism on the other. Public regulation of the market by a politically organized proletariat can serve as the transition from a petty-bourgeois economy dominated by small production to a socialism organized around modern large-scale industry. The final transition, from state capitalism to socialism, would be comparatively simple. It would depend on the ideological and political development of the proletariat and the progress of industrialization, for "when the working class has learned how to defend the state system against the anarchy of small ownership, when it has learned to organize large-scale production on a national scale along state-capitalist lines, it will hold, if I may use the expression, all the trump cards, and the consolidation of socialism will be assured."[20] The undeniable fact that the New Economic Policy would encourage capitalism would not harm the revolution *if it was organized by the workers' state*, a dictatorship which Lenin now defined as "the direction of policy by the proletariat."[21] "The whole problem," given Russia's social backwardness and her enfeebled working class, "is to find the correct methods of directing the development of capitalism (which is to some extent and for some time inevitable) into the channels of state capitalism, and to determine how we are to hedge it about with conditions to ensure its transformation into socialism in the near future."[22]

Establishing proper relations between the proletariat and the peasantry remained the revolution's fundamental political problem. These relations would have to be "proper" in view of communism's ultimate aim. "Agreement between the working class and the peasantry may be taken to mean anything. Unless we assume that, from the working-class standpoint, an agreement is possible in principle, permissible, and correct only if it supports the dictatorship of the working class and is one of the measures aimed at the abolition of classes, then, of course, it remains a formula on which all the enemies of the Soviet power, all the enemies of the dictatorship, operate."[23] Whether it was confronting counterrevolution, foreign intervention, and civil war or the landlords, bourgeoisie, and middle peasants, the dictatorship of the proletariat remained central to the revolution's prospects. As Marx and Engels had anticipated, it had become much more than the instrument to defend the still-vulnerable gains of October. It was becoming the revolution's heart and soul, its most dependable foundation. The dangers that this implied were as clear as were the opportunities, and questions of leadership figured prominently in both.

Class, Party, and Dictatorship

Marx and Engels had tended to emphasize the "self-activity" of the working class from the very beginning of their careers. The spontaneous character of the Paris workers' movement had deeply impressed them in 1871, and when they referred to the Commune's leadership at all it was almost always to point out its errors. A lifetime of theoretical and political struggles against the Blanquists, Jacobins, and other revolutionary sectarians were so central to their work that it has become commonplace to view Lenin's theory of the party as one of his most important anti-democratic departures from the spirit and letter of their work.

And yet, for all their well-known emphasis on the proletariat's independent activity, neither Marx nor Engels shared the anarchists' hostility to organization or to politics. As deeply as they believed that the workers' political independence would be the key to their success, they also developed a theory of leadership which was rooted in classical political thought and took account of the way capitalism had formed modern social classes. *The Communist Manifesto* was a party document, defined the communist movement as the fusion of the revolutionary intelligentsia's theoretical understanding with the proletariat's practical activity, and expressed the orientation toward politics which distinguished Marxism from its rivals. Marx and Engels's view was expressed in their claim that social classes act *as classes* only as they form political parties and orient themselves toward other classes and the state. If the bourgeoisie was able to defend capitalism's "distinction of classes" because it held political power, the proletariat's assault on that same distinction would likewise require the exercise of its political domination. This suggested that the workers would need a political party even after they had won power, "broken" the bourgeois state, and organized their own political structure.

Marx and Engels always had the dictatorship of the working *class* in mind and this required them to consider how the class would be organized. Many of their criticisms of Proudhon, Lassalle, Bakunin, and Mazzini were motivated by the failure of nineteenth-century revolutionism to distinguish between the dictatorship of a class and the dictatorship of an individual. The view that the workers could organize their *class dictatorship* only through their *class party* underlay Engels' frequent criticism of the pre-1871 activists. "Since Blanqui regards every revolution as a coup de main of a small revolutionary minority," he observed, "it automatically follows that its success must inevitably be followed by the establishment of a dictatorship—not, it should be well noted, of the entire revolutionary class, the proletariat, but of the small numbers of those who accomplished the insurrection and who themselves are at first organized under the dictatorship of one or several persons."[24] But if he and Marx attacked revolutionary vanity, they certainly did not attack working-class political organization. If the Commune has proven anything, he remarked shortly after its fall, it is that a divided and antagonistic society drives every class to seek exclusive political power. Like any class, the workers can formulate and implement their policy only through their political party. A class's struggle for exclusive political power is expressed as the struggle of its party for exclusive political domination:

> . . . the German Social-Democratic Workers' Party, just *because* it is a *workers' party*, necessarily pursues a "class policy," the policy of the working class. Since each political party sets out to establish its rule in the state, so the German Social-Democratic Workers' Party is necessarily striving to establish *its* rule, the rule of the working class, hence "class domination." Moreover, *every* real proletarian party, from the English Chartists onward, has put forward a class policy, the organization of the proletariat as an independent political party, as the primary condition of its struggle, and the dictatorship of the proletariat as the immediate aim of the struggle.[25]

Like Marx and Engels, Lenin had insisted for years that a workers' party could lead the rest of society only if it based itself on the activity of an ideologically developed and politically independent class. At the same time, the Russian revolution had produced the soviets as the authentic expression and vehicle of the revolutionary drive of the "laboring masses." The relationship between the party's guiding "consciousness" and coordination and the soviets' activity and control continued to occupy him as the revolution turned toward the New Economic Policy. His emphasis on peaceful matters was accompanied by a renewed accent on the importance of party unity, and it was no accident that it was at the Tenth Party Congress that he proposed both the New Economic Policy and the famous ban on factions.

The prospect of economic liberalization and a revival of trade combined with the reality of a decimated proletariat and an exhausted party to raise the possibility that the activity Lenin was trying to stimulate could quickly degenerate into uncontrollable chaos. This threat prompted the important "trade union debate," precipitated by Trotsky's proposal to militarize the trade unions and "tighten the screws of War Communism" in preparation for a renewed frontal assault on property. What appeared at first to be a limited debate about the relationship between the trade unions, the party, and the state developed into a debate about the character, structure, and tasks of the proletarian dictatorship long before a coherent economic plan was even a remote possibility.

Taking issue with the syndicalists who regarded the trade unions as the workers' most basic instruments, Lenin insisted that they were fundamentally different from the party in structure, scope, and role. Mass organizations which take in and speak for the entire proletariat in its economic struggles, they could not perform the tasks of a party which alone can organize the "vanguard's" political leadership of society. The proletariat cannot exercise its dictatorship through the unions precisely because the inclusiveness which defines them renders them incapable of functioning as instruments of coercion. A trade union "is an organization designed to draw in and to train; it is, in fact, a school: a school of administration, a school of economic management, a school of communism."[26] It can serve as an intermediate institution between the workers and "their" state and to that extent is essential to the exercise of the dictatorship of the proletariat. But a class expresses and exercises its leadership politically, through the state, and every class is led by its leaders. The October Revolution had been powered by the independent activity of the workers from below and the leadership of the Bolsheviks. The connection between coordination and activity was expressed as the relationship between their most important institutions:

> What happens is that the Party, shall we say, absorbs the vanguard of the proletariat, and this vanguard exercises the dictatorship of the proletariat. The dictatorship cannot be performed without a foundation such as the trade unions. These functions, however, have to be performed through the medium of special institutions which are also of a new type, namely, the Soviets.[27]

The dictatorship of the proletariat could succeed only as the dictatorship of a class, but no class ever rules directly or spontaneously. The Russian working class may have been the most advanced in the world because it was the only one which held state power, but the social circumstances of its victory made its party's guidance more important than ever. Since the economy was still dominated by private ownership and production, "the dictatorship of the proletariat cannot be exercised through an organization embracing the whole of that class, because in all capitalist countries (and not only over here, in one of the most backward) the proletariat is still so divided, so degraded, and so corrupted in parts (by imperialism in some countries) that an organization taking in the whole proletariat cannot directly exercise proletarian dictatorship. It can be exercised only by a vanguard that has absorbed the revolutionary energy of the class."[28] Lenin's certainty that things would get even more difficult made it particularly important that the party exercise what has come to be called its "leading role," for any concession to syndicalism would represent a dangerous "clean break with communism." Trotsky's suggestion that the trade unions be transformed into agencies of the Ministry of Labor clashed as directly with Lenin's views as did the anarcho-syndicalist claim that the unions could organize a socialist economy by themselves. Both misunderstood the continuing need for political leadership after October because they assumed that the workers' seizure of power would be a sufficient condition for the triumph of socialism. The general coordination which only politics can bring made the party as important after October as it had been before:

> Communism says: the Communist Party, the vanguard of the proletariat, leads the non-Party workers' masses, educating, preparing, teaching and training the masses ("school" of communism)—first the workers and then the peasants—to enable them eventually to concentrate in their hands the administration of the whole national economy.
>
> Syndicalism hands over to the mass of non-Party workers, who are compartmentalized in the industries, the management of their ministries . . . , thereby making the Party superfluous, and failing to carry on a sustained campaign either in training the masses or in *actually* concentrating in *their* hands the management *of the whole national economy.*[29]

At the same time, the unions would be more important after the turn to economic reconstruction than they had been before. Their role would be shaped as much by the workers' increasingly precarious position as by the need to gather and organize their resources in creating a new society. The market still shaped a social order whose bourgeois character stood in decided contrast to the proletarian state. Since the New Economic Policy marked a certain "return to capitalism," there was an increased likelihood that the workers would find themselves in conflict with "their" state. The measures which Lenin was advocating to jump-start the economy carried serious risks even if they were to be organized and implemented by a proletarian state. The backward pull of the social order would always tend to compromise the communist thrust of the state's activities, and this led Lenin to consider the future role of truly independent trade unions. Even if they could not do what only a political party could, they would remain basic instruments of the working class because they organized the workers at the point of production.

Even if he clearly marked his differences with the syndicalists and identified the party and the state as the workers' most important post-October institutions, Lenin did not ignore the unions. More than "schools of communism" and yet not a political party, they could help ensure the democratic organization of a modern economy. Bureaucracy could be combated only if the workers utilized every opportunity to directly intervene in public matters. The unions could provide an important avenue for this intervention even if they could not be state institutions. Lenin criticized Trotsky's proposal to subordinate them to the state as a bureaucratic and therefore antidemocratic response to a problem whose ultimate resolution lay in the sphere of politics rather than in organization. Independent trade unions were essential in maintaining "proper" relations between the leadership of the proletariat and the class as a whole. But the workers did not yet know how to run the state or the economy and, given that illiteracy had not even been eliminated yet, "the going will be slow." In the meantime, the workers need their "army of steeled revolutionary Communists" to govern. The backward drag of a petty-bourgeois society and the inexorable bureaucratic tendency of any state made it more important than ever to recognize the importance of leadership:

> It is common knowledge that the masses are divided into classes; that the masses can be contrasted with *classes* only by contrasting the vast majority in general, regardless of division according to status in the social system of production, with categories holding a definite status in the social system of production; that as a rule and in most cases—at least in present-day civilized societies—classes are led by political parties; that political parties, as a general rule, are run by more or less stable groups composed of the most authoritative, influential and experienced members, who are elected to the most responsible positions, and are called leaders.[30]

The transition from war to peace did not mean that things are going to get easier, Lenin warned the delegates to the Tenth Congress; all it meant is that the conditions of an intricate and difficult class struggle had changed. None of the revolution's most basic questions had been answered. The workers did not know how to organize an economic plan, how to begin socialist construction, or how to manage relations between different classes. Engels may have been right when he called politics the "concentrated expression of economics," but for Lenin the revolution's progress now depended on mastering the petty and mundane tasks of economic construction. The absence of much theoretical and practical experience now meant that the continuing debate about the trade unions was making it difficult to guide the practical work which had once again become so necessary. The interests of the revolution now demanded that "general party talk" stop and that renewed attention be paid to painstaking, deliberate, boring—and indispensable—"production work." Like every democratic upheaval before them, the Revolutions of 1848 and the Paris Commune had reached a point where it had become necessary to suspend democracy in order to defend it. Permanent crisis had brought the Russian Revolution to a similar point:

> There would be nothing to fear from a slight syndicalist or semi-anarchist deviation; the party would have swiftly and decisively become aware of it, and would have set about correcting it. But it is no time to argue about theoretical deviations when one of them is bound up with the tremendous preponderance of peasants in the country, when their dissatisfaction with the proletarian dictatorship is mounting, when the crisis in peasant farming is coming to a head, and when the demobilization of the peasant army is setting loose hundreds and thousands of broken men who have nothing to do, whose only accustomed occupation is war and who breed banditry. At the Congress, we must make it quite clear that we cannot have arguments about deviation and that we must put a stop to that. . . . The atmosphere of the controversy is becoming extremely dangerous and constitutes a direct threat to the dictatorship of the proletariat.[31]

Lenin's warning about party unity stemmed from his concern about the revolution's difficult political and economic situation. His proposed ban on "factionalism"—"the formation of groups with separate platforms, striving to a certain degree to segregate and create their own group discipline"— expressed his view that legitimate disagreement was going over to *de facto* sabotage. He had always encouraged the free and open debate which strengthens a healthy party, but decisions had to be made and implemented. Proletarian politics could not be like the bourgeoisie's "talking shop" and society could no longer tolerate open organizing against a democratically agreed-upon party position. The emergency had become so severe that it was necessary to subordinate everything, including internal party democracy and the formal rights of party members, to the larger democratic interests of the revolution.[32] "Clearly, in a country under the dictatorship of the proletariat, a split in the ranks of the proletariat, or between the proletarian party and the mass of the proletariat, is not just dangerous; it is extremely dangerous, especially when the proletariat constitutes a small minority of the population."[33] Russia's enormous peasantry made it as important as ever to draw a sharp distinction between the Revolution's core classes and maintain a proletarian point of view. In the present environment,

> only the political party of the working class, i.e., the Communist Party, is capable of uniting, training and organizing a vanguard of the proletariat and of the whole mass of the working people that alone will be capable of withstanding the inevitable petty-bourgeois vacillations of this mass and the inevitable traditions and relapses of narrow craft unionism or craft prejudices among the

proletariat, and of guiding all the united activities of the whole of the proletariat, i.e., of leading it politically, and through it, the whole mass of the working people. Without this the dictatorship of the proletariat is impossible.[34]

The workers had developed many institutions but none could attain the party's comprehensiveness of view. The trade unions were their basic mass organizations and served to link them to their state in the area of production. The soviets were the basic mass organizations of all "toilers" and linked them to the party in the sphere of the state, while the cooperative societies were the basic mass organizations of the peasants and provided the vehicle through which the party could draw the rural population into socialist construction. But the workers' party is and must be the leading and coordinating force in the drive to build a new society. Proletarian politics would continue to drive economics even if the revolution seemed to have become reduced to administration and organization.

Under these circumstances, Lenin acknowledged, the "dictatorship of the proletariat" might boil down to the dictatorship of its politically organized minority. But while he affirmed this "in general," he was careful to note that the dictatorship of the proletariat must be carried out by a party which is accountable to the workers through the democratic soviets. In that case, the party is implementing the dictatorship of the *proletariat*. The party may be the most comprehensive form of class organization but it is not the same as the class, and Lenin continued to insist on the distinction between them so each could act.[35] The soviet republic remained the instrumentality through which the workers' party could organize the proletarian dictatorship—even if it was not yet clear how the nonparty workers would supervise its work:

> The state is a sphere of coercion. It would be madness to renounce coercion, especially in the epoch of the dictatorship of the proletariat, so that the administrative approach and "steerage" are indispensable. The Party is the leader, the "vanguard" of the proletariat, which rules directly. It is not coercion but expulsion from the party that is the specific means of influence and the means of purging and steeling the vanguard. The trade unions are a reservoir of the state power, a school of communism and a school of management.[36]

The undeniable need for expertise and the equally unavoidable requirement that it be democratically controlled continued to shape Lenin's thinking. The revolution's dangerous bureaucratic proclivities were rooted in the atomized and scattered character of a huge mass of impoverished and illiterate small rural producers. Left to itself, the petty bourgeoisie spontaneously tended to reestablish the market, and the market always tends to generate bureaucracy. The drive to control the mortal threat to socialism in the countryside's tendency to reproduce the social relations of an economy of small production and exchange was a precondition of the proletarian revolution's struggle against the state. But the contradictory character of the New Economic Policy forced the workers' state to momentarily strengthen the same small production which irresistibly generated bourgeois social relations and bourgeois politics. Under the circumstances, everything depended on the proletarian dictatorship's ability to turn the New Economic Policy's concession to the past to the benefit of the future. In the long run, only the proletarian character of the state could enable the workers to use "their" bureaucracy to defeat bureaucracy and "their" New Economic Policy's concessions to the market against the market:

> The New Economic Policy introduces a number of important changes in the position of the proletariat and, consequently, in that of the trade unions. The great bulk of the means of production in industry and the transport system remain in the hands of the proletarian state. This, together with the nationalization of the land, shows that the New Economic Policy does not change the nature of the workers' state, although it does substantially alter the methods and forms of socialist development for it permits of economic rivalry between socialism, which is now being built, and capitalism, which is trying to revive by supplying the needs of the vast masses of the peasantry through the medium of the market.[37]

The transition from the old capitalist market of small-scale peasant production to the new socialist planned economy of state-owned large-scale industry now lay through the New Economic Policy, proletarian dictatorship, and state capitalism. When Marx and Engels had spoken of "state capitalism" they had been describing a variety of capitalism. But state capitalism in a country where the proletariat has won "the battle of democracy" is another thing altogether. Given working-class state power, it could serve socialism even if it remained capitalism. But this did not end the revolution's difficulties—if anything, it defined them more sharply. The "commanding heights" of the economy were in the hands of the workers' state but the direct producers remained separated from the unmediated ownership of the means of production, the distinctions between mental and manual labor and between town and country were becoming more intense, and other remnants of the past continued to exert a backward pull on the economy and the polity. Even as it helped create the conditions for communism, state capitalism "represented" capitalism. Even as it had to be encouraged, it had to be controlled. Only a proletarian state could make it possible for a state capitalism which had served capitalism under the political rule of the bourgeoisie to serve communism under the political rule of the working class.

In some ways Lenin was describing little more than a capitalism democratically and publicly regulated by a proletarian state. But there was more than one danger hidden in this complicated situation, for if the communist goal of social ownership of the means of production was now taken to be state ownership of the means of production, then the "withering away of the state" would not seem as important in practice as it had been in theory. Lenin's famous definition of socialism as "electrification plus soviet power" testified to the identification of the social with the political, of the withering away of the state with the reappropriation of the means of production by society as a whole. His emphasis on proletarian state power was partly a reaction to emergency but also illustrated contradictory tendencies inherent in both the political theory of Marxism and the socialist project itself. An association of free producers would make possible the resolution of these contradictions in the interests of the whole society. The problem was no longer how to get there but how to *begin* to get there.

The Culture of Communism

The end of War Communism precipitated an important shift in the revolution's direction and in the accompanying thrust of the workers' state. Victory over the open counterrevolution made it possible to begin addressing some of the problems of communism. "Now," said Lenin to the Party's Eleventh Congress, "it is not a matter of possessing political power, but of administrative ability, the ability to put the right man in the right place, the ability to avoid petty conflicts, so that state economic work may be carried on without interruption. This is what we lack; this is the root of the mistake."[38] The peasants will no longer respond to heroic ideological or patriotic appeals, he warned; the old "campaign style" will no longer work with them. They can be won over only on the basis of their experience and their material interests, and an immediate improvement in their living conditions had become the revolution's most important priority. He knew that it would not be easy to organize the economy, for communists now had to learn how to trade and how to be businessmen—activities for which even the most experienced of revolutionaries were not particularly equipped. The turn to indirect methods of struggle against capitalism meant that even the party's monopoly of political power might not be enough to contain the danger even as it clearly remained indispensable. Principles were fine, but real life had a way of reducing the most heroic of communist tasks to the most mundane and apparently noncommunist level:

> We need a real test. The capitalists are operating alongside us. They are operating like robbers; they make profits; but they know how to do things. But you—you are trying to do it in a new way; you make no profit, your principles

are communist, your ideals are splendid; they are written out so beautifully that you seem to be saints, that you should go to heaven while you are still alive. But can you get things done? We need a test, a real test . . . [39]

Such a test was not hard to find, for the revolution's contradictory course meant that it would be necessary to build the economic foundations of communism with the tools of capitalism. There were enormous dangers in such a difficult enterprise and to manage them required a level of theoretical and practical sophistication which Lenin feared the party did not have. "We have sufficient, quite sufficient political power," he said; "we also have sufficient economic resources at our command, but the vanguard of the working class which has been brought to the forefront to directly supervise, to determine the boundaries, to demarcate, to subordinate and not be subordinated itself, lacks sufficient ability for it. All that is needed here is ability, and that is what we do not have."[40]

Lenin was worried by more than the backwardness of the country, the weakness of the class, and the inexperience of the party. The revolution had turned out to be extraordinarily complex and laced with unprecedented difficulties. Constructing communism demanded a certain emancipation of capitalism. Communists had to free some of the market's most chaotic forces in order to establish the links between town and country which would permit the planned organization of economic affairs. Two antagonists remained locked in an exceedingly complicated struggle and their mutual dependence clouded the outcome. As if all the earlier difficulties had not been enough, communist construction had come down to the struggle against Russia's notorious laziness, slovenliness, passivity, and instability—all of which Lenin was increasingly inclined to view as a legacy of her enormous petty bourgeoisie.

He was clear about the solution. Business matters had to be recognized and treated as such; the revolution no longer depended on seizing and consolidating state power, negotiating the peace of Brest-Litovsk, organizing a Red Army, or winning the civil war. Now the task was to organize the peaceful work of economic reconstruction and get the right people in the right place. This was the only way the party could draw the masses of the productive population into political, administrative, and economic affairs and ensure that both the promise of the Paris Commune and the future of socialism were served. If anything, he told the party, the situation was more intensely dangerous now than it had ever been:

. . . after the greatest political change in history, bearing in mind that for a time we shall have to live in the midst of the capitalist system, the key feature now is not politics in the narrow sense of the word (what we read in the newspapers is just political fireworks; there is nothing socialist in it at all), the key feature is not resolutions, not departments and not reorganization. As long as these things are necessary we shall do them, but don't go to the people with them. Choose the proper men and introduce practical control. That is what the people will appreciate.

In the sea of the people we are after all but a drop in the ocean, and we can administer only when we express correctly what the people are conscious of. Unless we do this the Communist Party will not lead the proletariat, the proletariat will not lead the masses, and the whole machine will collapse.[41]

It was the proletariat's weakness and Russia's backwardness which forced Lenin to turn to the party and the state. He knew the risks he was running. The scientific work of engineers and agronomists must now replace the ideological and political sophistication of propagandists and agitators. The heroic and very "leftist" expectation that the workers could immediately build socialism by themselves had made it more important than ever to understand the difficult relationship between theory and the world. Using bourgeois experts did not signify a surrender to capitalism by itself any more than fortifying the workers' state represented an embrace of the statism against which Marx and Engels had always fought. But turning both to the workers' advantage would require an extraordinary degree of political understanding and organizational skill. Administration need not degenerate into bureaucracy, but the party would have to learn how to bring proletarian politics to life:

> Men's vices, it has long been known, are for the most part bound up with their virtues. This, in fact, applies to many leading Communists. For decades, we had been working for the great cause, preaching the overthrow of the bourgeoisie, teaching men to mistrust the bourgeois specialists, to expose them, deprive them of power and crush their resistance. That is a historic cause of world-wide significance. But it needs only a slight exaggeration to prove the old adage that there is only one step from the sublime to the ridiculous. Now that we have convinced Russia, now that we have wrested Russia from the exploiters and given her to the working people, now that we have crushed the exploiters, we must learn to run the country. This calls for modesty and respect for the efficient "specialists in science and technology," and a business-like and careful analysis of our numerous *practical* mistakes, and their gradual but steady correction. Let us have less of this intellectualist and bureaucratic complacency, and a deeper scrutiny of the practical experience being gained in the center and in the localities, and of the available achievements of science.[42]

By the end of War Communism it had become clear that a lengthy and unstable transitional period would come before the foundations of a socialist economy could be established. With the benefit of a little bit of hindsight,

Lenin could now see that War Communism and the New Economic Policy were transitions themselves, internally contradictory, temporary and unstable resolutions of crises which had matured as the revolution had moved forward. The October triumph of the socialist proletariat had brought the democratic revolution to a successful conclusion, and War Communism had damaged the rural economy and nearly destroyed the proletariat as it had defended the revolution and begun expropriating the landlords and the bourgeoisie. One aspect of state capitalism—which stimulated the development of a free market and led away from communism—coexisted with its socialist counterpart, public regulation of the market by a proletarian state. The turn toward the NEP reinforced private property in agriculture so it could be transcended, and the immediate motion of the soviet republic violated many of the Paris Commune's egalitarian lessons. The bourgeois-democratic revolution had gone over to the first stages of the socialist revolution without a break but with considerable difficulty, each contradictory stage limited only by the progress of an intensifying class struggle which provided the revolution's motive force and drove it forward:

> The first develops into the second. The second, in passing, solves the problems of the first. The second consolidates the work of the first. Struggle, and struggle alone, decides how far the second succeeds in outgrowing the first.
>
> The Soviet system is one of the most vivid proofs, or manifestations, of how the one revolution develops into the other. The Soviet system provides the maximum of democracy for the workers and peasants; at the same time, it marks a break with *bourgeois* democracy and the rise of a *new*, epoch-making *type* of democracy, namely, proletarian democracy, or the dictatorship of the proletariat.[43]

The process had gotten more complicated and its contradictions more intense as the revolution had developed. Lenin seems to have been surprised that peaceful economic matters had turned out to be so much more complex and dangerous than the relatively simple political seizure of power and military defeat of the counterrevolution. The party's accumulated experience had enabled it to mobilize the enthusiasm of an exhausted population, but communists would now have to learn how to apply methods of administration and organization in the service of communism which the bourgeoisie had developed and used in the service of capitalism. The basic contradiction of the entire transitional period was still that between a socialism which was emerging but weak and a capitalism which was on the defensive but remained powerful. The completion of the revolution's earlier stages signified only that it would be necessary to find new methods of waging the class struggle. The old ways were no longer appropriate to a situation which would take a long time to approach, much less realize. The objective situation had changed, and Lenin told the party in no uncertain terms that communists would have to change as well:

> Borne along on the crest of the wave of enthusiasm, rousing first the political enthusiasm and then the military enthusiasm of the people, we expected to accomplish economic tasks just as great as the political and military tasks we had accomplished by relying directly on this enthusiasm. We expected—or perhaps it would be truer to say that we presumed without having given it adequate consideration—to be able to organize the state production and the state distribution of products on communist lines in a small-peasant economy directly as ordered by the proletarian state. Experience has proven that we were wrong. It appears that a number of transitional stages were necessary—state capitalism and socialism—in order to *prepare*—to prepare by many years of effort—for the transition to socialism. Not directly relying on enthusiasm, but aided by the enthusiasm engendered by the great revolution, and on the basis of personal interest, personal incentive and business principles, we must first set to work in this small-peasant country to build solid gangways to socialism by way of state capitalism. Otherwise we shall never get to communism, we shall never bring scores of millions of people to communism. This is what experience, the objective course of the development of the revolution, has taught us.[44]

If the New Economic Policy was a compromise with capitalism, it was also part of the dictatorship of the proletariat and a stage in the development of communism. It did not signify an end or even a relaxation of the class struggle but guaranteed that it would continue in new forms and at new levels. The Russian bourgeoisie may have been "defeated" but was still quite powerful, and the absence of socialist revolutions in the West would only encourage further instability in the newly enlarged and ever-more important petty bourgeoisie. A weakened proletariat had to exercise its "dictatorship" as it became a smaller island in an ever-larger peasant ocean. As if the trials of earlier periods were not enough, "upon the proletariat, enfeebled and to a certain extent declassed by the destruction of the large-scale machine industry, which is its vital foundation, devolves the very difficult but paramount historic task of holding out in spite of these vacillations."[45] Its dictatorship had to be exercised as much against the hesitancy of its allies as against the hostility of its enemies but it could serve communism only if it simultaneously served democracy:

> For the first time in history there is a state with only two classes, the proletariat and the peasantry. The latter constitutes the overwhelming majority of the population. It is, of course, very backward. How do the relations between the peasantry and the proletariat, which holds political power, find practical

expression in the development of the revolution? The first form is alliance, close alliance. This is a very difficult task, but at any rate it is economically and politically feasible.

How did we approach this problem practically? We concluded an alliance with the peasantry. We interpret this alliance in the following way: the proletariat emancipates the peasantry from the exploitation of the bourgeoisie, from its leadership and influence, and wins it over to its own side in order jointly to defeat the exploiters.

The Menshevik argument runs like this: the peasantry constitutes a majority; we are pure democrats, therefore, the majority should decide. But as the peasantry cannot operate on its own, this, in practice, means nothing more nor less than the restoration of capitalism. The slogan is the same: Alliance with the peasantry. When we say that, we mean strengthening and consolidating the proletariat.[46]

Lenin described the New Economic Policy as a concession and a temporary defeat as often as he characterized it as an advanced form of the class struggle and a step toward communism. By 1923 it was clear that it was the profoundly contradictory strengthening of both capitalism *and* socialism. Making the former serve the latter would depend on the workers' monopoly of state power, even if having that power guaranteed nothing by itself. Marx and Engels had attributed the failure of the 1848 democrats to their failure to "break" the state and their tendency to think of revolution as replacing bad ministers with good ones. That insight had found concrete expression in Lenin's view that the soviet republic was the Russian counterpart of the Paris Commune. Civil war, foreign intervention, and intractable backwardness had compelled him to place more of his immediate trust in the rudimentary structures of the proletarian state than he might have in different circumstances. It would take longer than he had initially thought to finish the political revolution begun in October and "really" establish a workers' state, much less lay the foundations of a classless society. A great deal had been accomplished in the past five years, but many difficulties lay ahead and proletarian control of the state was more essential now than it had ever been.

So were proletarian politics. "We still have the old machinery," Lenin said to the Moscow Soviet near the end of his life, "and our task now is to remold it along new lines. We cannot do so at once, but we must see to it that the Communists we have are properly placed. What we need is that they, the Communists, should control the machinery they are assigned to, and not, as so often happens with us, that the machinery should control them."[47] NEP Russia was not yet socialist Russia. As the unfamiliar tasks of economic construction imposed themselves it would become even more important to improve the standards and performance of the state. Politics were more important than ever. Engels had expected the proletarian state to "wither away" as communist society emerged, but for the moment at least Lenin saw no alternative to strengthening it so it could assist in the unfolding of a society whose foundations were barely in the process of formation. "What elements have we for building this apparatus?" he asked in his last work.

> Only two. First, the workers who are absorbed in the struggle for socialism. These elements are not sufficiently educated. They would like to build a better apparatus for us, but they do not know how. They cannot build one. They have not yet developed the culture required for this; and it is culture that is required. Nothing will be achieved in this by doing things in a rush, by assault, by vim or vigor, or in general, by any of the best human qualities. Secondly, we have elements of knowledge, education and training, but they are ridiculously inadequate compared with all other countries.[48]

The October revolution was less than seven years old when Lenin died in 1924. The heroic seizure of power and defense of the revolution had yielded for the moment to the prosaic job of organizing and administering economic affairs. The repressive side of the proletarian dictatorship was not as prominent now as it had been earlier, but in some ways Lenin knew that its peaceful economic future might be even more difficult than its violent and "political" past had been. His late emphasis on streamlining and reducing the governmental machine accompanied his understanding that the revolution would require a strong state for some time. His hope that the soviets would enable the workers to supervise the state accompanied his continued reliance on the guiding and leading role of a vanguard party which would have to assist a ravaged proletariat reconstitute itself. His conviction that socialism could be the work of only an enlightened working class underlay the late emphasis on the education and "culture" to which he had paid so much attention over the years. He also knew that the proletariat was not yet equal to its task but that history would not wait very long for it to rise to the occasion. The bourgeoisie had been defeated by a revolution which now stood on the verge of moving into uncharted areas, but compromises with property were necessary if class society was to be eliminated. State capitalism politically organized by the workers could be part of the transition to the "first stage" of communism described in *The State and Revolution* but the coexistence of these mutually contradictory social formations meant that each would have to function in direct violation of its own rules. Given the complexities and the newness of the situation it is not surprising that Lenin's thinking should have revealed deep internal contradictions. They were the contradictions of real life and they had rested at the heart of the Marxist theory of the proletarian dictatorship for the better part of a century. How the theory of the dictatorship of the proletariat could contribute to the workers' ability to realize their "ultimate general result" of a classless society remained to be seen.

NOTES

1. V. I. Lenin, "Report on the Substitution of a Tax in Kind for the Surplus-Appropriation System," *Collected Works* (Moscow: Progress Publishers, 1960–72), 32:214–28. Unless otherwise noted, all subsequent references will be to this edition.

2. "New Times and Old Mistakes in a New Guise," 33:23.

3. "The New Economic Policy and the Tasks of the Political Education Departments," 33:66.

4. *Ibid.*, 73.

5. "The Peasant Question in France and Germany," *Selected Works in Three Volumes*, 3:460.

6. Engels, "Introduction to the 1892 Edition of *Socialism: Scientific and Utopian*", *ibid.*, 105.

7. "Conspectus of Bakunin's Book *State and Anarchy*," *Anarchism and Anarcho-Syndicalism*, 148. See also "The Nationalization of the Land," in *Selected Works in Three Volumes*, 2:288–90.

8. "The Peasant Question in France and Germany," *Selected Works in Three Volumes,* 3:464.

9. *Ibid.*, 470.

10. *Ibid.*, 461.

11. *Ibid.*, 463.

12. *Ibid.*, 471.

13. See Albert Soboul, *The French Revolution 1787–1789* (New York: Random House, 1975), Part Two, chaps. 4–5.

14. "Report on the Political Work of the Central Committee of the RCP (B)," 32:185.

15. *Ibid.*, 187.

16. "Report on the Substitution of a Tax in Kind for the Sur-plus-Appropriation System," 184–85.

17. *Ibid.*, 215.

18. *Ibid.*, 217.

19. *Ibid.*

20. "The Tax in Kind," 32:333.

21. *Ibid.*, 341.

22. *Ibid.*, 345.
23. "Report on the Tax in Kind Delivered to the Tenth All-Russia Conference of the R.C.P. (B)," 32:404.
24. "Programme of the Blanquist Commune Emigrants," *Selected Works in Three Volumes*, 2:381.
25. "The Housing Question," *ibid.*, 2:356.
26. "The Trade Unions, the Present Situation and Trotsky's Mistakes," 32:20.
27. *Ibid.*
28. *Ibid.*, 21.
29. "The Party Crisis," 32:50.
30. "Left Wing Communism, An Infantile Disorder," 31:41.
31. "Report on the Political Work of the Central Committee of the RCP (B)," 32:178.
32. "Once Again on the Trade Unions, the Current Situation and the Mistakes of Trotsky and Bukharin," 32:71–80.
33. *Ibid.*, 75.
34. "Preliminary Draft Resolution of the Tenth Congress of the RCP on the Syndicalist and Anarchist Deviation in Our Party," 32:246.
35. "Purging the Party," 33:39–41.
36. "Once Again on the Trade Unions, the Current Situation and the Mistakes of Trotsky and Bukharin," 32:97–98.
37. "The Role and Functions of the Trade Unions Under the New Economic Policy," 33:184.
38. "The Political Report of the Central Committee of the RCP (B)," 33:300.
39. *Ibid.*, 273.
40. *Ibid.*, 279.
41. *Ibid.*, 304.
42. "Integrated Economic Plan," 32:145.
43. "Fourth Anniversary of the October Revolution," 33:54.
44. *Ibid.*, 58.
45. "Third Congress of the Communist International," 32:460.
46. "Report on the Tactics of the RCP Delivered at the Third Congress of the Communist International," 32:485.
47. "Speech at the Plenary Session of the Moscow Soviet," 33:442.
48. "Better Fewer, But Better," 33:488.

Conclusion

Chapter 8

The "Main Point"

Its extension of democracy into society stimulated modern communism's early development and continues to provide the foundation of its political theory. Framed by the requirements of a uniquely comprehensive social revolution, Marxism's theory of the dictatorship of the proletariat took shape during the 1840s, was largely in place by 1848, and matured in connection with the events of subsequent decades. Developed and applied by Lenin in circumstances which neither Marx nor Engels could have anticipated, it rests at the heart of a theoretical orthodoxy which is unintelligible without it. More than the name of an unfortunate if necessary instrument in service to a noble purpose, it describes the entire transition from capitalism to communism and is therefore at the center of what Marxism signifies.[1] Means cannot be separated from ends any more than politics can be separated from economics, and the theory rests on the claim that a historically unique transition can be directed successfully only by a consistently revolutionary and proletarian-led popular democracy organized from below. Whatever future direction the communist movement takes, its current crisis makes it more essential than ever that this claim be taken seriously.

If it describes Marxism's understanding of democracy, the theory simultaneously defines a transitional process of unprecedented complexity. Shaped by the unstable but unavoidable coexistence of two antagonistic systems in

173

conditions of permanent emergency, the dictatorship of the proletariat became increasingly important to Lenin as an immediate matter after the October Revolution. The leading role of the proletarian state had been at the heart of Marx and Engels's communism from the 1840s on, but they had never been forced to consider the practical implications of the profound backwardness which confronted Lenin. The Left had identified "the people" as the laboring majority for many years and the Paris Commune's assault on the state had infused democracy with an entirely new and inherently revolutionary meaning, a meaning which was enriched by the Russian workers' later discovery of the soviets. Lenin's understanding that the contemporary incarnation of the commune state would be a soviet republic represented his preservation and development of the Marxist theory of the revolutionary state and of socialist democracy. He shared with Marx and Engels the conviction that the dictatorship of the proletariat would be both the political expression of an intensifying class struggle and the contradictory transition to a classless society which would finally dispense with the state, the dictatorship, and the democracy which had helped bring it into being.

The Politics of Transition

Theory led Marx and Engels to anticipate that politics would lead economics during the entire struggle against a capitalism whose roots they expected to remain in place for some time after the proletariat's apparent victory. Their long-run goal of a free association of producers expressed the Left's traditional hostility to the state, but they were limited by the fact that history offered them only one brief opportunity to observe how the workers would organize their assault on private property. Indeed, their continuing inclination to regard political power as the decisive immediate weapon against class society seemed to leave them open to the same statism with which they had charged many of their opponents over the years. The theoretical and ideological battles which marked the history of the First International quickly became practical problems for Lenin, and the particular features of the Russian Revolution could not fail to color the way he thought of the workers' state.

Its tenacity a function of its deep social roots, bourgeois society not only confronted the newly victorious proletariat immediately upon its October "victory" but remained very powerful for some time after the bourgeoisie and the landlords had been expropriated. The petty bourgeoisie's small property had been strengthened by the campaign against the large capitalists and landlords and was officially encouraged by the New Economic Policy. Many forces came together to produce an environment in which the workers' state and the socialist sectors of the economy, said to be the most advanced in the world and the harbinger of the future, were weaker than and besieged by their supposedly "obsolete" antagonists. The shattered industrial base and extremely backward agricultural sector challenged all naive expectations that the seizure of state power and public ownership of the economy's "commanding heights" would be enough to guarantee rapid social transformation. The revolution's most immediate economic task was to industrialize, and this would shape its politics for the better part of two decades.

Marx, Engels, and Lenin knew that the workers would have to be patient with a powerful petty bourgeoisie which had become essential to a socialism it did not yet want and of whose benefits it was not yet convinced. Democracy may mean the rule of "the people," but when Lenin died in 1924 the vast majority of the Russian "people" were small propertied peasants. Yet all three men had spent many years arguing that neither democracy nor socialism could be built on the slogans of the petty-bourgeois democrats whose support was now so important and whose small property was such a problem for the "commune state." Democracy and communism seemed to demand that a socialist proletariat satisfy the short-run desires of a decidedly nonproletarian and nonsocialist petty-bourgeois majority.

The struggle between a workers' state and a bourgeois society on the one hand and between the relatively weak elements of communism and the persistent structures of capitalism on the other had given practical meaning to Marx's theoretical understanding of the need to "break" the bourgeois state as the condition of building a proletarian one. Stronger than its predecessors because it rested directly on a popular insurrection and would lead a social revolution of unparalleled depth, the new state's democratic character would be a stage on the road to its own dissolution. Marx and Engels's opposition to Lassalle and his "free people's state" mirrored their opposition to the anarchists' intention to "abolish" the state immediately after the overthrow of the bourgeoisie. "The whole talk about the state should be dropped," said Engels in 1875, "especially since the Commune, which was no longer a state in the proper sense of the word."[2] The Commune had substantiated their earlier theoretical expectation that the state would begin to disappear immediately upon its consolidation, but it had not lasted long enough for the full implication of this development to become clear.

It proved significantly easier to proclaim all this in theory than to organize it in practice. An ever-sharpening class conflict compelled the new state to discharge many of the same repressive functions of its predecessors, and it was obliged to do so in much the same fashion. Its primary task during War Communism had been defending the soviet republic against counterrevolution. In the absence of either advanced productive forces or developed proletarian social relations, only a workers' state could block a still-powerful bourgeoisie from overthrowing an apparently victorious but comparatively weak proletarian revolution. The early prominence of its "negative" and repressive functions meant that the new state bore a certain similarity to bourgeois states even if it was built on and controlled by a democratized republic of soviets. This anomaly was modified but not eliminated during the New Economic Policy, a continuation of the class struggle whose ultimate object was to abolish the same property and market on whose temporary support it was built. Lenin was forced to reserve an important role to a socialist state whose transformation, he acknowledged toward the end of his life, had barely begun.

Even so, he was as convinced as Marx and Engels had been that the socialist state was fundamentally different from the bourgeois "machine" it seemed to resemble. It was a repressive apparatus first and foremost, but it was an apparatus in the hands of the majority—and that made all the difference. Coercion is not the same everywhere, he argued, nor is it inimical to democracy everywhere; a repressive proletarian republic can serve democracy and communism just as a repressive bourgeois republic once served democracy and capitalism. In a backward society the proletariat might have no choice but to use "bourgeois" measures in support of communism, but such measures would have a wholly different meaning than they had when taken by a bourgeoisie in support of capitalism. Taylorism, one-man management, competition, toleration of the market, encouragement of the peasants' personal interests, and the like could serve communism *if undertaken and organized by a workers' state*. In the long run, their bourgeois past could serve the communist future only because they were organized by soviet power. "Representative institutions remain," Lenin observed of the Paris Commune, "but there is *no* parliamentarism here as a special system, as the division of labor between the legislative and executive, as a privileged position for the deputies. We cannot imagine democracy, even proletarian democracy, without representative institutions, but we can and *must* imagine democracy without parliamentarism, if criticism of bourgeois society is not mere words for us."[3] This "socialism" was neither an autonomous mode of production nor a political system organized for its own sake but a phase of the continuing struggle between communism and capitalism.

It was much more than a simple transition from one to the other, however, for the break in continuity represented by the October Revolution guaranteed nothing by itself. Socialism is communism at an early stage of development, and its consolidation would signify only that the transition to a classless society had begun. The birth of the new neither required nor implied the immediate death of the old; capitalism would remain stronger than the embryonic structures of communism for some time in the conditions of "socialist" Russia's numbing backwardness. Lenin knew that efforts to consolidate the world's first socialist revolution would intensify all the contradictions which Marx and Engels had anticipated theoretically. The understanding that the past would continually exact its price from the present is what forced all three men to the contradictory suggestions that the workers could use their market against the market, their bureaucracy against the bureaucracy, their state against the state, and their class dictatorship against class society.

Marx described the effects of capitalism's backward pull in uncharacteristic detail as he evaluated Lassalle's 1875 proposal that German Social-Democrats organize their party program around the distribution of "the undiminished proceeds of labor" to "all members of society." As ancient and popular as this demand was, Marx criticized it as a romantic and retrograde position rooted in a series of economic and logical errors. The "undiminished proceeds of labor" simply cannot be returned to "everyone." If socialism means anything, he said, it is that ownership no longer governs distribution. No socialist can seriously propose that Lassalle's "everyone" include a bourgeoisie which does not work because it owns. The "undiminished proceeds of labor" will not be available in any event because deductions from the total social product must be made for economic expansion and investment, public administration, social necessities, insurance, and welfare before any distribution to individuals can take place. Socialism would mean considerably more than equitable distribution to individuals in the absence of social appropriation of the means of production and their fruits.

Marx expected that the free market and private ownership of the "commanding heights" of the economy would disappear during the "first phase of communist society," but wage labor and commodity production and exchange would remain. The distribution of the "proceeds of labor" would therefore be regulated by the same exchange of equivalents which governs commodity production and circulation everywhere. The bourgeois sense of justice as equal treatment defined such exchange as "fair" within the boundaries of capitalist society. The abolition of private property will ensure that applying the same standard will produce dramatically "fairer" results in socialism.

> Accordingly, the individual producer receives back from society—after the deductions have been made—exactly what he gives to it. What he has given to it is his individual quantum of labor. For example, the social working day consists of the sum of the individual hours of work; the individual labor time of the individual producer is the part of the social working day contributed by him, his share in it. He receives a certificate from society that he has furnished such and such an amount of labor (after deducting his labor for the common funds), and with this certificate he draws from the social stock of means of consumption as much as costs the same amount of labor. The same amount of labor which he has given to society in one form he receives back in another.[4]

This socialist principle of distribution according to work is an advance over the bourgeois principle of distribution according to ownership but nevertheless remains limited by the past. Work can be measured by only its intensity and duration—but it was the application of a single standard to different cases which had organized the capitalist market and accelerated the social differentiation of owners from workers even as it expressed their legal equality. An undoubted advance over feudalism's explicit legal preferences, it might be necessary at an early stage of communism but is still a "stigma." Its tendency is to transform unavoidable differences between people into the very class divisions whose elimination is socialism's *raison d'être*. This may not have mattered very much when the material conditions for a classless society did not exist, but the possibility that communist society could now be built made "bourgeois right" as dangerous to socialism in the long run as it was necessary to it in the short. Marx's early hostility to a liberal rights-based conception of democracy had started him on the road to a comprehensive theory of "human emancipation." That criticism was amplified thirty years later as he offered an assessment of how socialist distribution would be limited by the bourgeois past from which it arose but which it no longer served:

> But one man is superior to another physically or mentally and so supplies more labor in the same time, or can labor for a longer time; and labor, to serve as a measure, must be defined by its duration or intensity, otherwise it ceases to be a standard of measurement. This *equal* right is an unequal right for unequal labor. It recognizes no class differences, because everyone is only a worker like everyone else; but it tacitly recognizes unequal individual endowment and thus productive capacity as natural privileges. *It is, therefore, a right of inequality, in its content, like every right.* Right by its very nature can consist only in the application of an equal standard; but unequal individuals (and they would not be different individuals if they were not unequal) are measurable only by an equal standard in so far as they are brought under an equal point of view, are taken from one *definite* side only, for instance, in the present case, are regarded *only as workers* and nothing more is seen in them, everything else being ignored. Further, one worker is married, another not; one has more children than another, and so on and so forth. Thus, with an equal performance of labor, and hence an equal share in the social consumption fund, one will in fact receive more than another, one will be richer than other, and so on. To avoid all these defects, right instead of being equal would have to be unequal.[5]

Even in a workers' state, equal rights reflect and encourage inequality and will become unnecessary as classes disappear. But if the road to equality lies through the recognition of inequality, the disappearance of private profit and exploitation will not eliminate the need to organize socialist exchange on bourgeois foundations. Equal amounts of labor will have to be exchanged for equal amounts of labor for some time; reward according to work describes the distributive principle of a controlled market which organizes a "first stage" of communism even as its own development simultaneously undermines it. This implied that some form of market mechanism would regulate socialist distribution for some time after the seizure of political power. "But these defects are inevitable in the first phase of communist society as it is when it has just emerged after prolonged birth pangs from capitalist society," Marx knew. "Right can never be higher than the economic structure of society and its cultural development conditioned thereby."[6] The transition he was describing was shaped by his understanding that the past would weigh on the present with the force of centuries. The only instrument the "victorious" proletariat held to block the still-powerful bourgeoisie was the state. Neither the productive forces nor the social relations of communist society were in place, and the use of public power to create them has defined a good deal of contemporary communism's theoretical and practical history.

Future Freedom

Marx and Engels certainly shared the nineteenth-century's optimistic view that increased production could create the material conditions for human emancipation. So central was this confidence that by 1848 their initially moral indictment of capitalism had come to rest in *The Communist Manifesto*'s announcement that it was the "fettering" of its productive forces which marked the limits of its historic possibilities. Indeed, communism would be such a fruitful advance over all earlier social formations that scarcity would become a thing of the past as human emancipation became a real possibility.[7] For Lenin, Marxist theory and Russian backwardness came together to make increasing production the October Revolution's chief economic project. "Only at a certain level of development of the productive forces of society, an even very high level for our modern conditions, does it become possible to raise production to such an extent that the abolition of class distinctions can be a real progress, can be lasting without bringing about stagnation or even decline in the mode of social production," said Engels in an 1875 essay which theoretically anticipated some of the difficulties the Bolsheviks would face forty-two years later.[8] But Russia's backwardness was so pronounced that Lenin would have to start at the very beginning. Only the production of the means of production themselves could give concrete force to *The State and Revolution*'s hopeful suggestion that the state would become unnecessary as the productive forces developed and it became possible to apply a more developed principle of distribution than the bourgeois one of equal right.[9] But what would this new principle be? Granted Marx and Engels's reluctance to describe the future, it was their understanding of "freedom" which ultimately rested at the heart of their political theory and provided the measure by which everything connected with socialism could be evaluated.

Even if he had thought of freedom as consciousness, Hegel had embraced the Greek conception of it as the uniquely human capacity for intentional action. Marx and Engels shared this orientation; what they rejected was Hegel's idealistic path to it, and this had led them to regard the development of society's productive forces as the path by which people could systematically accomplish what they intend. The view that knowledge and conscious mastery of the social life they create separate humans from animals and define man's capacity for freedom was an ancient root of nineteenth-century social theory. "We pre-suppose labor in a form that stamps it as exclusively human," said Marx in a characteristically optimistic passage. "A spider conducts operations that resemble those of a weaver, and a bee puts to shame many an architect in the construction of her cells. But what distinguishes the worst architect from the best of bees is this, that the architect raises his structure in imagination before he erects it in reality. At the end of every labor-process, we get a result that already existed in the imagination of the laborer at its commencement."[10] Engels elaborated on this a decade later in his classic presentation of freedom as conscious control over nature made possible by social organization. The full development of man's social and individual power, which had rested at the center of his and Marx's thinking for a third of a century, required a communism which was now within reach:

> With the seizing of the means of production by society, production of commodities is done away with, and, simultaneously, the mastery of the product over the producer. Anarchy in social production is replaced by systematic, definite organization. The struggle for individual existence disappears. Then for the first time man, in a certain sense, is finally marked off from the rest of the animal kingdom, and emerges from mere animal conditions of existence into really human ones. The whole sphere of the conditions of life which environ man, and which have hitherto ruled man, now comes under the dominion and control of man, who for the first time becomes the real, conscious lord of nature, because he has now become master of his own social organization. The laws of his own social action, hitherto standing face to face with man as laws of nature foreign to, and dominating him, will then be used with full understanding, and so mastered by him. Man's own social organization, hitherto confronting him as a necessity imposed by nature and history, now becomes the result of his own free action. The extraneous objective forces that have hitherto governed history pass under the control of man himself. Only from that time will man himself, with full consciousness, make his own history—only from that time will the social causes set in movement by him have, in the main and in constantly

growing measure, the results intended by him. It is humanity's leap from the kingdom of necessity to the kingdom of freedom.[11]

Often accused of representing communism as a static Platonic utopia, Marx and Engels certainly knew that this "freedom" would not come easily. Even if it tended toward the elimination of classes and their resulting conflict, the "state of constant flux and change" which drives all social formations would characterize a classless society as well.[12] The theory of the dictatorship of the proletariat is nothing more—and nothing less—than Marxism's account of the full transition from blind necessity to conscious freedom.[13]

The uncontrolled chaos of the bourgeois market had brought nature's blindness into human affairs as a governing force, and Marx and Engels were not alone when they argued that freedom required its transcendence by planned production for use. The automatic mechanisms of the market allocate surplus in capitalist society, and they spontaneously generate bourgeois relations of production as they do so. Only a socialist state could control the destructive effects of this mechanism in the short run, even if the ultimate communist solution to this dilemma was the conscious organization of social life by freely associated producers. But this "human emancipation" would also require repressive political power in the hands of the working class.

However much he defended the New Economic Policy from his "leftist" critics, Lenin was deeply suspicious of the socialist hybrid which Russia's backwardness had compelled him to organize. A powerful proletarian state was necessary if the public was to control the market's tendency to spontaneously generate capitalism. But this implied that the tension between state and society would characterize socialism as it had capitalism and that the workers' state might be trying to do the impossible. Lenin knew that the NEP could serve communism only if it set the conditions for the direct attack on the same private property which it was temporarily strengthening. The coexistence of communism and capitalism could survive for only a short period of time, the growing antagonism between the public and private regulated by a powerful state which was supposed to gradually disappear. Yet Lenin's seemingly Jacobin expectation that a capitalism founded on private property and sustained by market relations could be used "against itself" if guided by a proletarian state seemed to collide with Engels's observation that capitalism was not brought into being by force and could not be eliminated by it either:

In other words, even if we exclude all possibility of robbery, force and fraud, even if we assume that all private property was originally based on the owner's own labor, and that throughout the whole subsequent process there was only exchange of equal values for equal values, the progressive development of production and exchange nevertheless brings us of necessity to the present capitalist mode of production, to the monopolization of the means of production and the means of subsistence in the hands of one, numerically small, class, to the degradation into propertyless proletarians of the other class, constituting the immense majority, to the periodic alternation of speculative booms and commercial crises and to the whole of the present anarchy of production. The whole process can be explained by purely economic causes; at no point whatever are robbery, force, the state or political interference of any kind necessary.[14]

The deepest economic contradiction of the dictatorship of the proletariat was revealed during the New Economic Policy because the attempt to make capitalism serve communism violated each system's most basic tendencies. It had been clear from the very beginning that simple repression would not be enough to resolve this contradiction and this is why expropriating the bourgeoisie, defeating the counterrevolution, and regulating the market described only one aspect of Marxism's theory of the revolutionary state. The creative tasks of the "expansive" proletarian dictatorship remained and they would have to work in tandem with their "negative" opposites. The link between them could only be the democracy on which the proletarian dictatorship rested, but Lenin was aware that it would not be easy to ensure that the workers would be able to continuously control "their" state.

"Active social forces work exactly like natural forces: blindly, forcibly, destructively, so long as we do not understand, and reckon with, them. But when once we understand them, when once we grasp their action, their direction, their effects, it depends only upon ourselves to subject them more and more to our own will, and by means of them to reach our own ends," said Engels as he described the freedom he thought would come with communism.[15] The "we" to whom he referred were "the producers working together," and he was confident that the rapid development of society's productive forces would interact with communist social relations to usher in the human emancipation of which he and Marx had spoken for many years. Lenin shared his confidence but Russia's backwardness forced a realization that nothing was guaranteed. After the spectacular and heroic victories of War Communism, he repeatedly warned, socialism had come down to the mundane and decidedly unheroic struggle to master economic affairs. The old order could be dismantled and the new constructed only if "real," substantive democracy enabled the people to supervise every aspect of public life, from routine daily administration to the grandest matters of state. But it was equally clear that the workers were not ready to undertake this, and the unavoidable compromises with both capitalism and the lessons of the Paris Commune carried long-run risks even if Lenin hoped that they would save the revolution in the short run. International isolation, grinding backwardness, an exhausted and decimated proletariat, an "ocean" of peasants, and a thousand other factors forced him to fall back on the soviet state and the Communist Party to supervise the most basic work of industrializing the country. The revolution was compelled to start at the very beginning, with the production of the means of production. Rapid development should propel socialism forward, but there were limits to how much could be asked and it would take much longer than Lenin had ever imagined before the state could even begin the famous transformation which Engels had described:

> When at last it becomes the real representative of the whole of society, it renders itself unnecessary. As soon as there is no longer any social class to be held in subjection; as soon as class rule, and the individual struggle for existence based upon our present anarchy in production, with the collisions and excesses arising from these, are removed, nothing more remains to be repressed, and a special repressive force, a state, is no longer necessary. The first act by virtue of which the state really constitutes itself the representative of the whole of society—the taking possession of the means of production in the name of society—this is, at the same time, its last independent act as a state. State interference in social relations becomes, in one domain after another, superfluous, and then dies out of itself; the government of persons is replaced by the administration of things, and by the conduct of processes of production. The state is not "abolished," it *dies out*.[16]

Marx and Engels had always known that the fullest measure of democracy ultimately implied the abolition of classes. Even if fettered by the "defects" associated with socialism's transitional character, their democracy was based on the ancient idea that "all men, as men, have something in common, and that to that extent they are equal."[17] Equality of needs unites all people, and Engels's 1891 proposal that the German Social-Democrats include an extended set of democratic demands in their program gave shape to his renewed criticism of the market's politics. "Instead of 'for equal rights for all,' " he said, "I suggest: 'for equal rights and *equal duties* for all,' etc. *Equal duties* are for us a particularly important addition to the bourgeois-democratic *equal rights* and do away with their specifically bourgeois meaning."[18] "No rights without duties, no duties without rights," declared Marx in a similar vein."[19]

As relatively advanced as it was, then, distribution according to work could not be communism's full social democracy. By the time Lenin died in 1924 Soviet citizens were becoming "equal" in their legal relationship to the means of production but he knew that equal participation in state affairs was a long way off. He expected that quantity would go over to quality at some point and that the conscious administration of the state by the majority would precipitate its reabsorption by society described by Engels. "The more complete the democracy," he had declared on the eve of October, "the nearer the moment when it becomes unnecessary. The more democratic the 'state' which consists of the armed workers, and which is 'no longer a state in the proper sense of the word', the more rapidly *every form* of state begins to wither away."[20] Toward the end of his life he had come to realize that it would be a long time before this happened. In the meantime, socialism's deeply contradictory tendency toward the abolition of classes and the state would require the dictatorial rule of the proletariat organized in a powerful state. The young Engels had thought that it would be "a trifling matter *to regulate production according to need.*" The "real, practical" emancipation whose outlines he and Marx had sketched decades earlier came full circle in the latter's classic description of communist "freedom." Based on the most basic thing that all people share, it expressed the fundamental equality of human needs, connected them to the abolition of classes, and thereby provided the standard against which socialism and its proletarian dictatorship would rise or fall:

> In a higher phase of communist society, after the enslaving subordination of the individual to the division of labor, and therewith also the antithesis between mental and manual labor, has vanished; after labor has become not only a means of life but life's prime want; after the productive forces have also increased with the all-round development of the individual, and all the springs of co-operative wealth flow more abundantly—only then can the narrow horizon of bourgeois right be crossed in its entirety and society inscribe on its banners: From each according to his ability, to each according to his needs![21]

Marxism's theory of the dictatorship of the proletariat is its political account of the entire transition from capitalism to this "higher phase of communist society" and the conscious satisfaction of human needs. It has been so important to contemporary life partly because successful socialist revolutions have turned out to be strategies of state-directed industrialization. Although the specific circumstances vary from country to country, the social backwardness which has precipitated such transformations has only intensified the intractable problem which any proletarian revolution will inevitably confront: to create communism in a hostile environment in which *the social basis for its development does not exist.*

The contradictions engendered by the impossible yet unavoidable coexistence of a proletarian state and a bourgeois society dominated every aspect of Lenin's thinking from the October Revolution until his death. His emphasis on the production of the means of production reflected the specific conditions of Russian backwardness but has had some general relevance as well because much of modern socialism has unfolded as a course of modernization and industrialization. If he thought of the state as the potentially decisive weapon with which the proletariat could defend itself against a still-powerful bourgeoisie, he was no less certain that the communist social relations which Marx had begun to outline would develop in the context of a politically driven economy based on steel. For Lenin the dictatorship of the proletariat was more than a series of measures the workers' state would have to take in defense of the revolution. It also summarized the positive steps required for the planned construction of a classless society.

Lenin made his contributions to Marxism because the course of the Russian Revolution forced him to address the dictatorship of the proletariat as an immediate, practical matter rather than as a theoretical possibility. If he conceived it as the full transition to communism, he also understood that its form would change even as its class content was preserved. The dictatorship of the proletariat is nothing but the working class in possession of state power—but that is everything. Lenin expected it to take different forms in different societies and to evolve over time, but orthodox Marxism's political theory continues to insist that as long as classes exist the only alternative to the dictatorship of the bourgeoisie is the dictatorship of the proletariat. This did not prevent Lenin from warning against the tendency to regard everything the Russians had done as intrinsic elements of a workers' state. A one-party system, War Communism's requisitions, the New Economic Policy, and other elements of the October Revolution may be of limited applicability in other environments, but there were certain elements which he clearly regarded as having general relevance. The seizure and subsequent use of political power required suppressing the bourgeoisie and breaking its state. When all is said and done, this is the core of the Marxist theory of the revolutionary state and of socialist democracy. It culminated in Lenin's understanding that a soviet republic would guide Russia's industrialization, and its manifestations continue to be so important and so controversial because communists have not yet been forced to consider what the dictatorship of the proletariat might look like in a society which has moved beyond industrialization and steel to one organized around electronics.

The same has been true of the leadership of the Soviet Union for some time. Having narrowed the dictatorship of the proletariat to the unfortunately necessary politics of socialist industrialization, it has tried to freeze in time what Lenin regarded as the ever-changing and always-dynamic content of the entire transition to a classless society. That transition will doubtless pass through successive stages, and the shape of the workers' state can be expected to change as its tasks change. But the October Revolution has become temporarily blocked, and the contradiction between its bureaucratically hardened state and the objective requirements of its increasingly postindustrial society has become so acute that it can no longer be managed without a dramatic theoretical, political, and economic advance. The crisis of "actual existing socialism" is its momentary failure to make the turn which the logic of its own development will eventually compel it to make.

Having effectively denied that contemporary Marxism has any class content at all, its putative leaders have come to articulate a bureaucratic and non-partisan view of its political tasks. Managing the economy to satisfy as many sectors as possible, ensuring distribution according to work performed and defending the moral interests of "humanity" figure prominently in their self-described agenda. The social transformations of which Marx, Engels, and Lenin spoke are presumed to have ended with industrialization and the collectivization of agriculture. Gorbachev and his advisors claim that *perestroika* and *glasnost* represent a social revolution and repeatedly invoke Lenin to support this contention, but their hostility to the state and their commitment to what they call social "self-management" effectively sever them from what Marxism offers by way of guidance.

The root of socialism's current crisis lies in too little politics rather than in too much. The state took the lead in forging a modern social order but the absence of democratic accountability has strengthened a bureaucracy which is entangled in and seeks to preserve a soviet society stuck in an industrial phase of development. It is so involved with production, with the party, and with virtually every area of public life that it seems to have become synonymous with socialism. Gorbachev understands how suffocating, un-democratic, and parasitical it has become, but privatization and marketization can only exacerbate the problem. The fundamental lesson of the Paris Commune remains as central to socialist politics now as it was a century ago. The only way to control a bureaucracy which is as necessary to modern society as it is dangerous to democracy is through continuous mass revolutionary supervision from below. The Marxist name for this is "the dictatorship of the proletariat," and for a time it was exercised by soviets whose very existence was incompatible with the political power of the bourgeoisie and with class society as such. If the Paris Commune and 1917's "dual power" signified anything at all, it was that the workers had to take up the struggle against the bourgeois state *as soon as* they organized themselves in soviets. The same is likely to characterize the developing struggle against the prerogatives of a bureaucracy whose existence conflicts with the purpose and the direction of the socialist society from which it arose and which it is supposed to serve.

The worldwide transition from an economy based on steel to one organized around electronics is relentlessly undermining the relationship between what remains of socialism's economics and its politics. Even as an end to scarcity becomes possible, the bureaucracy intensifies its resistance to restructuring society around the new instruments of production. Yet reliance on the market will not reinvigorate a postindustrial socialist economy. Everyone recognizes that economic reorganization is necessary—but this also requires a political battle which can be waged successfully by only a strengthened and revolutionized workers' state. *Glasnost* expresses Gorbachev's limited understanding that political reform must accompany economic restructuring, but destroying the privileges of the bureaucracy and making the leap to a public power rooted in technology and electronics are very different from the current infatuation with privacy, individualism, and the market. Gorbachev and his advisors may point to the New Economic Policy as Lenin's model of socialism, but Lenin thought of it as nothing more than a temporary expedient. It did not express the totality of socialism any more than did War Communism, and the fact that he died in 1924 cannot blind us to the flexibility of his understanding that communism can emerge only gradually and in stages. The problems of communism can no longer be solved with the tools of capitalism, particularly if proletarian politics are read out of the picture. Socialism's crisis is the crisis of an antipolitical bureaucracy in power desperately trying to hold back a qualitative leap which is as inevitable as it is dangerous.

Claims to theoretical orthodoxy or to innovative modification notwithstanding, the "dictatorship of the proletariat" which plays such a vital role in classical Marxism has failed to animate communism's political theory for at least as long as it has been abandoned by it in practice. The undoubted difficulties to which its contradictory history has given rise render its declared relationship to democracy especially important and problematical. In the long run this may turn out to be more a matter of practical life than of theoretical refinement, but continuing struggles about the role of the party and the state have intensified the debate about whether the Left's current difficulties derive from its past embrace of the theory or from its more recent abandonment of it. The collapse of what remains of the communism of the Third International is creating more confusion and stimulating more intense disputes about fundamentals than has been seen in many years. Marxism has been a theory of communism as much as a critique of capitalism since 1917, and the theory of the dictatorship of the proletariat has been so central to both its accomplishments and its difficulties that a serious appraisal of its implications is more important than ever. Such an examination must be applied as equally to what passes for the contemporary Left as to capitalism's democratic pretensions. As always there will be passionate controversy about what Marx, Engels, and Lenin had to say on the subject and even more about whether their thinking has anything to offer a world which is very different from the one they knew. I have tried to contribute to this discussion by reasserting the orthodox claim that the theory is a democratic one, that it rests at the heart of the socialist project, and that it cannot be easily abandoned even as its concrete meaning must be reassessed. If Marxism is to be taken seriously it must take itself seriously, and further repudiation of its theoretical underpinnings will only intensify a crisis whose long-run solution is more socialism rather than less. Their "bourgeois" character notwithstanding, democratic liberties and social rights were torn from the bourgeoisie only by protracted and costly popular struggles. Socialism's current crisis is mirrored by that of democracy, for it remains as true as ever that both can grow stronger only if they enrich each other. Capitalism has not undergone some sort of miraculous transformation over the last decade or so; its contradictions and driving forces are the same as they were when Marx, Engels, and Lenin were alive. The theory of the dictatorship of the proletariat still describes the democratic and revolutionary politics of its only alternative.

NOTES

1. Hal Draper, *The "Dictatorship of the Proletariat" From Marx to Engels* (New York: Monthly Review Press, 1987); Richard N. Hunt, *The Political Ideas of Marx and Engels*, vol. 2, *Classical Marxism, 1850–1895* (Pittsburgh: Pittsburgh University Press, 1984); and George Lichtheim, *Marxism: An Historical and Critical Study* (New York: Columbia University Press, 1982) are among many works which present the theory of the dictatorship of the proletariat in a different light from this interpretation.

2. Letter to A. Bebel of 18–28 March 1875, in Marx and Engels, *Selected Works in Three Volumes*, (Moscow: Progress Publishers, 1969), 3:35.

3. "The State and Revolution," 25:429.

4. Marx, "Critique of the Gotha Programme," *Selected Works in Three Volumes*, 3:17–18.

5. *Ibid.*, 18–19.

6. *Ibid.*, 19.

7. C. B. Macpherson's *The Real World of Democracy* (New York: Oxford University Press, 1972) is a recent example of this orientation.

8. "On Social Relations in Russia," *Selected Works in Three Volumes*, (Moscow: Progress Publishers, 1960–72), 2:387.

9. 25:471–72.

10. *Capital* (New York: International Publishers, 1967), 1:178.

11. "Anti-Duhring," 25:270.

12. Engels letter to Otto Von Boenigk, August 1890, *Selected Works in Three Volumes*, 3:485. See also his letter to C. Schmidt, 5 August 1890, *ibid.*, 484.

13. See Hal Draper and Richard N. Hunt for two of the best presentations of the dictatorship of the proletariat as a temporary emergency measure.

15. *Ibid.*, 266.
16. *Ibid.*, 268.
17. *Ibid.*, 95.
18. "A Critique of the Draft Social-Democratic Programme of 1891," *Selected Works in Three Volumes*, 3:432.
19. "General Rules of the International Working Man's Association," *Selected Works in Three Volumes*, 2:20.
20. "The State and Revolution," 25:479.
21. "Critique of the Gotha Programme," *Selected Works in Three Volumes*, 3:19.

Bibliography

ARTICLES

Adamiak, Richard. "The 'Withering Away' of the State: A Reconsideration." *Journal of Politics* 32: 1 (Feb. 1970): 3–18.

Avrich, Paul. "Russian Factory Committees in 1917." *Jahrbucher für Geschichte Osteuropas* 11 (1963): 161–82.

Barfield, Rodney. "Lenin's Utopianism: State and Revolution." *Slavic Review* 30: 1 (March 1971): 45–56.

Bender, Frederic L. "The Ambiguities of Marx's Concepts of 'Proletarian Dictatorship' and 'Transition to Communism.' " *History of Political Thought* 11 (1981): 525–55.

Blackburn, Robin. "Marxism: Theory of Proletarian Revolution." *New Left Review* 97 (May–June 1976): 3–35.

Block, Fred. "The Ruling Class Does Not Rule: Notes on the Marxist Theory of the State." *Socialist Revolution* 7: 3 (May–June 1977): 6–28.

Bloom, Solomon. "The Withering Away of the State." *Journal of the History of Ideas* 8: 1: 113–21.

191

Claudin, Fernando. "Democracy and Dictatorship in Lenin and Kautsky." *New Left Review* 106 (1977): 59–76.

Cunliffe, John. "Marx, Engels and the Party." *History of Political Thought* 2: 2 (June 1981): 349–67.

Daniels, Robert. "The State and Revolution: A Case Study in the Genesis and Transformation of Communist Ideology." *American Slavic and East European Review* 12: 1 (February 1953): 22–45.

Draper, Hal. "Marx on Democratic Forms of Government." *Socialist Register 1974*. Ed. Ralph Miliband and John Saville. (London: Merlin Press, 1974): 101–24.

———. "The Principle of Self-Emancipation in Marx and Engels." *Socialist Register 1971*. Ed. Ralph Miliband and John Saville. (London: Merlin Press, 1971): 81–106.

———. "The Death of the State in Marx and Engels." *Socialist Register 1970*. Ed. Ralph Miliband and John Saville. (London: Merlin Press, 1970): 281–307.

Ehrenberg, John. "Karl Marx and the Dictatorship of the Proletariat." *Research in Political Economy*. Ed Paul Zarembka. 12 vols. Greenwich, Conn: JAI Press, 1990. 12: 187–208.

———. "The Politics of Materialism." *Contemporary Marxism* 9: 4 (December 1984): 44–59.

———. "Dialectics of Dictatorship: Marx and the Proletarian State." *Social Praxis* 7: 1–2 (1980): 21–39.

Emmanel, Arghiri. "The State in the Transition Period." *New Left Review* 1979: 111–31.

Frankel, Jonathan. "Lenin's Doctrinal Revolution of April 1917." *Journal of Contemporary History* (April 1969): 117–42.

Gilbert, Alan. "Salvaging Marx from Avineri." *Political Theory* 4 (1976): 9–34.

Harris, Abram L. "Utopian Elements in Marx's Thought." *Ethics* 60: 2 (Jan. 1950): 79–99.

Kain, Philip J. "Estrangement and the Dictatorship of the Proletariat." *Political Theory* 7: 4 (November 1979): 509–20.

Keep, John. "1917: The Tyranny of Paris Over Petrograd." *Soviet Studies* 20 (July 1968): 22–35.

McLellan, David. "Marx's View of the Unalienated Society." *Review of Politics* 31 (1969): 459–65.

Miliband, Ralph. "The State and Revolution." *Monthly Review* 21: 11 (April 1970): 77–90.

Menasche, Louis. "Demystifying the Russian Revolution." *Radical History Review* (Fall 1978): 142–54.

Mewes, Horst. "On the Concept of Politics in the Early Work of Karl Marx." *Social Research* 43 (1976): 276–94.

Miller, Richard. "Marx and Aristotle: A Kind of Consequentialism." *Canadian Journal of Philosophy*, suppl. 7 (1981): 323–52.

Moore, Stanley. "Marx and Lenin as Historical Materialists." *Philosophy and Public Affairs* 4 (1975): 171–94.

Ollman, Bertell. "Marx's Vision of Communism: A Reconstruction." *Radicalism in the Contemporary Age*. Ed. Seweryn Bialer. *Radical Visions of the Future*. Boulder: Westview Press, 1977: 2: 35–83.

Rubel, Maximilien. "Notes on Marx's Conception of Democracy." *New Politics* 1: 2 (1962): 78–90.

Schonfeld, William. "The Classical Marxist Conception of Liberal Democracy." *Review of Politics* 38 (1971): 360–76.

Sirianni, Carmen. "Production and Power in a Classless Society: A Critical Analysis." *Socialist Review* 59 (Sept.–Oct. 1981): 33–82.

Sowell, Thomas. "Karl Marx and the Freedom of the Individual." *Ethics* 73 (June 1963): 119–25.

Spencer, Martin. "Marx and the State: The Events in France Between 1848–1850." *Theory and Society* 7 (Jan.–Mar. 1979): 167–98.

Wright, Eric Olin. "To Control or to Smash Bureaucracy: Weber and Lenin on Politics, the State, and Bureaucracy." *Berkeley Journal of Sociology* 19 (1974–75): 69–188.

BOOKS

Aganbegyan, Abel, ed. *Perestroika 1898*. New York: Scribner's, 1988.

Anarchism and Anarcho-Syndicalism: Selected Writings by Marx, Engels, Lenin. New York: International Publishers, 1972.

Anweiler, Oskar. *The Soviets: The Russian Workers', Peasants', and Soldiers' Councils, 1905–1921*. Trans. Ruth Hein. New York: Pantheon, 1974.

Avineri, Shlomo. *The Social and Political Thought of Karl Marx*. London: Cambridge University Press, 1968.

Balibar, Etienne. *Sur la Dictature du Prolétariat*. Paris: Maspero, 1976.

Bender, Frederic L., ed. *Karl Marx: The Essential Writings*. Boulder: Westview Press, 1972.

Berlin, Isaiah. *Karl Marx*. 4th ed. New York: Oxford University Press, 1978.

Bernstein, Eduard. *Evolutionary Socialism*. Trans. Ruth Harvey. New York: Schocken, 1961

Bronner, Stephen Eric. *Socialism Unbound*. New York: Routledge, 1990.

Buchanan, Allen. *Marx and Justice*. Totowa, N.J.: Rowman and Littlefield, 1982.

Burke, John, Lawrence Crocker, and Lyman Lefters, eds. *Marxism and the Good Society*. New York: Cambridge University Press, 1981.

Campbell, Tom. *The Left and Rights*. London: Routledge, 1983.

Carnoy, Martin. *The State and Political Theory*. Princeton: Princeton University Press, 1984.

Carr, Edward Hallett. *A History of Soviet Russia*. 7 vols. New York: Macmillan, 1950–1964.

———. *The October Revolution: Before and After*. New York: Random House, 1971.

Chamberlin, William Henry. *The Russian Revolution 1917–1921*. Vol. 1. *From the Overthrow of the Tsar to the Assumption of Power by the Bolsheviks*. New York: Macmillan, 1987

Chang, Sherman. *The Marxian Theory of the State*. New York: Russell and Russell, 1965.

Cliff, Tony. *Lenin*. 4 vols. London: Pluto Press, 1975–79.

Cohen, Marshall, Thomas Nagel, and Thomas Scanlon, eds. *Marx, Justice, and History*. Princeton: Princeton University Press, 1980.

Cohen, Stephen, and Katrina vanden Heuvel, eds. *Voices of Glasnost: Interviews With Gorbachev's Reformers*. New York: Norton, 1989.

Corrigan, Philip, Harvie Ramsay, and Derek Sayer. *Socialist Construction and Marxist Theory: Bolshevism and Its Critique*. New York: Monthly Review Press, 1978.

Cummins, Ian. *Marx, Engels and National Movements*. New York: St. Martin's Press, 1980.

Cunningham, Frank. *Democratic Theory and Socialism*. Cambridge: Cambridge University Press, 1987.

Draper, Hal. *The "Dictatorship of the Proletariat" from Marx to Lenin*. New York: Monthly Review Press, 1987.

———. *Karl Marx's Theory of Revolution*. 3 vols. New York: Monthly Review Press, 1977–86.

Draper, Hal, ed. *Karl Marx and Friedrich Engels: Writings on the Paris Commune*. New York: Monthly Review Press, 1971.

Felix, David. *Marx As Politician*. Carbondale, Ill: Southern Illinois University Press, 1983.

Fischer, Louis. *The Life of Lenin*. New York: Harper and Row, 1964

Gilbert, Alan. *Marx's Politics: Communists and Citizens*. New Brunswick, N.J.: Rutgers University Press, 1981.

Gorbachev, Mikhail. *Perestroika: New Thinking for Our Country and the World*. New York: Harper and Row, 1987.

Harding, Neil. *Lenin's Political Thought*. 2 vols. New York: St. Martin's Press, 1977–81.

Harding, Neil, ed. *The State in Socialist Society*. Albany: SUNY Press, 1984.

Hibbin, Sally, ed. *Politics, Ideology and the State*. London: Lawrence and Wishart, 1978.

Hobsbawm, Eric. *The Age of Capital 1848–1875*. New York: New American Library, 1975.

Hunt, Richard N. *The Political Ideas of Marx and Engels*. 2 vols. Pittsburgh: Pittsburgh University Press, 1974–84.

Jessop, Bob. *The Capitalist State*. New York: New York University Press, 1982.

Kolakowski, Leszek. *Main Currents of Marxism*, 3 vols. Oxford: Oxford University Press, 1978

Lange, Oskar and Fred Taylor. *On the Economic Theory of Socialism*. Ed. Benjamin E. Lippincott. New York: McGraw Hill, 1964.

Lenin, V. I. *Collected Works*. 45 vols. Moscow: Progress Publishers, 1960–72.

Levin, Michael. *Marx, Engels and Liberal Democracy*. New York: St. Martin's Press, 1989.

Levine, Andrew. *The End of the State*. London: Verso, 1987.

Lewin, Moshe. *Lenin's Last Struggle*. New York: Monthly Review Press, 1968.

Lichtheim, George. *Marxism: An Historical and Critical Study*. New York: Columbia University Press, 1982.

———. *The Origins of Socialism*. New York: Praeger, 1969.

Lukacs, Georg. *Lenin: A Study on the Unity of His Thought*. Cambridge, Mass.: MIT Press, 1971.

Lukes, Stephen. *Marxism and Morality*. New York: Oxford University Press, 1985.

Luxemburg, Rosa. *The Russian Revolution and Lenin or Marxism?* Ann Arbor: University of Michigan Press, 1977.

MacGregor, David. *The Communist Ideal in Hegel and Marx*. Toronto: Toronto University Press, 1984.

Macpherson, C. B. *The Real World of Democracy*. New York: Oxford University Press, 1972

————. *The Political Theory of Possessive Individualism: Hobbes to Locke*. Oxford: Oxford University Press, 1962.

Marx, Karl. *Capital*. 3 vols. New York: International Publishers, 1967.

Marx, Karl, and Frederick Engels. *Collected Works*. 50 vols. New York: International Publishers, 1975– .

————. *Selected Works in Three Volumes*. Moscow: Progress Publishers, 1969–72.

————. *Selected Works in One Volume*. New York: International Publishers, 1968.

McLellan, David. *Karl Marx: His Life and Thought*. New York: Harper and Row, 1973.

Mehring, Franz. *Karl Marx: The Story of His Life*. Ann Arbor: University of Michigan Press, 1973.

Miliband, Ralph. *Marxism and Politics*. Oxford: Oxford University Press, 1977.

Moore, Stanley. *Marx on the Choice Between Socialism and Communism*. Cambridge, Mass.: Harvard University Press, 1980

Nicolaievsky, Boris, and Otto Maenschen-Helfen. *Karl Marx: Man and Fighter*. Hammondsworth: Penguin, 1976.

Nove, Alec. *The Economics of Feasible Socialism*. London: Allen and Unwin, 1983.

————. *An Economic History of the USSR*. New York: Penguin, 1969.

O'Rourke, James J. *The Problem of Freedom in Marxist Thought: An Analysis of the Treatment of Human Freedom by Marx, Engels, Lenin and Contemporary Soviet Philosophy*. Dordrecht, Holland: D. Reidel, 1974.

Padover, Saul, ed. *Karl Marx on Revolution*. New York: McGraw Hill, 1971.

Page, Stanley, ed. *Lenin: Dedicated Marxist or Revolutionary Pragmatist?* Lexington, Mass.: D. C. Heath, 1970.

Parkinson, G. H. R. ed. *Marx and Marxisms*. Cambridge: Cambridge University Press, 1982.

Paul, Ellen Frankel, Jeffrey Paul, Fred Miller and John Ahrens, eds. *Marxism and Liberalism*. Oxford: Basil Blackwell, 1986.

Pennock, J. Roland, and John Chapman, eds. *Marxism*. New York: New York University Press, 1983.

Polan, A. J. *Lenin and the End of Politics*. Berkeley: University of California Press, 1984.

Rabinowitch, Alexander. *The Bolsheviks Come to Power: The Revolution of 1917 in Petrograd*. New York: Norton, 1978.

Reed, John. *Ten Days That Shook the World*. New York: International Publishers, 1934.

Riazanov, David. *Karl Marx and Friedrich Engels*. New York: Monthly Review Press, 1973.

Rosenberg, Arthur. *A History of Bolshevism*. New York: Russell and Russell, 1965.

Rubel, Maximilien, and Margaret Manale. *Marx Without Myth: A Chronological Study of His Life and Work*. New York: Harper and Row, 1976.

Shirokov. M., ed. *Textbook of Marxist Philosophy*. San Francisco: Proletarian Publishers, n.d.

Shub, David. *Lenin*. Baltimore: Penguin, 1966.

Sirianni, Carmen. *Workers' Councils and Socialist Democracy: The Soviet Experience*. London: Verso, 1982.

Soboul, Albert. *The French Revolution 1787–1789*. New York: Random House, 1975.

Teeple, Gary. *Marx's Critique of Politics 1842–1847*. Toronto: Toronto University Press, 1984.

Theen, Rolf. *Lenin: Genesis and Development of a Revolutionary*. Princeton: Princeton University Press, 1979.

Thomas, Paul. *Karl Marx and the Anarchists*. London: Routledge, 1980.

Tucker, Robert. *The Marxian Revolutionary Idea*. New York: Norton, 1969.

Ulam, Adam. *The Bolsheviks*. New York: Macmillan, 1965.

Van den Berg, Axel. *The Imminent Utopia*. Princeton: Princeton University Press, 1988.

Venturi, Franco. *Roots of Revolution: A History of the Populist and Socialist Movements in Nineteenth-Century Russia*. Chicago: University of Chicago Press, 1983.

Wilson, Edmund. *To the Finland Station*. New York: Doubleday, 1953.

Wolfe, Bertram. *Three Who Made a Revolution*. New York: Dell, 1948.

Wolin, Sheldon. *Politics and Vision*. Boston: Little, Brown, 1960.

Index